The Best Years of the
Century

The Best Years of the
Century

Richard Watson Gilder, *Scribner's Monthly*,
and the *Century Magazine,* 1870–1909

ARTHUR JOHN

UNIVERSITY OF ILLINOIS PRESS
Urbana   Chicago   London

LIBRARY OF CONGRESS CATALOGING IN PUBLICATION DATA

John, Arthur W   1913–
The best years of the Century.

Bibliography: p.
Includes index.
1. Century illustrated monthly magazine.   2.   Gilder,
Richard Watson, 1844–1909—Biography—Careers.
I.   Title.
PN4900.C46J64   051   80-25841
ISBN 0-252-00857-X

For Beryl, Jeffrey, and Barbara

———

Contents

Preface

This study is basically the story of a great American magazine in its greatest years—the magazine that began as *Scribner's Monthly* in 1870 and became *The Century Illustrated Monthly Magazine* in 1881 . The dominant figure in the magazine's history was Richard Watson Gilder, who largely set the tone for *Scribner's Monthly* after about 1875 and who edited the *Century* from 1881 until his death in 1909.

The *Century*, which many contemporary critics considered the best general periodical in the world during its great years, was essentially a projection of Gilder's ideas and ideals. In this book I attempt to explain these ideals by showing how they were applied in the magazine to American literature, fine arts, public life, and society during the late nineteenth and early twentieth centuries. It was the hopeful assumption of Gilder and his editorial colleagues that the American middle class, if sufficiently exposed to the traditional culture and traditional values that supposedly embodied ideal standards, would move to a higher plane of appreciation for literature and art, would impose morality on American public life, and would create a just, ordered, and gracious society. The dazzling success of the *Century* over two decades is linked to the apparent acceptance of these standards by educated Americans; its ultimate decline, to the erosion of these standards brought about by industrialization, science and technology, power politics, the democratization of taste assisted by the mass media, and the growing inclination among artists, writers, and intellectuals to reject traditional forms and values.

The phrase "genteel tradition" has become so overworked and pejorative that I have avoided its use, but in his aims and his values, Gilder was unquestionably one of the genteel critics and reformers.[1] Too many critics, however, have equated his gentility with prudish repression of frank literary expression and with nothing else.[2] In addition to being one of the most lovable of men and most helpful of editors, Gilder was a zealous citizen and patriot who worked every day of his adult life, both in his magazine and apart from it, to make a better America according to his lights.

The note of patriotic nationalism was struck consistently throughout Gilder's career with the magazine. *Scribner's Monthly* was a leading force in urging reconciliation of North and South during the latter half of the Reconstruction era, and it was a pioneer in providing postwar southern writers with a national audience. Gilder as editor showed an evangelical zeal in glorifying America's past and her heroes. An idealized image of the United States was an integral part of the national culture he promulgated.

The history of the magazine reflects two major transitions in American intellectual life. *Scribner's Monthly* began as a general periodical of evangelical Christian flavor under Josiah Gilbert Holland. Within a few years, largely under the influence of Gilder and with Holland's acquiescence, it had begun to speak to a more secular America. Increasingly, its pages stressed culture rather than religion. Improved engraving and printing processes were used to exploit a new middle-class interest in art and objets d'art and to promote the "new art" that had sprung up among young, European-trained American painters. *Scribner's* won fame for its illustrations and tried through them to educate the taste of its middle-class readers.

With Gilder in full command after 1881, the religious note was muted, although there was some continuity of Christian outlook as exponents of the social gospel played a prominent part in the critique of American public life and society which Holland had begun and Gilder continued. The ideals that Gilder projected for American letters, arts, and society were not based on Christianity, however, but on the Keatsean conception that truth and beauty are one.

Gilder, an agnostic in his later years, had no difficulty in adjusting to the increasing secularization of American life, especially among intellectuals. But Gilder's ideals were fixed; they could not be reconciled with the relativism and pragmatism that took root in the late nineteenth century and flowered before World War I. The *Century's* decline in circulation, noticeable in the 1890s and swifter after 1900, was brought about by a revolution in magazine production that threw up a host of new, inexpensive periodicals with an appeal that the older monthlies could not match. Enriched by advertising rates keyed to a mass circulation, they were able to outbid Gilder for famous writers. Gilder's insistence on clinging to ideal standards for his monthly, in illustration as well as in content, accelerated the decline. In their journalistic thrust, in their appeal to readers outside the cultivated upper middle class, the new magazines not only undermined the older monthlies like the *Century*; they helped to erode the structure of nineteenth-century cultural and moral values.

Gilder died in 1909, before the defeat of ideality was final, and this narrative ends with his death. By then the challenge to absolute values and ideal standards was clear, and the *Century* was fated to go down with them.

The incentive to complete and revise this study with a view toward publication came from the encouragement offered by Winton U. Solberg, professor of history at the University of Illinois. Additional support came from Professor Theodore Peterson, also of the University of Illinois, and it was especially welcome since he is a recognized authority as a historian of American magazines. The subject had initially been suggested by the late Arthur Schlesinger, Sr., and I had done research on the topic during my governmental career.

Many librarians and library employees have assisted me in the research for this book. I am especially grateful to the staffs of the New York Public Library and of the Houghton Library, Harvard University. Letters in the William Dean Howells Papers, the Edmund Gosse Papers, and the Thomas A. Janvier Papers are cited or quoted by permission of the Houghton Library. I thank the Manuscripts and Archives Division of the New York Public Library for permission to publish material from the Century Collection, the R. W. Gilder Papers, the R. R. Bowker Collection, the Galaxy Correspondence, and the Josiah G. Holland Papers.

I am grateful to Charles Scribner, Jr., for his permission to publish from materials in the archives of Charles Scribner's Sons, which are now in the Princeton University Library.

I am glad to express my thanks to Miss Rosamond Gilder,

daughter of Richard Watson Gilder, who was helpful as early as 1950 and as late as 1978 in making available letters of her father and in sharing her memories of him. I owe a special debt to the late Rodman Gilder, son of the editor, who in personal conversation and written notes gave me the benefit of his firsthand knowledge of *Century* personnel and their working environment, and who made a professional and good-humored critique of my initial draft.

The late Mrs. Theodora V. W. Ward, daughter of Josiah Gilbert Holland, not only talked to me at some length about her father and his characteristics but lent me many letters dealing with the earliest years of *Scribner's Monthly.*

Dana H. Ferrin, when executive vice-president of Appleton-Century-Crofts, Inc., kindly shared with me some recollections of the Century Company, of which he had earlier been an official.

I thank Susan L. Patterson for her conscientious copyediting, which saved me from a number of errors, both stylistic and typographical.

Finally, I want to pay grateful tribute to Stephen J. Campbell and the late J. Stewart Hunter, my old and dear friends, who read the manuscript and made constructive suggestions for its improvement.

NOTES

1. John Tomsich in *A Genteel Endeavor: American Culture and Politics in the Gilded Age* (Stanford, Calif., 1971) deals with eight writers as representative of genteel aims and values. In addition to Gilder, they are Richard Henry Stoddard, Thomas Bailey Aldrich, George Henry Boker, Bayard Taylor, George William Curtis, Charles Eliot Norton, and Edmund C. Stedman. Gilder was the youngest of this group. While Gilder was an exception to some of Tomsich's perceptive generalizations about this group—notably, despite moments of despair, in his persistent optimism and his enthusiasms—he was quite representative in his alienation from much of contemporary American life in his later years and in his preoccupation with the past.

2. Alfred Kazin has remarked that Gilder was "a very amiable man whom some malicious fortune set up as a perfect symbol of all that the new writers were to detest." *On Native Grounds* (New York, 1942), 56.

1

Richard Watson Gilder

One October evening in 1883, George W. Cable, newly famous for his tales of Creole life in New Orleans, called on Richard Watson Gilder in New York. Gilder, then thirty-nine, and his gracious, artistic wife, Helena, lived with their two children in a picturesque house on East Fifteenth Street, just off Union Square. Known as The Studio, the residence had been remodeled from a stable and carriage house by a friend of the Gilders, twenty-one-year-old Stanford White. On the evening of Cable's visit, the other guests included E. L. Godkin, editor of the *Nation*; John Burroughs, the nature writer; the Reverend (later Bishop) Henry C. Potter; the great sculptor, Augustus Saint-Gaudens; Joe Jefferson, then at the peak of his fame as an actor; Andrew Carnegie; and a distinguished visitor from England, Matthew Arnold. "It was a night to remember all one's days," Cable wrote his wife.[1]

The Gilders were "at home" every Friday evening in the large, square room that took up the entire ground level of The Studio. The company gathered around an open fireplace in which a large kettle hung from a crane, and over which was a bas-relief portrait of the Gilder family by Saint-Gaudens. Helena Gilder served tea, chocolate, and biscuits and kept the atmosphere warm and informal. Cable remembered more than one evening when Clara Louise Kellogg, the rising young American soprano, performed Negro songs, accompanying herself on the banjo, yielding time now and then for Cable to sing his Creole numbers. Helen Modjeska, the Polish-American actress, was a frequent guest and could easily be persuaded to recite, sometimes in Polish.[2]

Such gatherings went on for many years, in The Studio and in the larger homes to which the Gilders moved as their family increased—ultimately to five children—and the celebrities kept coming: Rudyard Kipling, John Singer Sargent, General William Sherman, William James, Eleanora Duse. Gilder was passionately fond of music, and if Adele Aus der Ohe or later the young Ignace Paderewski were to be among the guests, their host made sure to have a concert grand piano available for the evening. It was typical of Gilder's relations with people that the Messrs. Steinway refused to accept a rental fee from him for this service.[3]

When conversation replaced music, it was likely to be about literature and the arts. Both Gilder and his wife believed that the arts represented what he called "ideality," a showing forth of beauty that was indistinguishable from truth. This shared passion had brought them together. Helena de Kay, who had been a friend and neighbor of Henry James in summers at Newport, came from a cultivated, well-known New York family. When Gilder met her, she was a young student of painting, one of the growing number of American artists who had studied in Europe, where she had learned German, French, and Italian. Before her marriage to Gilder in 1874, their courtship had centered around concerts, art exhibits, lectures, the study of Dante, and the reading of Edward Fitzgerald's version of *The Rubáiyat*—a work as yet little known in the United States. As a young wife, Helena continued to paint and to study. She was one of the founders of the still-flourishing Art Students League of New York. Her talents and her connections were helpful to her husband's career. She illustrated his first book of poems, *The New Day*, published in 1875. She helped form the taste in art which became one of his hallmarks as an editor, and she was a continuing influence on his artistic judgments.[4]

While they were genteel, the Gilders were—what a later generation sometimes forgets was possible for gentility—passionate in their feelings and warm in their friendships. Walt Whitman remembered that "at a time when most everybody else in their set was throwing me down they were nobly and unhesitatingly hospitable . . . without pride and without shame." Cable, exploring the city's literary and publishing world, found that "Gilder is . . . the sweetest, gentlest, manliest, most interesting fellow I see."[5]

In addition to being a lovable man, Gilder was a popular poet, but his influence in the world of art and letters arose from his role as editor of *The Century Illustrated Monthly Magazine*, a position he filled from 1881 to 1909. Gilder's home and his magazine were opposite ends of the same cultural axis. Most of his friends either wrote for or were written about in the *Century*, which, in the 1880s, he was making into what many contemporaries regarded as the best general periodical in the world.

Gilder was a man of slight stature, with dark hair and drooping mustache, large, lustrous eyes, and the poet's carelessness of dress. His life and character presented interesting paradoxes. He was, for example, a romantic who championed classical norms and models. Like other genteel critics, he wanted to restore a sense of repose and serenity to a disorderly and raucous age. But while talking of repose, he lived his life on the run. When expressing their fondness for Gilder, many of his friends stressed his unworldly air. To Carnegie, he was "one of the sweetest, saintliest, yet most heroic souls I have ever been privileged to know and love." Burroughs said he had never encountered anyone in person or in books who made "such an impression of pure spirit." Yet Gilder was an activist and man of affairs. The Society of American Artists and the Authors Club of New York were both organized in his home. He was a bundle of selfless energy, forever enthusiastic about some piece of literature, work of art, or person, spending himself in civic and cultural causes, tireless in helping his friends. He persuaded President Daniel Coit Gilman of Johns Hopkins University to give Cable a much-needed job as lecturer and later to offer William Dean Howells a professorship—Howells was tempted, but declined. Gilder was unworldly only in that he lacked guile; he went after what he wanted openly and persistently, displaying, in the words of one who knew him well, a "tactical hardihood" and a dauntless spirit.[6]

His friend Burroughs thought Gilder's life lacked continuity, that he fluttered about too much from cause to cause. In part this opinion probably reflected the contrast between the world of nature, where Burroughs lived, and the swift tempo of the metropolis, where Gilder lived and worked. Gilder did extend himself too far in too many directions and periodically worked himself into a state of nervous exhaustion. Still there was continuity, even a unity in his life that came from his driving idealism, the core of his nature from which all his activities stretched out.[7]

It will become apparent, in the course of this study, how Gilder expressed his ideals in and through his magazine, but it will be useful at the outset to note the intensity of his idealism, which was not philosophical but intuitive and unreflective. He carried through life the kind of euphoric faith in the good, the true, and the beautiful that most of us experience briefly as teenagers. In his youth this intense feeling was identified with religious experience; the adolescent Gilder responded so emotionally to evangelical appeals that he once had to be sent to the country to recover his equilibrium.[8] As his religious faith waned in his maturity, he simply transferred his devotion to patriotism and the arts. In its bent and in its intensity his idealism was religious. His veneration of great men, for example, extended to the relics of their existence; he cherished the bronze cast of Abraham Lincoln's hands, the death mask of John Keats. In its essence, his life was that of a missionary.

Not only his energy and zeal but the circumstances of his age had given Gilder a powerful voice in the literature, culture, and morals of late nineteenth-century America. His arrival on the New York scene coincided with the city's emergence as the cultural capital of the United States and the gateway through which foreign luminaries of arts and letters entered the country—often to be seized by Gilder as guests, contributors, or both. There were new movements in art which he was able to promote and a growing public taste for things artistic which he hastened to exploit. And once Gilder had brought the *Century* to the top, he was in a position, along with the editors of *Harper's Monthly* and *Scribner's Magazine*, to exercise a dominant influence on American literature; these three periodicals were the great markets for writers at a time when few literary men could survive by publishing only books.

Gilder was not solely responsible for the success of the *Century*; he inherited a sound concern from the magazine's founders. But he commanded the *Century* in its years of glory and gave it the distinctive tone that made it an ornament of its time and one of the great periodicals in American history.

"A happier boy I never saw," wrote Jane Nutt Gilder of her three-year-old "Watsey." Richard Watson grew up in an atmosphere of affection and security, adored not only by his parents but also by a doting aunt who was his "second mother." His real mother, whom Gilder recalled as "lovely" and "wonderful," came from a line of prosperous farmers. His father, the Reverend William Henry Gilder, was a "high-church Methodist" minister, a man of culture as well as faith, who edited religious journals that were also literary. The Reverend Gilder ran a private school in Bordentown, New Jersey, where Richard Watson was born in 1844, and later became proprietor of Flushing Female College on Long Island. Watsey at eleven was the only boy in the school and president of its literary association. At twelve he was hanging around the composing room of the Long Island *Times*, where he amused himself by publishing his own boyish newspaper.[9]

After a sound secondary education, young Gilder contemplated becoming a minister; he even read Hebrew and Greek for a time with that in mind. Later he decided to study law. But his father, commissioned a chaplain in the Union army, died in 1864 of smallpox incurred while ministering to the hospitalized men of his regiment. Gilder did not overvalue his own brief stint with the First Philadelphia Artillery in the Gettysburg campaign, but he was always proud of his father's death in line of duty. With his father's passing, Richard Watson was left as the chief support of his family, and he had to abandon hopes of college training. Six honorary degrees from leading universities, granted after he had achieved fame, did not diminish his regret over this necessary sacrifice; he missed college, he said, every day of his life.[10]

Following a term as a clerk in a New Jersey railroad office, he became a legislative reporter for the *Newark Daily Advertiser*. In 1869 he joined with a young friend, Robert Newton Crane—later to be Stephen Crane's uncle—in founding the *Newark Morning Register*, a venture that lasted several years but ended in financial failure, leaving Gilder with debts that he paid off only after years of hard work and saving.[11]

Meanwhile, he obtained a second job as editor of *Hours at Home*, a monthly magazine that was an appendage to the publishing house of Charles Scribner and Sons. This was a fortunate move. By 1869 he was editor-in-chief of this magazine; when it was absorbed into its more ambitious successor, *Scribner's Monthly*, Gilder stayed on as assistant editor of the new publi-

cation and became heir-apparent to its editor, the renowned Josiah
Gilbert Holland. So began a career that lasted nearly forty years
and that left a distinctive mark in the history of American
periodicals.

NOTES

1. Lucy L. C. Biklé, *George W. Cable, His Life and Letters* (New York,
1928), 103–4.
2. Arlin Turner, *George W. Cable: A Biography* (Baton Rouge, La.,
1966), 136–37; Rosamond Gilder, ed., *Letters of Richard Watson Gilder*
(Boston, 1916), 56–63, hereafter cited as Gilder, *Gilder*; William Webster
Ellsworth, *A Golden Age of Authors: A Publisher's Recollection* (New
York, 1919), 22, 148–50; L. Frank Tooker, *The Joys and Tribulations
of an Editor* (New York, 1924), 167–68.
3. Gilder to the Messrs. Steinway, Feb. 1, Feb. 8, and Oct. 26, 1887,
Richard Watson Gilder Papers, New York Public Library, hereafter
cited as GP, and Ellsworth, *Golden Age*, 148–50.
4. Gilder, *Gilder*, 56–57; undated memorandum [1950] from Rodman
Gilder to the author; Cecilia Beaux's tribute to Gilder in *Century*, Feb.
1910, p. 631; Lawrence Campbell to the author, Apr. 24, 1979. (Campbell is an editor with the Art Students League of New York and is
writing a history of that organization.)
5. Horace Traubel, *With Walt Whitman in Camden*, 3 vols. (New York,
1961), 2:119, and Turner, *Cable*, 146.
6. The phrase "tactical hardihood" was William M. Sloane's in *Century*, Feb. 1910, p. 636; see Carnegie's and Burroughs's tributes in same
number; Robert Underwood Johnson, *Remembered Yesterdays* (Boston,
1923), 88; Tooker, *Joys and Tribulations*, 51; Kenneth S. Lynn, *William
Dean Howells: An American Life* (New York, 1971), 271–72.
7. Clara Barrus, ed., *The Heart of Burroughs's Journals* (Port Washington, N.Y., 1967), 242.
8. Gilder, *Gilder*, 17.
9. Ibid., 5–6; Gilder to R. R. Bowker, Mar. 6, 1906, Bowker Collection, New York Public Library; Gilder to George Alfred Townsend,
Nov. 5, 1896, Houghton Library Autograph file, Houghton Library,
Harvard University, Cambridge, Mass.
10. Gilder, *Gilder*, 22–35 passim; undated memorandum [1950] from
Rodman Gilder to the author on his father's study of Greek and Hebrew;
Gilder to W. O. Atwater, May 12, 1887, GP. "I would give my head
to have had such a training as one can get in college." Gilder to Maurice
Thompson, Feb. 20, 1891, GP.
11. Gilder, *Gilder*, 35–43, and *Journalist*, 12 (Dec. 13, 1890):4.

2

Launching *Scribner's Monthly*

Hours at Home had been "designed to stand among our monthly magazines as the representative of the religious element of American literature."[1] Its successor, *Scribner's Monthly*, also began with a religious tone, for its founders—Dr. Josiah Gilbert Holland, Roswell C. Smith, and Charles Scribner—were all devout Christians. Of these three, Scribner played the smallest role in the history of *Scribner's Monthly*—he died in 1871—but he had a vital part in its birth, for he endowed it with his publishing name and good will and with its first circulation list.

As to Dr. Holland, no American writer in those years had a firmer grip than he on the heartstrings of the nation. His didactic poems, novels, and essays, to the amazement and disgust of sophisticated literary men, were widely read even in hinterland regions where Henry Wadsworth Longfellow, Ralph Waldo Emerson, and John Greenleaf Whittier hardly penetrated.[2] His readers revered him as "Timothy Titcomb," the sage adviser of young people, and they flocked to see and hear him on the lecture circuit. His composition, *Kathrina*, which eventually sold 100,000 copies, was one of the more popular narrative poems ever penned in America. However much critics might scorn this "apostle of the common place," his sentiments and his moral standards found a sympathetic response in thousands of American homes.[3]

Holland's moral earnestness, like that of many of his readers, stemmed from a New England inheritance. His father, a wool-carder at odds with the factory age, had apparently less influence on Holland than did his pious mother, who wanted him to be a minister and lamented that she could not afford to educate him for that calling. Yet all his writings were to be sermons, and he was to make his editorial chair a pulpit from which he reached an audience that a Henry Ward Beecher might envy.

Holland was born in 1819 near Belchertown, in western Massachusetts. Although he had to toil as chore boy and textile-mill
hand to help keep his family above the poverty line, he found
time to study at Northampton High School. As a young man
he won regional fame as a teacher of penmanship and elocution.
He used his earnings to attend Berkshire Medical College at Pitts-
field, but his diploma brought him little more than a title, for
his practice in Springfield was brief and unhappy. His attempt
to establish a weekly newspaper was no more successful. Having
married Elizabeth Chapin, an educated young lady of a comfortable Springfield family, the doctor turned teacher to support
her. In 1847 he took an appointment at a private school in Rich-
mond, Virginia, and a year later moved to Vicksburg, Mississippi,
where he was an effective superintendent of schools. He came
back to New England in 1849 with a certain sympathy for southern opinion which was to serve him well as an editor.[4]

From his outpost in Dixie young Holland had sent poems to
northern magazines, and some of them had been printed. On a
vacation visit to Louisiana he had gleaned material for some
"Sketches of Plantation Life," which he sold to the *Springfield
Republican*. That daily was already famous, and Holland, bent on
a literary career, sought a place on its staff. Its proprietor, the
second Samuel Bowles, made him his assistant. Although Holland
thought his boss heathenish, and the free-and-easy editor regarded
his right-hand man as something of a prig, their collaboration
raised the *Republican* to new heights of prosperity.[5]

With Bowles's encouragement, Holland wrote a series of moral
essays for the newspaper, signing them "Timothy Titcomb."
Three series of these lay sermons, addressed in turn to bachelors,
maidens, and young married couples, were eagerly read by earnest
New Englanders and brought a marked increase in the paper's
circulation. Holland then sought out Scribner in New York, who
agreed to bring out *Timothy Titcomb's Letters* as a book. Thus
began Holland's link with a national audience, and thus was
started his close relationship with Scribner, which culminated in
the founding of *Scribner's Monthly*.[6]

Holland's next literary efforts—a creditable history of western
Massachusetts and a colonial romance called *The Bay-Path*—also
appeared first in the *Republican*. Holland had acquired a one-

quarter interest in the newspaper, but in 1857 he sold it and resigned to become a free-lance author. In the following year he won national fame with *Bitter-Sweet*, a dramatic poem which, although attacked by the critics (as all his work was to be), sold 90,000 copies. With this triumph he began a series of lecture tours that took him to about 500 towns in the next twenty years and strengthened the bond between "Timothy Titcomb" and the inhabitants of the inland states.[7]

A succession of volumes—fiction, verse, and essays—all in the same moralistic vein, added to his reputation and made him one of the few Americans of his time to make a fortune out of literature. In 1868, when his friend Scribner asked him to take charge of *Hours at Home*, his popularity was at its crest. He was nearing fifty, a robust, handsome, warm-spirited man who loved work and loved praise, and he had no thought of retiring. But he was about to take his family on a tour of Europe, so he declined the magazine assignment.[8]

Scribner insisted on keeping the offer open until Holland returned. But Holland felt that *Hours at Home* was moribund. Reflecting on the matter, he began to think of an essentially new publication, which he could run on his own lines. At Geneva, Switzerland, he talked over this idea with his friend Roswell Smith, who became his enthusiastic partner.[9]

Smith, like Holland, was a Yankee who knew the far side of the Alleghenies. A tall, bulky, bearded man, he looked and behaved like a biblical hero, for to him the intervention of God in the affairs of people was a living reality. "Diligent in business, fervent in spirit, serving the Lord"—such was his precept, hung in gold letters over his office desk. And it was indeed a rare combination of work and Providence that had brought him, at the age of forty, into a comfortable fortune.

Born in Lebanon, Connecticut, in 1829, he was brought up by an uncle, Roswell Chamberlain Smith, author of a famous school grammar. Roswell the younger, serving his apprenticeship with the firm of Paine and Burgess, his uncle's publishers, acquired experience, a taste for books, and a belief in the power of the printed word. He completed the English course at Brown University, where his grades were consistently high, and then went to Hartford to study law. There he became a friend of Henry L. Ellsworth, a member of a notable Hartford family; when Ellsworth moved to Lafayette, Indiana, in 1852 to open a law and land-office business, Smith, on invitation, went, too.[10]

In the "West," however, Smith gained neither prosperity nor distinction in his early years. He developed consumption, and to fight it he went to Texas, where, as an abolitionist, he was unhappy. In the meantime, however, he married Ellsworth's daughter, Annie. When his father-in-law died, Smith inherited his considerable Indiana landholdings; and since the Lord had arranged that coal should lie under this property, he was able to turn over his business affairs to subordinates and depart for the East. His doctor had ordered a rest and a change, but after sixteen years Smith still felt himself a stranger among the impious Hoosiers, and he had no intention of returning to their midst.[11]

Smith was an austere man, hard as New England granite, whose quiet optimism found no outlet in charm or ebullience; he did not make friends easily. But when, as chairman of the local lyceum committee, he had welcomed the famous Dr. Holland to Lafayette, he had found a kindred New England spirit, one who could sympathize with his dislike of "dirty Indiana, where they are jealous of all Yankees and all Yankee influence." The two fellow Christians came quickly to a state of mutual affection and trust. In 1868, a year of pause and reflection for both, they planned to bring their families together and sail as one party for Europe.[12]

Some unrecorded event altered that scheme, but the two men arranged to meet later on the Continent. Smith had an idea for a publication; Holland was weighing Scribner's offer. Conferring at Geneva, as they looked down on the rushing Rhone, they decided to join forces on a new magazine. Holland was to be editor; Smith the business manager; and Scribner, they hoped, would lend his prestige and some of his resources to the project.

In midsummer of 1869 Smith returned to New York and called on Scribner, with a letter of introduction from Holland, to broach the subject. Scribner was cautious at first in dealing with the bearded stranger. He doubted the expediency of bringing a third salaried executive into an enterprise that two men might handle, and furthermore he was reluctant to see his tidy little *Hours at*

Home embarked on a more venturesome course than he had plotted for it. But after a few talks with Smith, he found himself agreeing with Holland that there was room aboard for a business pilot of such obvious fertility of mind and knowledge of people. It would mean an extra split in the profits, but "we must hold out to ourselves no other result than . . . a great success and we will be more likely to secure that if we have an efficient business organization."[13]

No sooner had Smith reached this level of confidence with Scribner than he was forced to mediate between his two partners on the issue most serious to both—religion. Holland had no reverence for theological abstractions and no patience with sectarian dogma. In Springfield he had expressed such liberal views to his Bible class that the church deacons convened to consider whether he was a heretic. He had taken the lead in establishing the evangelical but nondenominational Springfield Memorial Church. Such deviations from established Christianity troubled the devout and conservative Scribner. He was not willing to give the editor free rein, insisting that he must participate in determining general policies governing the selection of writers and materials.[14] Holland had a different idea:

> I would have nothing to do with the magazine, unless I should be at liberty to say what I should feel moved to say, on any subject whatever. The magazine must be an aggressive, free speaking thing with a flavor of vitality about it. . . . Harper's monopolizes the market for harmless and inoffensive literary pap. We have no field there—but a magazine that would boldly lead in the denunciation of social, and political abuses from the Christian standpoint . . . irrespective of the prejudices and opinions of men, would at least stand a chance to live. I am afraid Mr. Scribner does not wish to have his name associated with such a magazine as this, and to trust its conduct to me without the wish to question, or the power to veto.[15]

Smith, who conveyed these words to Scribner, tried to soften their bite. He himself had great faith in Holland's prudence. "I *know* that he is sound in the faith once delivered to the saints . . . I *know* that he is *not* such a terrible radical as many think him."[16]

Meanwhile, Smith was evidently successful in soothing Hol-

land's pride. "You and I never had any difficulty in dealing face
to face," Holland wrote Scribner, "and we are not likely to
have."[17] By the close of 1869 the general plan of a new magazine
was accepted as an accomplished fact; the details would be worked
out by the triumvirate on Holland's return to the United States
in the spring.

The final arrangements were made in an atmosphere of mutual
trust which left undefined—so far as the records show—not only
the degree of Holland's editorial authority but also the larger
question of how far the magazine was to be independent of the
Scribner book firm. Scribner seemed to have thought of the
project as an extension of *Hours at Home* and therefore as closely
linked to his publishing business. Holland and Smith wanted the
Scribner label with only so much Scribner control as was warranted by the book firm's financial interest in the periodical itself.
They insisted on, and got, a separate concern, Scribner and Company, to produce the magazine—a partnership in which Scribner,
in exchange for his name and good will and the subscription list
of *Hours at Home*, got a 40 percent interest. Holland and Smith
put up cash for the remaining 60 percent of the stock, which they
divided equally between them.[18] This division was crucial, for
when a policy dispute arose with Scribner's heirs a decade later,
this majority of the shares gave Smith the leverage to break away
from the Scribner interest entirely, taking the magazine with him.
The initial joint cash investment by Smith and Holland was apparently $7,200.

Holland and Smith, the active partners in the magazine, agreed
to draw equal salaries, but the editor thought he ought to get
"a certain consideration . . . at the start *from somebody*" for his
literary prestige. Smith heartily concurred; whether Scribner did
is not recorded.[19]

Holland reached New York in the spring of 1870 and prepared
to launch his magazine. He found a favorable environment for
his new enterprise. Like steel and other commodities, literature
for the first time was about to find a truly national market. With
the end of the slavery issue, the former Confederacy was a part
of this market, and the New South was to provide themes and
writers, and in time, readers, for the magazines of the eastern
seaboard. The growing West added to the expansion of the na-

tion's intellectual lifestream. The railroads were gathering the regions together. Advances in printing, stereotyping, and engraving processes were underway. Distribution techniques kept pace with production innovations; the American News Company, founded in 1864, assured a wider and more economical sale of periodicals by taking from the publishers the problems and credit risks of doing business with newsdealers in all parts of the country. Under these favorable circumstances, American periodicals, exclusive of newspapers, grew from about 700 in number in 1865 to more than 1,200 in 1870.[20]

This "mania of magazine-starting" did not mark any clear gain for American letters, for many of the new ventures were pallid miscellanies, specialized journals, or catchpenny reprints. Before 1870 no first-class literary monthly had established itself as a serious challenger to the prewar leaders, *Harper's Monthly* and the *Atlantic Monthly*. The best of them had been unable to overcome the two main problems now facing Holland: the dearth of American writers and the formidable competition of *Harper's*. Founded in 1850 as a "feeder" to the book-publishing house of Harper and Brothers, *Harper's Monthly* had reached a circulation of 150,000 by 1870 and represented the closest approach to a family magazine for the American people. But *Harper's* had won its way by serializing the novels of famous British authors—a policy that brought good Victorian literature into American homes but did little to develop American talents and themes.[21]

The *Atlantic Monthly*, founded in 1857 with James Russell Lowell as editor, and with the blessings of Emerson, Longfellow, Whittier, and Oliver Wendell Holmes, had not needed to look to England for its material. In the first fifteen years of its existence, two-thirds of its contributors, as of its readers, were New Englanders. While William Dean Howells later recalled that as editor of the *Atlantic* he was eager to discover outlying talent, New York writers complained that they could not scale the provincial barriers to this Olympus.[22]

Lippincott's Magazine, which began publication in 1868, developed a striking list of native American writers and was admired for its distinctive flavor, but it was not a financial success. Besides, it was a Philadelphia publication, and literary people generally agreed in the post–Civil War years that New York was the natural center for the new magazine that they felt was needed. "The metropolis, many-sided, all-embracing," said Edmund C. Stedman, must surely wrest the literary scepter from New England, and a Boston editor admitted that New York, with its publishing houses and great newspaper enterprises, was drawing to itself the writers who would give it primacy.[23]

Before *Scribner's Monthly* came to help fulfill these prophecies, Manhattan writers relied on the *Galaxy* and *Putnam's Magazine*. The former gained retrospective critical esteem by printing early stories of Henry James and contributions from Mark Twain and Walt Whitman. But its peak circulation, reached in 1871, was less than 25,000, and the *Galaxy*, when it was sold to the *Atlantic* in 1878, had less than 5,000 paying readers—the result, one must suppose, of competition from *Scribner's Monthly*.[24] *Putnam's* prided itself on being completely American. The Putnam book firm, emulating its publishing rivals, had begun the monthly before the war and re-established it in 1868 with the declaration that American writers, "like the gold in the gulches of the Rocky Mountains . . . are only waiting for a little adventurous prospecting to bring them to light." But competitors were now sifting the same native ore, and *Putnam's*, with a circulation of only 15,000, could shortly afford no nuggets: at the close of 1870 it was absorbed by the new *Scribner's Monthly*, passing along its tradition of independent comment on politics and social life to reinforce a policy already announced by Holland.[25]

In entering *Scribner's Monthly* as the latest challenger to *Harper's*, Holland found that his most pressing concern was the problem of finding good writers. They were not plentiful, and those who were established often had professional or sentimental ties to other publications. He looked abroad for one answer to this problem. He personally solicited novels from Charles Kingsley and George Eliot; he authorized the American journalist and diplomat William James Stillman to act as agent for *Scribner's* in England, commissioning him to seek contributions from John Ruskin, Thomas Hughes, William Morris, Algernon Charles Swinburne, and other eminent Victorians.[26]

But Holland was to learn that the way of the newcomer was hard. In the absence of international copyright, British publishers of celebrated authors usually sold advance sheets of their work to reputable American publishing houses for American reprinting. There was a gentlemen's agreement among American publishers not to tamper with the transatlantic business connections that were already established. Because the House of Harper had printed the past work of Wilkie Collins, for example, it was considered by "trade courtesy" to have first call on his future novels. Under these circumstances the only foreign prize *Scribner's* captured for its first volume was a preachy serial by the Reverend George MacDonald, a Scotchman who, like Holland, emphasized the moral more than he adorned the tale.[27]

From Europe, Holland had urged Scribner to look for American writers, especially for a promising young novelist. To bring other important contributors into the fold he was relying on his own energies and reputation. "I propose by personal effort to rally around the magazine the best Christian writers of the country—to do this by making my house a social center, by awakening so far as I am able an interest among the productive minds of the country in myself, by paying a good living price for work, and by so making the magazine the delight of the people and the exponent of the best thinking and creating, as to have every writer feel that he or she is honored by being reckoned among its contributors."[28]

Brave talk! But Holland had a problem—the very men who were bringing literary life to New York were hostile to him. Thomas Bailey Aldrich and Stedman had joined Howells earlier in declaring war on the sentimental literature of which Holland was perhaps the leading male practitioner. Howells, then on the staff of the *Nation*, had attacked "Timothy Titcomb" in 1865 as a writer whose success proved that "an order of mind has been allowed to flourish up into a thistly rank in our literature fit only to browse donkeys." He later condemned Holland's *Kathrina* as "puerile."[29]

These assaults, of course, preceded Holland's emergence as an editor with the power of the purse, and in the end these critics, even Howells, either accepted Holland's money or were won over by Gilder, who could talk their language. But at the outset Holland had to rely on the nucleus of authors he inherited from *Hours at Home* and *Putnam's*, which had been purchased by Scribner and Company in time to add impetus to the start of Holland's magazine—its manuscripts on hand were turned over to its successor. In the first number of *Scribner's*, every major article or story, with the exception of MacDonald's serial and Holland's own contributions, was produced by a former contributor to one or the other of these predecessors. The lead entry was a sixteen-page narrative poem by "An Old Fellow"—a thin disguise for the editor himself.[30]

Holland's retrospective assertion that his magazine began "without a single subscriber" was literally true but misleading, for the 9,000 regular purchasers of *Hours at Home* would hardly object to exchanging it for a bigger and better monthly at the same price.[31] The incorporation of *Putnam's* had brought another 12,000 buyers into *Scribner's Monthly*'s orbit.[32] But this total still added up to a feeble circulation for a magazine that aspired to be a national organ.

Understanding that his magazine would only gradually acquire distinction as he could lure good writers, Holland determined to rely at the start on visual impact. He would give his customers a new cover, faultless print, and better paper. "While I would make it more popular in its materials, I would make it more elegant in its externals. I would make it as handsome a magazine as America produces." He asked Scribner to hold back improvements on *Hours at Home* so that *Scribner's* could make a more dramatic contrast.[33]

In his early planning, Holland was strangely indifferent to the one feature that caught the public eye from the first number of *Scribner's*—its illustrations. He thought the heavy expense of art work might better be applied to improve the format and content, and Scribner agreed. Fortunately, at some prepublication meeting they reversed their stand—influenced perhaps by Gilder and Smith, and almost certainly by the conviction of both the editor and publisher of *Putnam's* that no magazine without engravings could succeed. Promotional advertisements promised that *Scribner's Monthly* would be *"profusely illustrated."*[34]

While insisting on an impressive appearance, Holland was counting more heavily on his renown as an author to make the initial appeal to readers. The prospectus, stressing that "Timothy Titcomb" himself was behind the new creation, declared that Holland's name was a symbol of success. "His books are everywhere, and his friends are with his books." On this middle-class Protestant note, Volume 1, Number 1 of *Scribner's Monthly: An Illustrated Magazine for the People* rolled forth, in late October 1870, to 40,000 homes.[35]

Scribner's Monthly, Dr. Holland boasted, took no magazine for its model but was "conducted from the first by an ideal standard." The editor of *Harper's Monthly*, on the other hand, thought that his upstart competitor would never have succeeded had it not adopted the plan of his publication "from beginning to end, even in its editorial departments."[36] There was some truth in both of these contradictory claims, for while Holland included in his monthly the standard ingredients of established periodicals, of which *Harper's* was the prototype, his complete formula had a flavor of its own. Even those features that he borrowed he usually adapted to his own ends.

The chief staple in the monthlies of the 1870s was the serial novel, two or three of which generally ran in a single issue. Scattered as side dishes around this main course were perhaps equal numbers of short stories and sketches. Holland followed the general rule that fiction was needed to float the heavier contributions, but he made the magazine carry a weightier load of nonfiction than did his competitors. In 1871, novels and short stories made up one-third of the reading matter in *Harper's*, only one-fifth in *Scribner's*.[37]

Another dependable feature of family entertainment that *Scribner's* borrowed from its predecessors was the illustrated article of travel and adventure. Typically this was a leisurely ramble through some historic quarter of the Old World or a glimpse of a remote, exotic land. But in the years after the Civil War the eyes of readers were turned increasingly toward the "Wild West" of their own country. This new focus brought an element of journalistic timeliness into periodicals, for in the early 1870s no less than seven scientific explorations of the trans-Mississippi area were in progress.[38] *Scribner's* published authoritative accounts of three of them. In 1871 Governor N. P. Langford of Montana told of his recent expedition to the Upper Yellowstone in two articles that created nationwide interest. Professor F. V. Hayden led a U.S. Geological Survey into the same region and described it for the magazine soon afterward. In 1875 Major John W. Powell related the highlights of his famous exploration through the canyons of the Colorado in five classic articles. Thus *Scribner's* early exhibited a penchant for chronicling significant events in the words of their chief participants.[39]

Within a decade the West, as seen in Dr. Holland's magazine, changed from a landscape to a burgeoning society with peculiar characteristics and problems. The mining booms in Colorado and the Black Hills of South Dakota could be pictured as colorful spectacles, but the presence of Indians in the path of settlement was a problem rather than a quaint exhibit, as Helen Hunt Jackson pointed out. Even John Muir's word paintings of the grandeur of the Yosemite, begun in the 1870s, were a prelude to the struggle for conservation of California's natural and scenic resources.[40]

Compared to its competitors, *Scribner's* was at first sparing in the use of another standard commodity, the historical or biographical article, but the monthly could not continue to neglect the kind of feature that offered such fruitful opportunities for illustration. In Holland's late years *Scribner's* published the first of the exhaustive appraisals of past men and events for which it was to become famous. Eugene Schuyler's "Peter the Great," begun in 1880, was an innovation in the periodical world, praised for the thoroughness of its documentation and the magnificence of its engravings. The *New York Evening Post* called this biography the "most notable event in modern magazine literature."[41]

The decade in which *Scribner's* began was notable for the impact of science on American life and thought. Specialized journals appeared, of which E. L. Youmans's *Popular Science Monthly* was the leader, and the columns of newspapers and magazines had accounts of the latest discoveries and their applications. In 1868 the *Atlantic*, in its subtitle, avowed itself to be a periodical of science as well as of literature, art, and politics; *Harper's* in 1869 started its "Editor's Scientific Record." Holland at first decided against a special department for this new interest, but in 1872 he went along with the trend and announced a regular feature called "Nature and Science," to be conducted by the eminent Professor John C. Draper, who held the chair of natural history at the City College of New York. Draper's monthly contribution was a miscellany which never struck the right balance between readability and true significance, and it was dropped in 1875. Regular coverage of science continued in "The World's Work," written in more popular, if less scholarly, fashion by Charles Barnard, which lasted until 1883. Its contents covered science rather superficially, but it was hardly less distinguished than similar columns of competitors.[42]

In feature articles *Scribner's* gave its readers thorough accounts of outstanding technological achievements. Simon Newcomb, the country's leading astronomer, described the new telescope at the National Observatory (November 1873). In "The Telephone and the Phonograph," George B. Prescott sketched the highlights of two American inventions that were exciting the wonder of the world (April 1878). Readers of the November 1878 issue spent a vicarious "Night with Edison" at his new laboratories in Menlo Park, New Jersey. A series of articles on that young wizard's work followed, culminating in a report that Edison himself, in a prefatory statement, termed the first "correct and authoritative account" of his invention of the electric light (February 1880).[43]

In marking off editorial departments in its back pages, *Scribner's* was following current periodical practice, but here, too, Holland geared his material to his purposes. Leading the parade was "Topics of the Time," penned every month until 1881 by Holland himself.[44] This was followed by Gilder's contribution, a "melange of gossip and sentiment" known as "The Old Cabinet," which was designed to sound a light, informal accompaniment to Holland's more ponderous themes. Gilder was no E. B. White, but now and then—when he described the delights of his Union Square neighborhood in summer, for example—a lyrical quality crept into his prose. Increasingly and sensibly Gilder wrote about his own interests, introducing comments on literature and the arts to the point where his chief feared the department was growing too specialized and beginning to exalt art for art's sake. But Gilder successfully resisted Holland's inclinations to drop the department, and "The Old Cabinet" was not closed up until 1878, when its author was being pressed more and more into the editor's role as Holland's health declined.[45]

Holland believed—no doubt correctly—that his magazine was read chiefly by women, and at Gilder's suggestion he began a unique feature aimed at feminine subscribers.[46] "Home and Society" offered advice on fashions, child rearing, gardening, house decoration, etiquette, and home-reading courses—on "everything which helps to make home attractive and delightful, and gives order and freedom and beauty to social intercourse." This department was so well appreciated by the admirers of "Timothy Titcomb" that it was enlarged in 1872. The humorist Frank R. Stockton, in charge of its contributions in its early years, supervised the work of various writers, among whom Sophie Bledsoe Herrick, a staff member, was especially prolific. Except for Holland's "Topics," no other department so well expressed the "improving" function of *Scribner's* as envisioned by its editor.[47]

The magazine's regular review of literature was expanded during its first year to embrace "Culture and Progress" of whatever sort, both at home and abroad. Numerous pens were called into service for book notices, while comments on art, music, and the theater, reflecting Gilder's pervasive influence, became increasingly prominent. "Progress" in this department was marked by reports on sociological as well as cultural events, always in the monthly's particular tone of uplift.

Finally, like a lecturer sending his audience home smiling, Holland closed his magazine with a potpourri of light verse, anecdotes, cartoons, and parodies collectively labeled first as "Etchings," then as "Bric-à-Brac," and, in later years, as "In Lighter Vein." More elastic in content than "The Editor's Drawer" of *Harper's*, this entertainment feature served most notably as a vehicle for early experiments in dialect verse and story. It held its place as tailpiece for more than forty years, surviving along with "Topics" when the other early departments were crowded out by the articles on the Civil War in the 1880s.

(It may be noted here that *Scribner's Monthly* was a pioneer in bringing humor out of departmental confines and putting it into its regular columns. "That anything funny should appear in a magazine except in the shape of short paragraphs had been unheard of."[48] In *Scribner's*, writers like Stockton, Charles Dudley Warner, and others found an opportunity for preliminary publication which, in turn, made it possible for them to bring out books.)

Scribner's Monthly gained distinction in the field of arts and letters as Gilder's influence came to overshadow Holland's. But

Holland made his own contribution to American periodical history by his serious critique of society and a tone of uplift that was unique in a major periodical.

NOTES

1. The quotation is the subtitle of *Hours at Home*, vol. 1. See also Roger Burlingame, *Of Making Many Books: A Hundred Years of Reading, Writing, and Publishing, MDCCCXLVI-MDCCCCXLVI* (New York, 1946), 191–92.

2. *New York Tribune* editorial, Oct. 23, 1881, and *New York Evening Post*, Oct. 13, 1881, cited in Mrs. H. M. Plunkett, *Josiah Gilbert Holland* (New York, 1894), 193–94.

3. *New York Tribune*, Oct. 13, 1881; Plunkett, *Holland*, 73, 195–96; H. H. Boyeson, *Literary and Social Silhouettes* (New York, 1894), 104–5.

4. H. H. Peckham, *Josiah Gilbert Holland in Relation to His Times* (Philadelphia, 1940), chs. 1, 2, passim, and Plunkett, *Holland*, 1–9, 13–27.

5. Plunkett, *Holland*, 26–27; George S. Merriam, *The Life and Times of Samuel Bowles*, 2 vols. (New York, 1885), 1:58–63; Richard Hooker, *The Story of an Independent Newspaper* (New York, 1924), 49–52.

6. Merriam, *Bowles*, 61–62; Peckham, *Holland and His Times*, 44–45; Plunkett, *Holland*, 39.

7. Peckham, *Holland and His Times*, 43–51, 127–28, and editorial, Mar. 1876.

8. Plunkett, *Holland*, 77, 195.

9. Editorial, June 1881.

10. George W. Cable, *A Memory of Roswell Smith . . .* (New York, 1892), 2–7, 11, 36; Washington Gladden, "Roswell Smith," June 1892; *Dictionary of American Biography*, s.v. "Smith, Roswell."

11. Cable, *Roswell Smith*, 15–17, and Gladden, "Roswell Smith."

12. Holland to Scribner, Oct. 26, 1896, Charles Scribner's Sons Archives, New York, hereafter cited as SC.

13. Scribner to Holland, Oct. 5, 1869, and Holland to Scribner, July 26, 1869, SC.

14. Plunkett, *Holland*, 110–11; 115–19, and Scribner to Holland, Oct. 5, 1869, SC.

15. Holland to Smith, Oct. 5, 1869, SC.

16. Smith to Scribner, Oct. 15, 1869, quoting Holland to Smith, n.d. [1869], SC.

17. Holland to Scribner, Dec. 18, 1869, SC.

18. Scribner proposed to sell Smith and Holland 60 percent of *Hours at Home* "on the basis of the purchase we have recently made of Mr. Sherwood's interest—that is $5000 for his 5/12." On this basis, the three-fifths share of Smith and Holland would come to $7,200 (of a $12,000 capitalization). There was to be a 7 percent preferred dividend on the

capital before Smith and Holland were paid their salaries. The remaining profits were to be divided pro rata. Since Scribner had already discussed this proposal with Smith before writing to Holland, this probably represents the final agreement for the partnership. Scribner to Holland, Oct. 5, 1869, SC.

19. Smith to Scribner, Oct. 25, 1869, and quote in that letter from Holland to Smith, Oct. 8, 1869, SC.

20. Frank Luther Mott, *A History of American Magazines*, 5 vols. (Cambridge, Mass., 1930–68), 3:5, and [American News Company], *Serving the Reading Public* (n.p., ca. 1944), pages not numbered.

21. Mott, *Magazines*, 3:5; J. Henry Harper, *The House of Harper: A Century of Publishing in Franklin Square* (New York, 1912), 84–85, 384; F. L. Allen, "The American Magazine Grows Up," *Atlantic Monthly*, 180 (Nov. 1947):78.

22. Allen, "American Magazine Grows Up," 78; M. A. DeW. Howe, *The Atlantic Monthly and Its Makers* (Boston, 1919), ch. 1, esp. 27–28; W. D. Howells, *Literary Friends and Acquaintances* (New York, 1911), 115–16; Laura Stedman and George M. Gould, eds., *Life and Letters of Edmund Clarence Stedman*, 2 vols. (New York, 1910), 1:449–50.

23. Stedman to Bayard Taylor, Dec. 25, 1873, in Stedman and Gould, eds., *Stedman*, 1:488–89; *Literary World*, 4 (Jan. 1874):120; Mott, *Magazines*, 3:396–99.

24. Mott, *Magazines*, 3:361–63; H. O. Houghton and Co. to W. C. and F. P. Church, Jan. 2, 1878, Galaxy Collection, New York Public Library. See also statements of sales in Galaxy Collection.

25. *Putnam's Magazine*, n.s., 1 (Jan. 1868):1–4 and 6 (Oct. 1870):464, and George H. Putnam, *George Palmer Putnam: A Memoir . . .* (New York, 1912), 362–63.

26. Kingsley to Holland, Sept. 2, 1870; G. H. Lewes to Holland, Aug. 21 [1870]; Stillman to Holland, Dec. 6 [1870]; Theodora V. W. Ward Collection. William James Stillman, *The Autobiography of a Journalist*, 2 vols. (Boston, 1901), 2:486.

27. Harper, *House of Harper*, 358, and MacDonald to Holland, May 27, 1871, Ward Collection.

28. Holland to Scribner, July 26, 1869, SC.

29. Edwin H. Cady, *The Road to Realism: The Early Years, 1837–1885, of William Dean Howells* (Syracuse, N.Y., 1956), 122–25.

30. *Putnam's Magazine*, 6:464; first editorial page (Oct. 1870); Holland to Scribner, Dec. 18, 1869, and Feb. 20, 1870, SC.

31. Editorial, June 1881, and Scribner to Holland, Oct. 5, 1869, SC.

32. This was the circulation when Putnam first offered his magazine to Scribner in 1869 for $15,000, but Scribner doubted its value, fearing that the new monthly might not retain the readers of *Putnam's*. Scribner to Holland, Oct. 5, 1869, SC.

33. Holland to Scribner, Oct. 26, 1869, SC.

34. Advertisement for *Scribner's Monthly* on back cover of *The Br*

Buyer, o.s. 3 (Sept. 1870); Holland to Scribner, July 26, 1869, and Scribner to Holland, Oct. 5, 1869, SC.

35. *Book Buyer*, o.s. 3 (Sept. 1870):back cover, and editorial, June 1881.

36. Editorial, Nov. 1880, and Henry M. Alden to Dr. Henry M. Field, May 18, 1894, in Harper, *House of Harper*, 601.

37. See ch. 3 for a content analysis of the two magazines.

38. Mott, *Magazines*, 3:58–62, and editorial, Oct. 1873.

39. Langford, May and June 1871; Hayden, Feb. 1872; Powell, Jan., Feb., Mar., Oct., and Dec. 1875.

40. "H. H." (Helen Hunt Jackson), "A New Anvil Chorus," Jan. 1878, and "The Wards of the United States Government," Mar. 1880. For Muir, see ch. 4.

41. *New York Evening Post*, quoted in advertising section, Mar. 1880, p. 8.

42. Mott, *Magazines*, 3:104–5; *New York Tribune*, Dec. 21, 1885; *The Critic*, 3 (Mar. 24, 1883):133.

43. The article was by Francis R. Upton, who was listed as "Mr. Edison's Mathematician."

44. Advertising section, Apr. 1871, p. 5; L. Frank Tooker, *The Joys and Tribulations of an Editor* (New York, 1924), 33; Rosamond Gilder, ed., *Letters of Richard Watson Gilder* (Boston, 1916), 53, hereafter cited as Gilder, *Gilder*.

45. Gilder, *Gilder*, 84; "The Old Cabinet," Nov. 1874; Herbert F. Smith, *Richard Watson Gilder*, Twayne U.S. Authors Series no. 166 (New York, 1970), 21–22.

46. Gilder, *Gilder*, 84–85.

47. Advertising section, May 1872, p. 5, and undated memorandum, "H. & S. Subjects," by Johnson, Century Collection, New York Public Library, hereafter cited as CC.

48. *Current Literature*, 2 (Jan. 1889):2.

3

Evangelism and Nationalism

The special aim of *Scribner's Monthly* at its beginning was to criticize American society from a Christian standpoint, and Josiah Gilbert Holland steadily pursued this aim through the turbulent decade of the 1870s. That his own faith was nonsectarian and nondoctrinaire gave him several advantages. It enabled him to make a broader evangelical appeal than the largely sectarian religious press could. It allowed him to take in stride the critical challenges to religious belief brought about by Darwinism and scholarly criticism of the Bible. It helped him to overcome prejudices, develop tolerance, and eventually acknowledge that all people of good will, not just professing Christians, could be his allies in improving American society. In the glow of his own success, and the cosmopolitan atmosphere of New York, his Puritanism thawed to the point where he welcomed the introduction of an aesthetic tone to his magazine. Holland's broadening outlook, in short, enabled him to accept the changes that would give *Scribner's* a growing national audience.

Disclaiming any wish to produce a strictly religious periodical, Holland yet planned to make *Scribner's* "as true to evangelical Christianity as the *Atlantic* has always been to Unitarianism and paganism."[1] Each number, Holland ordered, must contain at least one contribution of direct spiritual significance; "no man shall write a poem, or a story, or a review, or a disquisition who does not recognize Jesus Christ as the center and sum of our civilization." Not only were ministers of various denominations to write frequently for the magazine, but the business office and the editorial staff were to extend "the most considerate and generous treatment" to the clergy so that all of the evangelical sects should look on *Scribner's* as their literary organ.[2]

In seeking the support of church members and their leaders, Holland was not only expressing his own inclinations but was appealing to a wide segment of American opinion. Although the power of the churches in 1870 was not what it had once been, religion still held a strong grip on middle-class Americans. The clergy were among the foremost intellectual leaders of the land and spoke with an authority which, although modified by compromise with rising secular forces, was still respected by a large and sober following. Witnesses to the power of their voices were the more than 200 religious weeklies in the United States. The *Independent*, the *Churchman*, the *Christian Union*, the New York *Observer*, reaching into the same households to which *Scribner's* sought entry, were the earliest favored media for advertisers. These journals were militant critics of the social as well as the religious scene. Holland hoped to adapt this militancy to the literary monthly and to express it in less sectarian tones.[3]

Ever since his days on the *Springfield Republican*, where he had brought a social and moral accent to a newspaper press that had previously spoken largely in terms of politics and "general intelligence," Holland had conceived his life's mission in evangelical terms. The success of his Titcomb *Letters* and of his poems and novels, with their omnipresent religious sentiment, had confirmed in his heart the sense of a mission to the earnest people of America. In *Scribner's* he was simply mounting a higher platform from which to deliver his sermons.[4]

It was a moralist in his prime who ascended this rostrum. At fifty-one, Holland was a handsome, swarthy, six-foot figure with bright, dark eyes, a black mustache, and straight black hair that he wore long. A sonorous voice emphasized his aspect of seriousness and power. His egregious vanity was actually a childlike appetite for approbation, developed during his early years of poverty and obscurity. In a life "so full of loves and friends and successes," his sturdy Puritanism had mellowed year by year, and it thawed still further under the influence of the aesthetic, pure-spirited Richard Watson Gilder and the trusted friendship of Roswell Smith. The goads of critics and the sneers of sophisticates tortured him continually, but many New York artists and writers came to esteem him for the genuine aura of good will that, shining through his homilies, had long endeared him to his readers. On his part, the Yankee editor felt increasingly at home among the cultured of the metropolis. His view remained evangelical, but his horizon widened.[5]

The central pulpit from which he delivered his lay sermons through eleven years was his editorial department, "Topics of the Time." Its preparation was his principal and most delightful chore, for it brought him closest to his responsive readers.[6] There was no hint of charm or humor in his direct prose style, unadorned by illustration or metaphor, and his tone at times became downright truculent as he warmed to his preaching. He was one-sided in argument, but he was cogent and effective, for he always spoke out of conviction.

Holland's faith was simple and social. He believed in the necessity of Christ for the atonement of a person's sins and rescue from depravity, but he seldom spoke of salvation, nearly always of the formation of character and the good life. Christianity to him was the clue to personal happiness, the bond of human brotherhood, and the fount of civilization. His constant theme was that religion should be made more personal and less institutional, more an affair of the heart and less of the head. Such beliefs provided a firm base for a social Christianity. With few doctrinal barriers to confine it, Holland's religious outlook broadened in the latitudinarian urban environment. Ever-increasing tolerance marked the course of *Scribner's* through the eleven years of Holland's editorial rule.[7]

"When you run out of subjects, just attack the Romanists." The book reviewer in the first issue of *Scribner's* who quoted this advice of the old preacher to the young one did so only to scoff, but Holland made a militantly Protestant assault on the papacy in the same number of the magazine. His editorial "Papa and the Dogma" hailed the end of the pope's temporal reign and exulted that Europe was now ruled by Protestant powers made strong by "freedom from priestly domination," while the Catholic Church "has so sucked the life and manhood out of the other States, that they all sink into second and third rate powers." The anti-Catholic theme persisted through the early volumes of *Scribner's*, both in editorials and in articles, and even spilled over to its fiction; the subject of a short story called "Shane Finagle's

Station" in August 1872 was an Irish priest's cynical manipulation of his ignorant flock.

These assults on Catholicism diminished after 1875. Holland may have been learning not to antagonize a potential audience, but there is also evidence that he was overcoming his own prejudices in this and other respects. By 1878 the *Boston Pilot*, a Catholic weekly, could call the midwinter number of *Scribner's* "without qualification, the finest specimen of magazine-making ever issued."[8] Holland's publication took an unprecedentedly friendly tone toward a Catholic institution in 1880, when it included Georgetown College (later University) at Washington, D.C., in a series of articles on American centers of higher education. The magazine had moved noticeably toward its position of a few years later when it would champion the Catholic population against nativist discrimination.

If Holland at first criticized a church that interfered too much, he felt, between Christ and humans, he was equally bitter toward those who questioned the divinity of Jesus. Looking with a suspicious eye toward New England, he pounced on every manifestation of Unitarianism or lingering transcendentalism. "The dilettantism of Concord and Cambridge—the whole sloppy smash of philosophy, religion, infidelity and what not that emanates from Emerson and his worshippers is the abomination of my soul."[9] He despised Henry David Thoreau as the "Saint" of this infidel religion who, "instead of . . . striving with a great band of Christian workers to lift the multitude out of vice and crime and misery, refused to pay his poll-tax, and went out to see how little a man could live on, amusing himself, meanwhile, by poking around a pond."[10]

This stern front toward nonevangelical beliefs also softened with the years. As early as 1875 Holland spoke respectfully of Ralph Waldo Emerson in an editorial, and in February 1879 the Sage of Concord held the place of honor in the magazine's frontispiece. In 1878 *Scribner's* featured excerpts from the journals of Thoreau. Before the end of the decade Holland could assert that all lovers of truth, whatever their beliefs, should love and respect one another, for "truth is one, and . . . those who are earnestly after it, whether they deny Christianity or profess it . . . belong together, in one great sympathetic brotherhood of affection and pursuit."[11] By this time some of Holland's best friends were agnostics, although his own faith was as strong as ever.

Sects that tampered with the marriage relationship were outside the limits of Holland's tolerance. When Gilder visited a Shaker settlement and wrote a disparaging account of its celibate life, the magazine received a hot protest from the Shaker leader, but Holland brusquely advised the Shakers to "pair off, and go to separate house-keeping."[12] *Scribner's* also made the polygamy of the Mormons a repeated target.

With these exceptions, however, Holland's views were reaching a breadth that shocked and alienated some of his readers. The disaffection stemmed mostly from his war on sectarianism. Sects, he argued, existed "entirely in the minds of men" and not in the words of Christ. The doctor had anticipated remonstrances. "I have no sentiments of respect for the New York Grundies in religion," he wrote Smith when they were planning the magazine, "and I could not manifest any. I shall expect and intend to offend them."[13]

Seeds of distrust among the orthodox were planted in the very first number of *Scribner's* with the Reverend W. C. Wilkinson's protest against "The Bondage of the Pulpit," a charge concluded three months later in a second essay. These articles, said the *Methodist Recorder*, were more talked about than any that had appeared in the magazine world in eighteen months.[14] The articles indicted the clergy for lack of moral courage, manifested in an unseemly deference to their congregations and a reticence in rebuking sin.

Protests sprouted in 1873 when an anonymous minister charged in *Scribner's* that Protestant churches permitted no real freedom of thought or conscience; once bound to a denomination, the preacher dared not overstep the doctrine of the prescribed creed. The heresy-hunting religious press gave tongue. The *Christian Advocate* lamented that no American magazine met the requirements of evangelical Protestantism; its "faint hopes that *Scribner's* might answer to this felt want" had been disappointed.[15]

Scribner's next touched on clerical nerves already tense from the challenge of Darwinism to orthodox Christianity, when in three long-winded articles the Reverend Augustus Blauvelt warned that the clergy were mending insignificant doctrinal fences while a rising tide of unbelief washed at the foundations of the Christian faith. He admonished the church to drop its ineffectual theological defense and meet the challenge of naturalism on scientific grounds. This was not at all Holland's own view, of course, but he aggravated the anguish of his doctrinaire critics by endorsing Blauvelt's assertion that infidel truth was preferable to orthodox error and by declaring: "We fritter away our energies and waste our substance in building costly churches for the rich, in multiplying sects and . . . aping the wretched religious fooleries of the Old World."[16]

An anonymous writer in the New York *Observer*, the leading Presbyterian weekly, promptly accused *Scribner's Monthly* of hostility to Christianity itself. An unsigned article in the Baptist *Watchman and Observer* argued that *Scribner's* had been guilty of a breach of trust with its subscribers, who therefore had a right to a change in its management and to insist "that there should be placed upon its staff at least one man in whom the churches had confidence." Otherwise, the anonymous critic predicted, there would be a "stampede" of subscribers away from the magazine, "and there ought to be."[17]

But the editor of the *Watchman* disavowed the censures of his contributor, combining apology with words of praise which showed that the embattled Holland still bore the hopes of many Christians: "We count it a grand thing that a great popular magazine is trying to give its readers something worth thinking about, something that challenges a deeper interest and more vigorous thought than the love stories and the pictorial pages which make up the main staple of like periodicals. . . . As for ourselves we thank God for the many qualities in *Scribner's* magazine that, in our opinion, make it to be the purest, safest and best of all these monthly periodicals."[18]

Holland enjoyed his role as champion of religious freedom, and in the ensuing years frequently aligned himself with rebels of the cloth. In 1874, defending the eloquent preacher David Swing against charges of heresy, he cried, "Orthodoxy saves nobody; Christian love and Christian character save anybody." Two years later Blauvelt returned to the lists in *Scribner's* with a charge against "Protestant Vaticanism" (September 1876), his specification being that critics of Sabbatarianism within the evangelical churches were being throttled. For this article Blauvelt was suspended from his ministerial office by the Dutch Reformed classis, to which action Holland responded in an editorial: "We know of no reason why a theological dogma is any more sacred than a political dogma." (Since Holland was a firm Sabbatarian, his defense of Blauvelt was a measure of his tolerance.) When a Presbyterian minister was similarly dismissed from his pulpit for unorthodox views, Holland thundered that the theological "machine" that ousted such dissenters should be smashed.[19]

What gave a sense of urgency to Holland's efforts to place Christianity on broader ground was the challenge to religion presented by science and scholarship in these years. Charles Darwin's *The Descent of Man* reached the United States in the first year of publication for *Scribner's Monthly*. It destroyed any illusion that the children of Adam might be excepted from the evolutionary chain and thus directly controverted the doctrine of special creation. The ensuing conflict between scientists and theologians has been too thoroughly explored to demand review here. The pages of *Scribner's* reflected the passions that this hotly contested theory produced, but because Holland disregarded dogma, neither he nor his magazine was seriously shaken by the struggle. He permitted his clerical friends to view the new dictum of science with alarm in his columns or to see in it fresh evidence of God's grand design, while he continued to concern himself with a wider application of the Christian message. It is notable that writers in *Scribner's Monthly* after 1875—like Theodore T. Munger, who was to be a shining light of the "New Theology"—tended toward Holland's cheerful view.

Holland had an equally relaxed attitude toward the higher criticism that challenged the historical accuracy of the Bible. The main struggle in this field was to come in the 1880s, but in the early years of *Scribner's*, ecclesiastics were already embattled over the writings of David Friedrich Strauss and Joseph Ernest Renan, Continental thinkers who not only rejected the gospel as history but contended that Jesus was no more than a remarkable human being. Holland printed three sophistic articles by the ubiquitous Blauvelt, who tried to put the divinity of Christ on scientific grounds, and a counterargument by Lyman H. Atwater (February 1874), who argued against making belief an intellectual rather than a moral exercise. Unperturbed by the controversy, Holland calmly remarked, "There is a great deal of irrational reverence for the Bible." Those who saw God in it and nowhere else made it a sort of "fetich."[20]

To Holland, then, the crisis in religion was to be met not on the arid theological heights but on the plain of day-to-day living and practical ministry. He argued against the system of pew ownership, which discouraged the lowly from church attendance. He argued for more forceful preaching of the gospel message. *Scribner's* praised Henry Ward Beecher, Holland's old friend, on several occasions, defended him—although "coarsely blamed" for its stand—during the notorious Tilton adultery affair, and hailed his "exoneration" as the redemption of one of the country's greatest men. Holland also saluted the popular triumphs of the evangelists Dwight L. Moody and Ira D. Sankey.[21] Theological dispute largely disappeared from *Scribner's* in Holland's later years as editor, but the evangelical tone did not.

As confident a moralist as Holland might have hesitated to essay a critique of American society had he foreseen the myriad and unprecedented nature of the problems that arose in the 1870s. North and South were still not reconciled; the West had yet to be settled and governed. A new industrial order was transforming an agrarian nation, threatening old individualistic values, creating new wealth that bred corruption in both business and government as well as new pockets of poverty that poisoned the growing cities. New immigrants had to be assimilated. The worst panic and depression in the country's history scarred the decade and brought with it the onset of industrial violence on a major scale. And the religion that, diverse as it was, had provided the basis for cultural unity, was under challenge.

Holland's editorials, as well as articles in his magazine, engaged all of these problems, and while the editor was sometimes baffled to the point of despair, the range and force of his critique brought a new dimension to the popular periodical. The tone of uplift persisted through all the evils of the time and helped the magazine to keep its original subscribers and add new ones.

Besides developing a growing liberalism, Holland also had sound editorial instincts. Circumstances had helped to push *Scribner's* toward a more nationalist and distinctively American outlook, but Holland and his associates were quick to exert leadership in this direction, too, thus doing their part in trying to establish cultural unity.

On matters of personal conduct Holland was sure of his ground, and his confident criticism of manners and morals was a constant element in his editorials. His favorite subjects were temperance and the position of women. He proclaimed temperance to be the most important issue before the American people. "O Heaven! for one generation of clean and unpolluted men!— men whose veins are not fed with fire." He did not favor prohibition—that would only stamp the temperance movement with "the stigma of fanaticism." He did not regard social drinkers as evil men; he quarreled with them only because they set a bad example for the less temperate and because they were reluctant to take part in the temperance crusade. When moderate drinkers did take part in the great temperance drive of the late 1870s, Holland admonished abstainers to refrain from sulking and to accept their help.[22]

The Yankee editor, however, brought by his position into sophisticated circles, was distressed by the accepted practice of serving wine at social gatherings. "People in the country, in the ordinary walks of life, have no conception of the despotic character of this idea." Practicing what he preached, Holland gave nonalcoholic receptions at his Murray Hill home on Park Avenue, to the amazement of literati like the poet Richard Henry Stoddard who wandered around muttering, "Good heavens, boys, where's the whiskey!"[23] Throughout his life in New York, Holland endured a certain amount of social martyrdom because of his teetotal habits.

To end social drinking, Holland summoned the country's greatest moral force. Women, he said, could do more than legislators and reformers to make the nation temperate, and "they shall have *Scribner's Monthly* to help them."[24] The women he summoned as partners were, of course, the guardians of morals and character within the home, not that small minority of feminists who were renewing their quest for civil, economic, and social equality. In the smugness and speciousness of its arguments against women's suffrage, *Scribner's* was representative of its time. Its position was summed up by one woman contributor who asserted that America offered limitless opportunity for woman to become "all for which her nature and instincts fit her." There was no room for "that offensive weed known as woman's rights in this garden where she has no wrongs, except those common to our common humanity."[25] It is indicative of Holland's vehemence on the subject that, despite his tolerence of diverse opinions even in religion, no writer in *Scribner's* ever dissented from the editor's views on the subordinate political and economic status of women.

Scribner's did take a favorable view of higher education for women, provided that the curriculum was suited to their special role as future goddesses of the household. There were favorable articles on Vassar and Smith colleges. Holland, however, was uneasy about the abnormal confinement of girls to their own society, a practice that bred "diseases" of body and imagination. He advised Smith College to put its students in family units with a professor and his wife at the head of the household.[26]

Holland was aware that the nearest approach to an ideal society—as he defined it—was to be found in rural communities. Consequently he thought it one of the great evils of the times that youthful and energetic country people were abandoning farm life for the novel challenges and opportunities of the city. As this trend continued in the 1870s, he made the development of a healthier and more vital rural life one of his chief editorial aims. Realizing that loneliness prompted young people to push into the cities, and impressed by his observations of European farm organization, he advocated that future settlement be planned to center around farm villages.[27] Meanwhile, everything possible should be done to make existing communities more attractive. In an editorial of September 1876, he noted with gratification the formation "here and there" of village improvement societies, which not only worked toward a better physical environment but which could also serve as agents of culture by stimulating the growth of lyceums, reading clubs, and libraries.

This editorial brought so many requests for information that Holland commissioned Colonel George E. Waring, a public-spirited sanitary engineer (and creator of New York City's "white wings," street sweepers in white uniforms), to write a series of articles in 1877 on village improvement. Describing practical measures for drainage and beautification, Waring presented illustrations of model village layouts, one picturing an imaginary new settlement and another a settled farm region adapted to the village idea. Holland estimated that 1,000 villages would be stirred by these papers and his own editorials to form improvement societies, a prospect that seemed to him "one of the most encouraging and delightful in the social and domestic history of the time." He visualized the construction of "parks, fences, fountains—no end of things."[28] He proposed that young people form clubs for reading, the presentation of papers, musical performances, and the exhibition of local works of art. Meanwhile the department, "Home and Society," aimed especially at housewives, published hints for literary and sewing clubs, musicals, dances, and socials, and for the exchange of books where libraries were lacking.

From time to time Holland was pleased to note a response to his campaign. In November 1877 he said that he had direct testimony that many of the projects proposed by *Scribner's* had been taken up in "a great many towns throughout the length and breadth of the land." In fact, the response must have been quite limited; *Scribner's* hastened to note any concrete evidence that its proposals were taking hold, but there are few such notices. By December 1878 Holland had to admit that most rural communities remained "socially dead." But he was proud of his magazine's leadership in the effort to revitalize country life. He felt in 1880 that no editorial he had ever written had been so "prolific of beneficent results" as his original 1876 essay on village improvement.[29]

The industrial-urban environment was forcing Holland to deal with a more complex set of problems. Keeping its promise to consider sociological questions, *Scribner's* in its first number presented Mary E. Dodge's account of a visit to the New York Juvenile Asylum. In April 1871 there was a more comprehensive article on the evils of child labor, and still later (April 1875) there was an account of the trades injurious to workers' health, with a recommendation for closer public regulation.

While such obvious evils unmistakably violated the canons of

Holland's social Christianity, other aspects of the urban order were less susceptible to simple moral judgments. The work of the American Social Science Association, formed in 1865 with the object of discovering and applying "the immutable laws governing man in his social relations," offered an apparently more expert approach to these complex problems.[30] Although claiming to be scientific in its methods, the Association was strongly reformist in tone, and Holland found its studies an appropriate reinforcement of his private observations. Announcing in 1874 that it would concern itself with the progress of the infant social science, *Scribner's* frequently published articles and editorials that paralleled the program of the Association. Thus, when the social scientists made a special study of urban housing, an article in *Scribner's* described the financing of homes in Philadelphia through building and loan societies. The Association's concern with the care of the insane was reflected in two separate articles (September 1876 and February 1879), while topics such as prison reform, crime prevention, and pauperism were discussed in the magazine after they had appeared on the social science agenda.[31]

When he considered immigration, Holland allowed prejudice to triumph over both social science and his usual moral outlook. It was probably his anti-Catholic bias that prompted his hostility to the Irish, the dominant element at that time in the immigrant invasion. In "Bric-à-Brac," the magazine's humor department, the ignorance of the unassimilated Irish was constantly lampooned. Thus Paddy, a battered stovepipe hat on his head and his worldly belongings bundled under his arm, was pictured before a sign that read, "Pat. Agency Up Stairs," and was made to remark, "That's a quare name onyhow—I wondher if he's a Tipperary man."[32] Other contributors were less good-tempered, especially when addressing the inadequacy of the "barbarian" Irish as household servants.

The monthly's more sympathetic attitude toward Chinese immigrants was a reflex of its antipathy toward the Irish and labor unions, i.e., the Chinese appeared to have advantages as household servants and as strikebreakers. Then West Coast contributors were heard from, disputing the usefulness of the Chinese for these or any other purposes and urging their exclusion. Holland was reduced to acknowledging that "we want more light on the subject." He had been reminded that his was indeed a national audience.[33]

Holland addressed the central problem of the new industrial era, the conflict between capital and labor, with less prejudice. In fact, on this subject he frequently allowed his good heart and moral fervor to override his respect for the "science" of economics. *Scribner's* usually approved the classical economic "laws," including the iron law of wages. In the aftermath of the violent railroad strikes of 1877, Holland granted wage earners the abstract right to strike but argued that such a step was always useless and sometimes criminal, because labor would "always command its value—no more, no less." In October 1878 William Graham Sumner indicted socialism in the pages of *Scribner's*, championing the individualistic virtues of self-denial, thrift, and industry, and citing poverty and misery as the inevitable penalties of shiftlessness, extravagance, intemperance, and imprudence; when a reader wrote to complain, Holland took Sumner's side.[34]

But Holland recognized that strikes and unions were symptoms of a real discontent, and his magazine was no mere apologist for capitalism. As early as April 1871, an article surveying the strife in the anthracite coal fields concluded that monopolization of rail lines by a few producers was primarily to blame. In April 1873, a Holland editorial pointed to the giant railroad corporations and "their monopolies and combinations" as one of the great wrongs confronting the nation. On another occasion, the editor placed the onus of industrial peace on the capitalists; the Astors, Stewarts, Vanderbilts and Drews, he said, "bear mainly in their hands the responsibility of whatever difficulties may hereafter arise between wealth and labor in the United States."[35]

Holland said whatever he wanted in his "Topics," and when he was in the mood to disregard orthodox economic doctrine, he could fire off some startling proposals. In October 1877 he was in such a mood: "There is no question that the popular doctrine that the supply is always regulated by the demand, and that demand will always elicit supply, does not work with the requisite nicety or sensitiveness." He proposed that free enterprise give way to "regulated production" based on government reports of industrial capacity and estimates of annual demand.

At times *Scribner's* used language foreshadowing the muckraking era of a generation later, particularly when attacking corporate power and its abuse. In the second of two articles on life insurance (July 1877) Julius Wilcox assailed the fraud, autocratic control, and incompetence that had ruined most insurance companies and their policyholders. In October 1878 Holland wrote: "Few people are aware of the overshadowing power of corporations in this country." The "soulless" character of these giant organizations resulted in their using people like machines. In the following year Edmund C. Stedman, who worked at a brokerage when he was not writing essays and poetry, told the readers of *Scribner's* that the great capitalists had to be checked. "By their monstrous faculty of accumulation they gradually manage our governments, oppress . . . the public at large, build up a new feudalism."[36]

A moralist like Holland had no use for speculation. He denounced Wall Street as the worst gambling hell in the country. Holland's novel, "Sevenoaks," serialized in *Scribner's* during 1875, portrayed a scheming financier and oil speculator who was recognized as a fictional counterpart of Jim Fisk and who, like Fisk, came to a disastrous end.[37]

Looking back in the last year of his life over a decade of social upheaval, Holland, who had been willing to use the language of economics when it suited his purpose, was not ready to accept its dogmas as a substitute for moral responsibility. He saw labor unions, the Granger movement, cooperative experiments, and the antimonopoly party as signs of the struggle of the poor to win a better life. If they were denied recognition, Holland warned, they would "make the future a troubled and terrible one for our children and our children's children."[38]

Politics and government, like society, were in Holland's view subject to relatively simple moral standards. Morality was more important to a democratic electorate and its governors than wisdom; Abraham Lincoln had shown what heart and conscience rather than extraordinary intelligence could do. (One wonders how many of Holland's generation underrated Lincoln's intelligence because they preferred a moral interpretation of history.) In his first year as editor Holland was optimistic about his country. After all, the Americans, being a naturally religious people—

in contrast to the immoral French—were fit material for a republic.[39]

Disenchantment soon set in. The depredations of the Tweed Ring showed there was "moral rottenness in every quarter" of New York City. In Washington, President Ulysses S. Grant had been "used" by bad men, and he had been "entirely ready to be used." Political standards would be low until heads of government were chosen for their character as Christian gentlemen, and by this criterion there had not been a first-rate man in the presidential chair since John Quincy Adams.[40] The electorate had been ready to share in the dishonesty of politicians, through patronage and participation in shady financial deals. "The people of America," the editor concluded, "richly deserve the infliction of all the evils from which they suffer."[41]

Scribner's was nonpartisan in politics—morality had to be dispensed evenhandedly. Morality meant, among other things, sound money, and Holland found it hard to acknowledge that there were honest men in the South and the West who favored greenbacks or free silver. On the tariff issue, Horace Bushnell in the *Scribner's* of July 1871 took a mildly protectionist stand, but in 1877 Holland declared that protectionism was "played out" and came out solidly for a tariff for revenue only.[42]

But sound moral measures could not be expected from a Congress of "low-toned" men. Frequent editorial denunciations of the nation's lawmakers were climaxed in September 1878 when Holland attacked "The Terrible Congress" while Gilder in "The Old Cabinet" expressed his horror in verse:

> A sound of jackals ravening to and fro.
> Great God! And has it come to this at last!—
>   Such noise, such stench, where once, not long ago,
>   Clay's lightning flashed, and Webster's thunder rolled.

Along with most reformers of this era, *Scribner's* seized on reform of the civil service as the best hope for purifying the nation's politics. Editorials frequently urged adoption of the merit system for appointment and promotion, and the columns of the magazine featured a number of articles on the evils of the patronage system and the benefits of civil service reform. Holland realized that such reform was no panacea for the national ills, but he thought it was "the one medicine, at present, most needed."[43]

While *Scribner's Monthly* was only one of many editorial voices supporting the merit system, its record as advocate of North-South reconciliation was more distinctive. Sympathetic interpretation of the postwar South had begun in the pages of the *Nation*, the *Galaxy*, and *Lippincott's*, but it was *Scribner's* that most effectively dramatized the condition and prospects of the late Confederacy and spoke most influentially for its full partnership in the Union.[44]

Holland had not always been amicably disposed toward the former rebels. His short tenure as teacher and administrator in southern schools had given him some tolerance for the South's view of slavery, and in the years before the war he was unfriendly to the abolitionists. But he could not condone disunion. Writing privately in 1868, he termed the South "as thoroughly rebel today as it ever was. We ought to have hanged every leader, and confiscated property enough to pay the national debt." The South had learned nothing, he said, except contempt for those too weak to administer fit punishment for treason.[45]

No hint of this uncompromising view ever appeared in *Scribner's Monthly*. On the contrary, the magazine's earliest references to the South were in terms of tolerance and amity. The passage of time may have mellowed Holland's outlook on the rebels, but perhaps a more potent factor was his new responsibility as editor of a periodical that aimed to win a national audience. The shrewd Smith probably helped to influence this adjustment of vision, for it was he who inspired the magazine's first great project for interpreting the South to the country.

A series of twelve articles collectively entitled "The Great South" was written at Smith's suggestion and printed in 1873 and 1874; it sealed the magazine's bond of sympathy and mutual interest with the former Confederacy. It was a logical extension of the effort to achieve a national outlook already reflected in the descriptive accounts of the West that *Scribner's* had published. Although "The Great South" was not the most penetrating analysis of postwar Dixie to appear in print, its popular style and lavish illustration made it the most striking. With characteristic thoroughness, Smith spent $30,000 to send an expedition through the southern states with the object of portraying their "Life, Condition and Resources." Those states, said the publisher's announcement, were like another country to the North and West, so that "in painting the South to itself, and giving it a fair showing for its own satisfaction, we open a most interesting page to the whole country, and reveal our people at once to themselves and to one another."[46]

The author of the series was Edward King, an engaging young man of less than twenty-five, who was already a veteran journalist. Holland had known him as a boy in Springfield, Massachusetts, where he went to work for Samuel Bowles's *Springfield Republican*. Since then he had reported the Franco-Prussian War and the siege of the Commune in Paris, and when *Scribner's* hired him, he was the star correspondent of the *Boston Journal*.[47] With King traveled J. Wells Champney, already famous as "Champ" for his drawings in genre. Champney made over 400 sketches, while other well-known artists aided occasionally in the depiction of the journey.[48]

The expedition began at Sedalia, Missouri, where a large crowd watched King, Champney, and their aides embark in a luxurious hotel car on a special train of the Missouri, Kansas, and Topeka Railroad. Threading through cotton upland and delta country, through Florida swamps and Virginia tobacco land, visiting the new industrial belt of the Piedmont, penetrating into mountain regions where few northern men had ventured, the party aroused enormous interest. Arriving in a Tennessee mountain town on horseback, with baggage wagons trailing behind, they were thought to be a circus. When their tour was finished, having taken all of 1873 and the spring and summer of 1874, they had visited nearly every city and town of importance in the South and had traveled 25,000 miles, of which 1,000 had been covered in the saddle. When King's final article ran in December 1874, "The Great South" had filled more than forty pages a month in fourteen issues of the magazine and had been illustrated with more than 430 engravings.[49]

The response in the South was immediate and warm. As soon as the project was announced, offers to put information at King's disposal began to pour into the office of the magazine—a valuable complement to the eyewitness reports, as many of the South's libraries and commercial organizations had been broken up or destroyed by the war. While the articles won critical acclaim in all sections, the editors had "reason to know that the work has given great satisfaction to the region represented." King wrote back that *Scribner's Monthly* was gaining rapidly in southern readers. "In several towns that we have visited the sale is *one to every eighty or eighty-five inhabitants.*"[50]

This success encouraged *Scribner's* to extend its role as champion of sectional reconciliation, and a fortunate by-product of the "Great South" expedition hastened the process. Reaching New Orleans, King discovered George Washington Cable and induced him to send his exotic stories of the Creoles to *Scribner's*. These opened the way for a flood of local-color fiction from the South to the magazine.[51]

Holland used editorials to denounce carpetbag rule, deplore the perversion of military government to force the South to the radical political line, and salute President Rutherford B. Hayes for his removal of troops from the South. Southern views began to appear in contributions to the magazine. W. H. Ruffner, predicting that General Benjamin Butler's proposed civil rights bill would destroy public education in the South, explained that the moral state of blacks made them unfit to associate with white children.[52] The editors were cautious, though, in testing northern opinion. When "A Piece of Secret History," which eulogized General Robert E. Lee, was published in February 1876, they appended this note: "We publish the foregoing . . . in the language of sectional friendliness in which it reaches us. It will show, at least, how truly and earnestly one side regards as a pure patriot him whom the other side looks upon with condemnation, and will hardly fail to win sympathetic consideration for feelings and motives which opponents are too apt to ignore." Such tolerance was bound to win southern approval. The *Charleston News and Courier* informed its readers that *Scribner's* was not only superior to other magazines in style, variety, and thoroughness, but that it paid particular attention to southern life.[53]

But Holland did not hesitate to subject his new friends to the kind of social criticism that he addressed to his own section.

Indignant over the lawless cruelty to blacks that flared in the late 1870s, he wrote: "We wonder if the South knows how hard it is making it for its friends and those who would think well of its spirit and society." He called on the "better South" to assert itself. This editorial (June 1879) provoked "much intemperate railing" at the magazine.[54] Southerners also protested when Henry King in "A Year of the Exodus in Kansas" (June 1880) blamed conditions in Dixie for the emigration of 20,000 to 30,000 blacks. King told his critics that he had talked with the freedmen and that it was was idle to suppose they had fled without good cause.[55]

But on the whole, good will prevailed between *Scribner's* and the South, and the return of the southern tier into the living pattern of the states seemed to make Holland and his staff more aware of the grand mosaic of the nation they were addressing. As the centenary of the republic approached, Holland glowed with sentiment over the restored Union.[56] The editors in 1875 proclaimed that they were trying to make "an American magazine." Henceforth they would rely on American novels instead of British "society stories," and in their "philosophical and speculative discussion," too, "all the questions of the time . . . shall be treated from the American standpoint."[57] The new policy was apparent in the January 1876 number, which contained first installments on two historical essays, John F. Miner's "New York in the Revolution" and John Vance Cheney's "Revolutionary Letters"; Horace E. Scudder's "Cupid and Mars," a short story on the siege of Boston; a continuation of Bret Harte's novel, "Gabriel Conroy"; and the beginning of Edward Everett Hale's "Philip Nolan's Friends," a chronicle of early Louisiana.

As noted earlier, the policy of using American novels was to a large extent forced on *Scribner's* by the firm grip of competitors, notably *Harper's*, on leading English novelists. Nevertheless, the new policy did seem to give *Scribner's* a new buoyancy and interest, while Holland himself, who had been almost in despair at the state of the American nation and society, regained his optimism and hailed the centennial year as time of fresh departure toward a nobler future.[58]

At the close of the decade, and nearing the close of his life, Holland could feel that he had made good on his promise to make *Scribner's* a blunt critic of American life. At the end of its first year his magazine had already distinguished itself from its competitors, said the *Buffalo Courier*, by its "effective, aggressive campaigning in behalf of the good, the pure, and the true." In 1872 the *Cleveland Leader* noted that *Scribner's* had "a progressive, earnest spirit in all its editorial departments, which has had an important influence on other American magazines."[59]

Comparative content analysis supports such judgments (Tables 1 and 2). In 1871, the first calendar year of its existence, *Scribner's* devoted nearly 20 percent of its space to the problems of religion, education, women, manners, and similar sociological themes, while *Harper's* in the same year was spending only 1.5 percent of its pages on such topics. By 1880 *Scribner's* had broadened its

TABLE 1. Comparative Content Analysis of *Scribner's Monthly* and *Harper's Monthly*, 1871

Editorial Features	Scribner's	Harper's
Fiction	26	33
Travel and adventure	13	19
Science	9	10
Education	7	0.5
Fine arts	6	2
Literary essays and criticism	5	4
Public affairs	4	5
Religion	4	1
Editorial departments not otherwise classified[a]	4	3
History and biography	3	13
Verse	3	1
Women	3	0
Social life and manners	3	0
Social problems	2	0
Nature	2	0
Humor and entertainment	1	5.5
Miscellaneous	5	3

NOTE. Data are given as the percentage of space devoted to each editorial category. The percentages are based on a page count of the February, May, August, and November issues of each magazine, a cross-section that allows for seasonal variation. Where more than one category is represented by an article, a proportionate division is made. Illustrations are included in the categories to which they pertain.

[a]Principally "The Old Cabinet" and "Home and Society."

TABLE 2. Comparative Content Analysis of *Scribner's Monthly* and *Harper's Monthly*, 1880

Editorial Features	Scribner's	Harper's
History and biography	28	6
Fiction	15	34
Literary essays and criticism	10	5
Travel and adventure	6	27
Fine arts	8	4
Social life and manners	6	1
Public affairs	5	3
Science	4	0
Humor and entertainment	3	2
Theater	2	0
Editorial	2	4
Verse	2	2
Religion	2	0
Decorative arts	2	4
Nature	1	3
Education	0	1
Music	0	3
Miscellaneous	4	1

NOTE. Data are given as the percentage of space devoted to each editorial category. See the NOTE to Table 1.

coverage of literature and the arts and had developed a taste for elaborate, illustrated history and biography; these features had encroached on the space available for sociological topics, which now occupied only 8 percent of its columns. Still, this was four times as much coverage as *Harper's* gave these subjects in 1880. Public affairs occupied 5 percent of reading space in *Scribner's* that year, only 3 percent in *Harper's*. Qualitatively, the difference was even more striking. Holland's moral standard set the tone for his whole magazine, and *Harper's* offered nothing comparable to the blunt critique of public life and private morals that Holland attempted in his editorials.

So *Scribner's Monthly* had good grounds for its editor's contention that it had added a new function to the role of the popular literary periodical. *Harper's* virtually admitted this distinction in 1881 when it boasted that it had become "monarch of the monthlies" by giving its readers entertaining fare "without prosing, or preaching, or any kind of namby-pamby."[60] Its young competitor, however, had not found its more earnest pretentions an impediment to winning popular approval. By 1880 *Scribner's Monthly* had passed the 100,000 mark in circulation and was pressing the "monarch" ever more closely.[61]

NOTES

1. Holland to Charles Scribner, July 26, 1869, SC.
2. Ibid., and Robert Underwood Johnson, *Remembered Yesterdays* (Boston, 1923), 113.
3. Frank Luther Mott, *A History of American Magazines*, 5 vols. (Cambridge, Mass., 1930–68), 3:63–89, and Frank S. Presbrey, *The History and Development of Advertising* (Garden City, N.Y., 1929), 281–82.
4. Edward Eggleston, "Josiah Gilbert Holland," Dec. 1881, and L. Frank Tooker, *The Joys and Tribulations of an Editor* (New York, 1924), 27.
5. Holland to Scribner, July 26, 1869, SC; Johnson, *Remembered Yesterdays*, 85; Eggleston, "Josiah Gilbert Holland"; H. H. Boyeson, *Literary and Social Silhouettes* (New York, 1894), 104–5; *New York Tribune*, Oct. 23, 1881. Charles A. Dana of the *New York Sun* was perhaps Holland's most merciless critic.
6. Editorial, Nov. 1880.
7. Religion, Holland said in an editorial of Feb. 1877, "consists of love to God and love to man, and has its final result and grand consummation in character." For other editorials representative of Holland's faith, see the issues of Mar. 1875 and Feb. and May 1876.
8. Quoted in advertising section, Mar. 1878, p. 7.
9. Holland to Scribner, Feb. 20, 1870, SC.
10. Editorial, July 1871.
11. Editorial, Apr. 1879.
12. Editorial, Jan. 1874.
13. Holland to Smith, n.d. [Oct. 1869], quoted in Smith to Scribner, Oct. 15, 1869, SC; Mrs. H. M. Plunkett, *Josiah Gilbert Holland* (New York, 1894), 110.
14. Quoted in advertising section, Dec. 1871, p. 2.
15. Quoted in editorial, Sept. 1873.
16. Blauvelt: Aug., Sept., and Oct. 1873; editorial, Sept. 1873.
17. Editorials, Nov. and Dec. 1873.
18. Quoted in editorial, Feb. 1874.
19. Editorials, Aug. 1874 and Feb. and Aug. 1877.
20. Editorial, May 1875; Blauvelt: Mar. 1873, Apr. 1874, and Feb. 1875.
21. Editorial on pews, Jan. 1873; on Beecher, Oct. 1874 and Sept. 1875; on Moody and Sankey, Nov. 1875 and Apr. 1876.
22. Editorials, Apr. 1871 and July 1877.

23. Editorial, Mar. 1879, and Johnson, *Remembered Yesterdays*, 90.

24. Editorial, Jan. 1871.

25. Mrs. M. E. W. Sherwood, "What Has America Done for Women?" July 1873.

26. Editorial, Oct. 1873; Vassar, Aug. 1871; Smith, May 1877.

27. See, e.g., editorials, June 1872 and Apr. 1875.

28. Editorial, May 1877.

29. Editorial, Oct. 1880.

30. *Journal of Social Science*, 1 (June 1869):2–5.

31. An editorial of Feb. 1874 announced that such social science information that would be of interest to readers "will be briefly laid before them from month to month, adding another class of topics to those hitherto presented in these pages."

32. Cartoon, Dec. 1875.

33. Editorial, Jan. 1877.

34. Editorial, Dec. 1878.

35. Editorial, Mar. 1872.

36. "Aerial Navigation," Feb. 1879. Stedman hoped that aviation would break the railroad "monopoly."

37. H. H. Peckham, *Josiah Gilbert Holland in Relation to His Times* (Philadelphia, 1940), 150–51.

38. Editorial, July 1881.

39. Editorial, June 1871, and Plunkett, *Holland*, 52–53.

40. This statement evidently reflected disillusionment with Lincoln, probably induced by Colonel Ward Lamon's *The Life of Abraham Lincoln*. This book, published in 1872, authoritatively disputed Holland's contention that Lincoln was a practicing Christian. See David Donald, *Lincoln's Herndon* (New York, 1948), 269–70, for Holland's denunciation of Lamon's book, which nevertheless seems to have left its impression.

41. Editorial, Nov. 1875. See also editorials, Dec. 1871, Apr. 1872, Apr. 1873, and Feb. and May 1874.

42. Editorial on tariff, Dec. 1877; on sound money, Mar., May, and Nov. 1878.

43. Editorial, May 1881.

44. Mott, *Magazines,* 3:47–49, and Paul H. Buck, *The Road to Reunion, 1865–1900* (Boston, 1937), 221–23.

45. Holland to Scribner, Aug. 16, 1868, SC.

46. Publishers' department, Jan. 1873, p. 5; editorial, Dec. 1874; Mott, *Magazines*, 3:47–49; Edward King, *The Great South: A Record of Journeys* . . . (Hartford, Conn., 1875), dedication page; Johnson, *Remembered Yesterdays*, 97.

47. Publishers' department, Feb. 1873, p. 5, and Edward P. Mitchell, *Memories of an Editor: Fifty Years of American Journalism* (New York, 1924), 94–96.

48. Publishers' department, Feb. 1873, p. 5, and King, *The Great South*, preface, ii.

49. King, *The Great South*, preface, i; editorials July 1873, and Feb. and Dec. 1874; Tooker, *Joys and Tribulations*, 38. The series began in July 1873, but was then interrupted to resume with the new volume in Nov. 1873.

50. King's letter quoted in publishers' department, Apr. 1873, p. 5; advertising section, Apr. 1874, p. 6; editorial, Dec. 1874.

51. See ch. 4.

52. Editorials, July 1874, Aug. 1875, July 1877; Ruffner article, May 1874.

53. Quoted in advertising section, Feb. 1876, p. 6.

54. "Southern Civilization—A Southerner's View of the Situation," letter printed in Aug. 1879 issue, and Holland's answering editorial, same issue.

55. King letter, Dec. 1880.

56. Editorial, Aug. 1875.

57. Editorial, Nov. 1875.

58. Editorial, July 1876.

59. Publishers' department, Dec. 1871 and Dec. 1872, pages not numbered.

60. *Harper's Monthly*, 62 (Jan. 1881):303.

61. *N. W. Ayer & Son's Directory of Newspapers and Periodicals* (New York, 1880), 56.

4

A Literary Marketplace

While Josiah Gilbert Holland's zeal for moral reform of American society continued to show up in *Scribner's Monthly* until his death in 1881, the magazine was developing a more aesthetic tone that reflected Richard Watson Gilder's growing editorial influence. This influence showed most clearly in the monthly's growing reputation as an exemplar of the fine arts, but Gilder also played a key role in introducing into *Scribner's* a number of younger writers who favored a less didactic approach to fiction than Holland's.

Gilder's part in determining total editorial content was greater than Holland's from about 1875. Correspondence shows that in the early 1870s, Holland, even while on his frequent lecture tours, insisted on seeing proof sheets for each issue and had the final word on deletions or changes.[1] There are several reasons why Holland relaxed his editorial hold from about the mid-1870s. One was his increasing regard for Gilder, both as a person and an editor. "You have never failed me," he wrote his young associate in 1874. "You have been faithful to every duty by simply being faithful to yourself."[2]

Holland's failing health was another factor in Gilder's greater responsibility. He suffered from angina pectoris, which caused him to take long vacations at his "Bonnie Castle" retreat, in Thousand Islands, New York. Also, in the years 1873–78 Holland wrote three novels, which were serialized in *Scribner's*, and these, with his editorials, must have taken most of his energy.[3] The relationship between Holland and his assistant was happy, and both were involved in dealing with the many writers who came to *Scribner's* and helped to make it a success.

Scribner's Monthly began in a transition period for American literature. The creative powers of the revered New Englanders—

Ralph Waldo Emerson, James Russell Lowell, John Greenleaf Whittier, Henry Wadsworth Longfellow, and Oliver Wendell Holmes—did not flourish in the post–Civil War atmosphere, and the dean of New York letters, William Cullen Bryant, also acknowledged that "the poetical period of my life is with the past."[4] The rising figures of William Dean Howells, Mark Twain, and Henry James had yet to reach their zenith. Meanwhile, the noonday brilliance of England's great Victorians seemed to wither, rather than stimulate, the seedlings of a new American literature, for, in the absence of international copyright, the best foreign works could be sold to the public more cheaply than the products of lesser known native authors.

The salient characteristic of fiction in this period was its unreality. "Blood and tears" were the staples of American reading—melodramatic adventure stories, relished by veterans of the army camps, and saccharine domestic tales, cherished by their wives and sisters. Since the early days of the ladies' books, the magazines had been the special domain of the sentimental novel. This was distinctively the product of women writing for women, and in an age when, as Howells remarked, even the best authors were tainted with "ethicism," female writers carried the triumph of virtue to the extreme of incredibility. Popular monthlies like *Harper's Monthly*, explicitly designed for the family circle, served only to carry this emasculated fiction to a wider audience than the ladies' books had reached, although *Harper's* was enlivened by the genius of good English novelists.[5]

Scribner's Monthly, with its predominantly feminine readership, offered little promise in its early volumes of invigorating the nation's literature. Female writers accounted for thirty-five of the fifty-eight serials and short stories run by the magazine in its first two years. Frances Hodgson Burnett, Adeline Trafton, and Helen Hunt Jackson, representatives of the sentimental school, were mainstays of the contributors' list; Burnett and Trafton between them provided seven of the magazine's twenty-five serial novels during Holland's editorship.

The English-born Burnett, who was to become famous for her *Little Lord Fauntleroy* (1886), had served her apprenticeship in *Godey's Lady's Book* and *Peterson's Magazine*, two of the "Philadelphia sisterhood" of female periodicals. A warm friend of the

Holland family, she was welcomed as a protégée of *Scribner's* with the appearance of her first story for the monthly, "Surly Tim's Trouble," in 1872. It was Gilder thereafter who edited her work, much to her gratification. ("I am like that idiotic Alice in the song of Ben Bolt. I weep with delight when you give me a smile and tremble with fear at your frown."[6]) The tremendous popularity of her "Haworth's" and "That Lass o' Lowries," both serialized during the 1870s, was evidence that Holland's readers liked sentiment in large doses, and her son and biographer has testified that she purposely sweetened her stories to suit the taste of her public.[7]

Jackson, using the pseudonym "Saxe Holm," achieved a success nearly as great. Eleven of her short stories ran in *Scribner's* in the period 1871–78, and their wide popularity was enhanced by frequent newspaper speculation as to their authorship. As "H. H.," Jackson was also a regular contributor of verse and travel articles to the magazine. Such was her vogue with the public under both pseudonyms that Holland once toyed with the idea of filling an entire issue with her work. Yet her biographer has characterized her work as "formless, overintense, sentimental, and artificial." Like Burnett, she seems to have slanted her fiction to suit "Timothy Titcomb's" audience.[8]

Male authors like the Reverend George MacDonald and Holland himself similarly pictured the long suffering and ultimate vindication of the meek and virtuous, with the difference only that their protagonists were likely to be boys and young men rather than the heroines favored by the female writers. Holland's "Arthur Bonnicastle," begun as a serial in November 1872, created so much demand for an issue of *Scribner's* that extra editions containing his first installments had to be run.[9] The editor's "Sevenoaks" and "Nicholas Minturn," also serialized, were in the same didactic manner. The *North American Review* cordially recommended the latter novel to "either the infantile or the senile public," but its three reprintings in book form in the early twentieth century testify to the lingering appeal of sentimentality.[10]

In his editorials, Holland stated the philosophical basis for this homiletic fiction. "If a man's art is not a royal vehicle for the progress of the moral he desires to honor and convey, then he has no call to be a novelist."[11] This was a suitable explanation for the artificiality that enveloped the novel, for if the moral law were to determine the outcome of every story, its characters were doomed to serve as stereotypes. Writers of the time were schooled in this idea of literature as ethical illustration. Gilder in 1875 complained that *Scribner's* had to decline large numbers of manuscripts because of their sentimentality.[12]

Gilder, in fact, was beginning to insinuate his own set of values into the magazine's editorial judgments. The rising young poet, along with friends such as Edmund C. Stedman, Richard H. Stoddard, and Thomas Bailey Aldrich, was to carry on the tradition of ideality in American letters during the last third of the nineteenth century. Their theory of literature, which subtly inverted Holland's view, was well expressed in 1872 by a veteran of their school, Bayard Taylor. Chiding Holland for writing with a moral rather than a poetic inspiration, Taylor asserted that a poem, if it obeyed the laws of proportion and beauty, could not be immoral or irreligious, while art that ignored "the eternal requirements of Beauty" could not endure.[13] Gilder, commenting on Howells's "A Modern Instance" while it was being serialized in the magazine, declared: "If the author had forgotten his art under the stress of his moral message, he would have been untrue, not only to his own conscience but to life."[14]

To Gilder and his poetic friends, art in an era of materialism had its own high purpose. Holland, however, was suspicious of culture divorced from religion. Such a culture, he said, "works away at its own refinement and aggrandizement, but refuses to come down into the dusty ways of life, to point men upwards and to help them bear their burdens."[15] Protesting "the heresy that art is a master and not a minister," he charged that the literary class in the United States had formed a mutual admiration society bound up in themselves. "Why should the world be blamed for not overhearing what literary men and women say to each other? The talk is not meant for them."[16] This was, of course, the plaint of the outsider.

Nevertheless, the litterateurs Holland condemned in theory were infiltrating his citadel, giving his magazine the aesthetic tone his doctrine would have denied it. In addition to Gilder, another champion of ideality became an important figure in the early years of *Scribner's*. Stedman, known as "The Bard of the Exchange" because his main occupation was Wall Street brokerage, had first met Gilder in the office of the *Newark Advertiser*, and his close friendship with young Watsey linked him to *Scribner's* from its beginning.[17] His earlier criticism of Holland's writing gave way to tactful praise that won him the editor's gratitude and solidified his influence.[18] He not only became an important contributor but also identified his critical authority with the magazine so thoroughly that he became almost an ex-officio member of its staff.

Stedman's "Victorian Poets," a series of critical essays running in the years 1873–75, was the most ambitious literary project the monthly had yet undertaken. The spokesman for ideality had to use tact to get one of these essays through the editor's moralistic screen. Holland objected to Stedman's inclusion of Algernon Charles Swinburne, whose *Poems and Ballads* he considered offensive. Assuring Holland that he was unnecessarily worried, the critic pointed out that he had avoided "running amuck" among the poet's early work, which "the prurient would rush to read," and had considered only its technique. He was willing to have Holland register disapproval of his article in a footnote or an editorial.[19] In the end, the controversial essay ran without comment, Stedman in the text acknowledging that Swinburne had "fairly provoked censure," although "the outcry of the moralists may have been overloud."

A few years later, Stedman encountered even stiffer editorial opposition when he ventured to include Walt Whitman in his series on the "Poets of America." Holland had made Whitman one of his favorite whipping boys, denouncing him frequently in editorials; although these strictures were professedly directed at the poet's lack of artistic form, their tone was that of the outraged moralist. Holland went so far as to cut out every reference to Whitman in an article submitted by John Burroughs.[20] When Whitman had the temerity to submit one of his verses to *Scribner's*, it was rejected with what its author called "a note of the most offensive character." Whitman threw it into the fire and was later sorry he had not saved it as "a good specimen insult for the historian." (Whitman's dismissal of Holland some years later was itself a specimen: "Holland is a dead man—there's hardly anything of him left today: he had his strut and is passed on: he was a man of his time, not possessed of the slightest forereach.")[21]

Holland, therefore, was reluctant to agree when Stedman pointed out that he could not ignore Whitman in a discussion of American poets, and Stedman, before proceeding, had to promise to be judicious. In keeping with this injunction, he hailed Whitman as one of the foremost lyricists of his time, while stigmatizing some of his work as "too anatomical and malodorous."[22]

The protests that followed publication of this essay showed that Holland had been right to be careful. Yet it was a tribute to Stedman's diplomacy that the principals in the controversy were to a large degree satisfied. Whitman declared that Stedman's was the first article in a "conventional" magazine that fully recognized his genius and his aims—and in fact, the essay had a notable effect in gaining public acceptance for Whitman.[23] On the other hand, Holland thought Stedman's "treatment of Whitman's indecency is excellent, and the old wretch can no longer defend it. Without any plea for morality and purely on artistic grounds, he demolishes all the old man's defenses and leaves him without any apology for adhering to his early smut." The editor remained convinced that "Whitman does not in any measure deserve the great attention we are giving him."[24]

The conflict in literary philosophy appeared again in the magazine's attitude toward Edgar Allan Poe. In an editorial in January 1881, Holland declared that a man of Poe's bad character "could never write a poem . . . that possesses any intrinsic value whatsoever." But in the following issue, and without any written dissent from the editor, a reviewer remarked that "whatever may have been the shortcomings of Poe's life, the world willingly forgets and forgives. It knows that the order and harmony of the poet's verse have often no correspondence in his acts."

Such overt conflicts between the moralistic and aesthetic points of view were, in fact, exceptional. The warm personal relationship between the editor and his right-hand man helped to reconcile the standards of admission to the magazine. Holland, twenty-four years older than Gilder, took a fatherly interest in his young aide's personal and professional maturing, and Gilder, responsive by nature, developed an affection for his chief and an appreciation of his goodness that outweighed his awareness of the older man's limitations in literary and artistic taste.[25]

With Gilder's idealist friends, Holland's difference of principle was tempered by personal regard. The moralist secretly yearned for the acclaim of the literati he professed to scorn and responded with touching gratitude to the friendly compliments paid to him by men like Stedman. Responding to one letter from Stedman, Holland wrote: "I did not know until then, how, in the steeled life I have lived for fifteen years, I had been hungry for just those words. They melted me as if I had been wax, and I thanked God for you."[26]

Gilder and his friends, moreover, if they were more concerned with the artistic form of literature than Holland, were scarcely less concerned with its morals. Stedman was not merely being politic when he assured Holland that "I myself have no sympathy with any moral taint in art,"[27] and Gilder felt that the world needed the MacDonald kind of moralizer. To a friend in 1871 Gilder remarked: "Yes—there is a devil to fight in ourselves and in the world—there is something better than literary culture."[28] By standards of today Holland's squeamishness was at times fantastic: he struck out of one article a sentence contrasting cold mountain peaks to "the gentle bosom of a woman," and he objected to the proposed illustration of a poem that expressed the revery of a maiden in undress, on the grounds that readers would not understand how the artist could properly be present to make the sketch![29] Yet under Gilder's canon of ideality, excisions were frequently to be made for reasons that today seem equally prudish.

Eventually the mainstream of American literature was to follow neither the moralistic nor the idealistic channel, but the broader course of realism. The tendency to make fiction a more faithul reflection of life was already evident in the 1870s. A transition figure in this development was Rebecca Harding Davis, who in sketches such as "The Pepper-Pot Woman," "Dolly," and "The Poetess of Clap City" gave the readers of *Scribner's* brief but vivid portraits of actual characters in significant relationship to their environment.[30] The local-color writers who emerged in *Scribner's* and other periodicals during this period also displayed evidences of realism—in character and scene, although not in plot or denouement.

Both Holland and Gilder were hospitable toward such manifestations of realism, but both set strict limits beyond which fiction could not go in portraying unpleasant truths. Gilder rejected George W. Cable's story, "Posson Jone"—as did *Harper's* and other periodicals—because of a scene in which a drunken minister fought animals in an arena.[31] Edward Eggleston's "Roxy," although it was a "study of human conduct under moral stress," created such misgivings that Holland asked Gilder to edit the novel, balancing the author's boldness with his own prudence.[32] When *Roxy* appeared in book form, the reviewer for *Scribner's* (December 1878) might have been speaking for either of the two editors when he wrote, "It is not euphemism that is lacking, but mellowness—the sublimated treatment which in Hawthorne makes us content to dwell upon the disagreeable, even the morbid."

The first masters of realism to challenge the sentimentalism of American fiction incorporated such "sublimated treatment" of human nature and conduct into their method; hence their appearance in the magazine meant no clash with established standards. Holland thought highly of Henry James, whose early work had appeared in the *Atlantic Monthly* and the *Galaxy*, and exerted influence with that young author's father to add him to the contributors' list.[33] The younger James responded with a succession of short stories, five in all, beginning in 1874.[34] His "Confidence," which James's biographer has called a "feeble little novel," but for which he nevertheless collected $1,500 from *Scribner's*, was serialized in 1879 and 1880.[35]

Meanwhile the Continental realism which was to have an influence on American fiction was represented in *Scribner's* by the short stories of Ivan Turgenev. These were translated by H. H. Boyeson, the Norwegian-American professor of literature at Cornell University, who also wrote for the monthly an appreciation of Turgenev.[36] Boyeson himself was a regular contributor of realistic tales and in 1881 gave the magazine a novel, "Queen Titania." The ranks of the realists were augmented in the same year when the formidable Howells made his initial appearance in *Scribner's* with his novel, "A Fearful Responsibility."

Thus Holland and Gilder provided a foothold in their magazine for writers who did not necessarily agree with either of them as to the function of literature. This points up the true role of *Scribner's*—and the other periodicals—in the development of American fiction: they provided a marketplace in which a public slowly rising to an appreciation of good writing could choose from the products of an increasingly large and self-conscious American profession of letters. However much the editors might wish to—and often did—guide the taste of the magazine's audience or limit the creations of its contributors, they were helping to form a democracy of both readers and writers who would ultimately determine their own rules for the representation of life in fiction.

As noted earlier, there were not many good American writers in 1870, and Holland found difficulty in detaching even these from *Harper's* and the *Atlantic*, as well as from *Galaxy* and *Lippincott's*. The editors were so hard-pressed for fiction at the outset that they asked Eggleston to create their first short story almost overnight. At Gilder's importuning, he wrote "Huldah the Help"—his first fiction for adults—between a Friday evening and the next Monday morning.[37]

Holland's personal appeals for material brought a few affirmative responses. Charles Dudley Warner sent him his "Back-Log Studies," a readable series of informal essays in a style that was disappearing. Rebecca Harding Davis, acknowledging "an unpaid debt of gratitude to Timothy Titcomb," became a regular contributor. But James S. Parton, Rose Terry (later Cooke), and the prolific John T. Trowbridge all informed the editor that they had other commitments, while Parke Godwin and Elizabeth Stuart Phelps pleaded poor health. Bret Harte promised to try to send something, but he was soon tied to the *Atlantic* by the famous contract that gave him $10,000 for a single year's output.[38] Nor did Holland fulfill his promise to make his home a rallying point for authors; he gave only one reception each winter at his mansion on Park Avenue for "the general literary society of New York." At these nonalcoholic suppers were to be seen John Hay, Jackson, Burnett, Warner, and Harte.[39]

In his competition for contributors, Holland had one great asset: his readiness to pay good prices for manuscripts. He knew the danger of false economy in this respect, and Roswell Smith not only encouraged a liberal policy but by his enterprising business management brought in the revenues that made it possible. Smith sometimes handled directly the financial arrangements with popular authors that secured them for the magazine. Thus, *Scribner's* not only paid Harte $6,000 for the serial rights to his first novel, "Gabriel Conroy"—a sum "said to have been the highest ever paid for an American novel"—but, through Smith, obtained for Harte the entire proceeds of the magazine rights to the story in England. Harte jubilantly wrote his book publisher, James R. Osgood: "Smith the great! Smith, the well-born and hyphenly-connected, is my agent. I reject with scorn the small shafts and brutal sallies aimed in your note at that truly great man. One thousand pounds is the sum he is to get from the English publishers for me." When Harte left to take up a consular post in Germany in 1878, Smith arranged to take all of his writings, disposing of the ones that *Scribner's* could not use to other publications.[40]

Against such vigorous competition even the *Atlantic*, for all its prestige, struggled to hold its writers, even when strengthened by the accession of Howells as editor in 1871. Many authors doubtless agreed with Jackson, who declared that she would rather appear in the *Atlantic* than elsewhere, but could not afford to turn down the better rates offered by New York.[41] Stedman, who had a hard time breaking into the *Atlantic*, consoled himself in the knowledge that *Scribner's*, *Harper's*, or the *Galaxy* would "pay me double what Boston would," and even when Howells accepted a book review from him, he complained that "the magazine don't half pay for it."[42] In 1873 Stedman somewhat disingenuously told Bayard Taylor that he had "cut loose" from the *Atlantic* and had thrown "all my advice, influence, work, in favor of the 'coming monthly,' *Scribner's*."[43]

By 1875 Howells was pleading with James not to send any stories to *Scribner's*. That magazine, he said, was "trying to lure away all our contributors, with the siren song of Doctor Holland, and my professional pride is touched." Nevertheless James appeared frequently in Holland's magazine during the 1870s, while, however, saving his best work for the *Atlantic*. Warner was similarly unmoved when Howells, hearing that he was about to write a story for *Scribner's*, chided him with, "If it's true, it's a mean shame, and you will suffer for it." Adding to Howells's chagrin was his long-standing personal feud with Holland. This flared up again in 1874 when the *Atlantic* failed to review Holland's narrative poem, "The Mistress of the Manse." Holland was so annoyed that he refused to open his columns to Howells's biographical sketch of Aldrich. Gilder, whose own work had been praised in the *Atlantic*, tried to have Aldrich mediate the quarrel, assuring him that he personally would be glad to have Howells among his magazine's contributors, but not until 1878 did Howells and Holland make up "all old sorrows."[44]

With Gilder's increasing editorial power, relations between the two monthlies improved. Gilder assured Howells that he had never presumed on personal friendships with men like Lowell and Longfellow to lure them from the *Atlantic*. As long as they wrote exclusively for the Boston periodical, he was not inclined to approach them, but when their work began to appear in other magazines, he felt free to "beg hard" for their contributions.[45] By 1880 Howells himself, having resigned his editorship, began to send novels to *Scribner's*. Emily Dickinson later asked, "Doctor—How did you snare Howells?" The editor replied, "Money did it."[46] But Gilder's friendship with Howells was doubtless also a factor.

While the *Atlantic's* once semiprivate preserve was being invaded, the New York magazines, as well as *Lippincott's* of Philadelphia, hunted for good material in a wide-open field. The experience of S. G. W. Benjamin, a free-lance artist-journalist, indicates that the competition was for features as well as for writers. When *Scribner's*, in the winter of 1874–75, announced a forthcoming series of articles on the Channel Islands and the adjacent French coast, *Harper's* hired Benjamin to produce several papers on the same subject, with the stipulation that he must submit each installment in time to appear a month ahead of its counterpart in Holland's monthly. Within twenty-four hours Benjamin had sailed for Europe (having in the meantime arranged with the *Atlantic* to do three additional travel articles on other areas), and he turned out the manuscripts within the prescribed time limit.[47]

Growing numbers of magazine writers were emerging, and a reputation for liberality and fair dealing brought many of them to *Scribner's*. Lulu Gray Noble found that Holland was "one of those delightful editors who pay on acceptance." Davis was eager to meet the editor who could reject a manuscript "with such tact and cordiality as to satisfy the author quite as much as if he had accepted it." Holland's sympathy with writers was so strong that Gilder felt obliged to guard him against contributors who appealed more to his tender emotions than to his literary taste. "I do believe, Gilder," the editor would say, mildly, in such instances, "that you have an antipathy to any one who wants to write for this magazine." Sidney Lanier had high praise for Holland's "unusual generosity, warmth of heart, and goodness." The poet and humorist, H. C. Bunner, demanded of his brother-in-law, Walter Learned, "Why under the sun don't you write for *Scribner's*? You could not find more appreciative people."[48]

As the number of writers seeking entry to the magazine increased, the power of the editors grew correspondingly. Authors had no way of reaching the public, Lanier declared, except through men like Holland, and Holland "would not accept anything in the world which didn't please him, even if Homer, Shakespeare, Dante and Milton should go down on their eight knees and beseech him."[49] Magazine editors had a tradition of ruthless control over not merely the style and wording but even the substance of manuscripts that came into their hands. Holland sometimes demanded stylistic changes—for example, he asked the humorist, Henry Wheeler Shaw ("Josh Billings") to drop the deliberate misspellings from his aphorisms that, as "Uncle Esek's Wisdom," ran for several years in the monthly, beginning in 1880. Yet Holland, in spite of his occasional moral excisions and taboos such as women's suffrage and alcohol, prided himself on the freedom of expression he allowed to writers. Lanier felt "greatly obliged" to *Scribner's* for "a general reception of my little offerings far more hearty than I could expect in view of our wholly different way of looking at things."[50]

The combined efforts of Holland and Gilder to enlist good authors produced results within a few years. In contrast to the rather drab list of writers in the early numbers, the issue of

January 1874 contained contributions from T. W. Higginson, MacDonald, Harte, the historian J. A. Froude, Gail Hamilton, John G. Saxe, Warner, Stoddard, Hay, and Edward King. A more imposing array of names, said the *Literary World*, had "never distinguished an American magazine."[51] The roll of authors in the August 1876 number included Harte, Hamilton, and Stoddard again, and also Edward Everett Hale, Aldrich, Lanier, Burnett, Bryant, James, and Turgenev. In 1878, when the *Galaxy* ceased, *Scribner's* became the major place of publication for able writers such as Brander Matthews and Burroughs, whose work it had shared with that monthly.

But by the mid-1870s Holland had still not found a suitable source of supply for the most important element of fiction in the magazine, the serial novel. How essential this feature was to a monthly had been shown by the experience of *Harper's*. After the Civil War, that monthly fell off in circulation so sharply that the House of Harper considered ending its publication. But the serialization of Charles Dickens's "Our Mutual Friend" and Wilkie Collins's "Armadale" restored its prewar leadership.[52] The continued story was "all important," Holland pointed out, for inducing the large number of nonsubscribing readers to keep up regular purchases.[53] The shortage of good novels, however, was a matter of common remark. In May 1872, a reviewer in *Scribner's* declared that "we seldom come upon an American novel which is worth finding fault with. The sum of offense with most of them is that they exist at all."

As one solution to this problem Holland turned to Britain, whose great Victorians were then creating a remarkable and prolific literature. But, as already noted, he was balked by the "law of courtesy," which provided that the American publisher who had once issued a foreign author's work was entitled to first consideration of that writer's subsequent books. Through this trade custom, *Harper's* in particular had cornered many of the greatest names: Charles Reade, William Makepeace Thackeray, Anthony Trollope, George Meredith, Edward Bulwer-Lytton, Dickens, and Collins. Unfortunately for Holland's purpose, Charles Scribner had determined to keep his book house American. William James Stillman, Holland's agent in England, was deluged with offers from unestablished authors but was unable to contract for the work of the major figures. When Holland personally asked George Eliot for contributions, her husband and agent informed him that his wife must give "due regard" to her American publishers, Fields and Osgood.[54]

Scribner's in its early years secured only two British novelists of repute: MacDonald, whose "Wilfred Cumbermede" helped to launch the magazine, and Mrs. M. O. W. Oliphant, who contributed three serials to the monthly in its first two years. That these foreign features were emphasized in the magazine's advertisements and that these authors received virtually the only contributors' by-lines in *Scribner's* during this period indicated how eagerly the editors welcomed them.

It is probable, then, that Holland was making a virtue of necessity when in November 1875 he proclaimed that his monthly would thenceforth print only American novels. Three years had then elapsed since the magazine's last previous British serial had begun—a circumstance that adds to the presumptive evidence that the unavailability of good foreign material was largely responsible for the new policy of encouraging native works.[55]

Holland, of course, gave other, plausible reasons for his declaration of literary independence. He professed to believe that his readers were tired of the "English society novel," which, he said, was concerned with a "form of social life more conventional than our own, with scenery less grand and attractive, with personalities more feebly individualized, and with events and incidents as much less interesting than those of American life as the conditions of English life are more artificial than ours." He pointed out that the two leading novels in *Scribner's* for the forthcoming year— Harte's "Gabriel Conroy," and Hale's "Philip Nolan's Friends"— could "only have been written in America by Americans." The editor noted that his new policy would encourage native literature. *Scribner's*, he said, aware of the "evil effects" of foreign serials on the writers of its own land, "saw, at last, that it could do no better for its own countrymen and for American literature than to discard utterly the British novel, and get the best American novel it could, to take its place."

Regardless of its motivation, the new policy did widen somewhat the market for American writers, and Holland, in later years, felt that the encouragement of indigenous authors was among the leading elements of his magazine's success. As late as 1883 the *Critic*, in a survey of leading periodicals, counted only five serial novels by American writers currently appearing, of which three were in the *Century*, the continuation of *Scribner's*.[56]

In trying to encourage and publish American authors, the editors had to single the best out of a miscellaneous crop in which eager young women poets were prominent. Some of these came armed with the blessings of their elders and betters. Longfellow recommended a Cambridge protégée, Charlotte F. Bates, who became a regular in the magazine's female verse-writing contingent. Louise Chandler Moulton, another regular, had her first encouragement to write from Holland himself. But most tyros, Gilder pointed out, had served an apprenticeship, often anonymously, in the dailies, weeklies, and quarterlies.[57]

As increased stipends beckoned more and more aspiring writers to test their skills (sometimes failing), they began to complain that young genius was ignored in favor of authors of established reputations. Holland denied the charge. He admitted that periodicals preferred "great names," but assured young writers that his magazine was eager to find new talent, for "nothing kills a periodical so surely as 'a regular list of contributors.'"[58] Sometimes, indeed, the editorial sanctum was hard to reach—Robert Louis Stevenson, heading straight for *Scribner's* from an immigrant ship in 1879, was turned away by a clerk.[59] But more typical was the attitude of Robert Underwood Johnson, an assistant editor, in the same year. He read a statement by Whitman that the best promise of American literature lay in a group of young men just coming on the scene. "They have not yet begun to speak, because the magazines are in the hands of old fogies like Holland or fops like Howells." Johnson promptly asked Whitman to put him in touch with these voiceless young men, and Whitman replied, lamely enough, that he could give no names, for "I spoke mainly of a class, or rather of a leaven and a spirit."[60]

Alert for discoveries, the editors made one of their first within their own precincts. Frank R. Stockton was a slight, gentle young man who had been a writer for *Hearth and Home* before joining the staff of *Scribner's*. When in 1872 Scribner and Compny launched *St. Nicholas*, a magazine for children, he became its assistant editor. An expert creator of juvenile fiction, he turned to writing fantastic tales for adults. His "Rudder Grange," which appeared in *Scribner's* in November 1874, showed the style that was to characterize his long career, its essential feature being the narration of preposterous events in commonplace language. The incongruities resulting from this understatement produced a comic effect as typically American as the traditional exaggerations of the frontier tales—deadpan humor, it would be called today. The popular success of Stockton's first story led to a number of "Rudder Grange" sequels. Master of the short story and a key figure in the refinement of American humor, Stockton reached the summit of his fame with "The Lady, or the Tiger?" which appeared in the monthly after it had become the *Century*.[61]

Scribner's made its greatest literary finds in the school of regional fiction that rose to prominence in the 1870s and 1880s. At the time when Holland and his partners were founding their magazine, a new generation of writers began to record the provincialisms of American life that a postwar nationalism was tending to obliterate. Even as the first number of his monthly went to press, Holland tried to enlist the pen that had launched this local-color era, for Harte had already created a sensation in the East with his tales and ballads of the California mining camps. When he had finished his stipulated year of work for the *Atlantic*, the editors of *Scribner's* joined the quest for this literary lion, and in January 1873, he made his first appearance in their magazine with "After the Accident," a ballad about a mine disaster. His three-part story, "An Episode of Fiddletown"—which reportedly brought its author $1,000—began in August of the same year. By the end of 1874, three more of Harte's short pieces had appeared in *Scribner's*. In November 1875 his first novel, "Gabriel Conroy," began its serial run with much fanfare. In it Harte aimed to present in grand panorama all aspects of California life, but despite some brilliantly evocative passages, it failed badly in construction and credibility. Financially, however, it was a triumph for the author.[62]

Far removed both in character and locale from Harte's melodramatic episodes of the Far West were Eggleston's unadorned pictures of rural Indiana, where he had spent his early manhood as a Methodist circuit-rider. Turning to literature, Eggleston had traveled to the East to serve as book critic and superintending editor of the *Independent*, and later as editor of the weekly, *Hearth and Home*. He contributed literary reviews to the first number of *Scribner's* as well as its first short story. "Huldah the Help" was followed by four additional sketches within a year, of which "Ben: A Story for May-Day" and "Priscilla" were especially significant for their realistic treatment of incidents and character in a midwestern village. Eggleston left *Hearth and Home* after his serialized novel, "The Hoosier Schoolmaster," had given that weekly a new lease on life, and—through the 1870s and beyond—his leonine figure became a familiar sight in the offices of *Scribner's*. His most important contribution to Holland's monthly in its first decade was his novel, "Roxy," which, in spite of editorial fears that its realism was too vivid, brought many favorable comments to the magazine.[63]

Scribner's tapped its richest vein of local color when King made his tour of the South. Reaching New Orleans, King encountered Cable, a sensitive, religious man who had been a private in the Confederate army and was now a clerk in a cotton factor's warehouse. A fascinated student of New Orleans history, Cable had begun to write about its Creole society of an earlier generation. He already had a good local reputation as a newspaper writer and in 1871 had sent the Scribner book firm a number of clippings from his column in the *New Orleans Picayune*, but that publishing house, perhaps dubious about encouraging a recent rebel, had not been forthcoming. King sent two of Cable's stories to Holland, and in October 1873, *Scribner's* ran his "Sieur George," the first of his Creole tales to reach print in a periodical. Although the magazine rejected his next three stories, King and Gilder became Cable's enthusiastic promoters, inserting in New York newspapers accounts of his work that described him as a southern counterpart of Harte. By 1878 his short stories in Holland's magazine, marked by a delicate style and an exotic flavor that was reflected in their titles—" 'Tite Poulette," "Belles Demoiselles Plantation," "Jean-ah-Pouquelin," "Café des Exilés"—had impressed the northern public so strongly that the Scribner book firm was glad to bring them out in a volume, *Old Creole Days*, which continued to find an audience for many years. In 1879 Cable's first novel, "The Grandissimes," written at the invitation of the editors, began a serial run in *Scribner's*. His novelette, "Madame Delphine," was also serialized, beginning in 1881.[64]

Cable was the forerunner of a group of southern writers who were either discovered or first exploited by *Scribner's* and the *Century*. Throughout the 1870s, *Harper's*, possibly restrained by its staunch Republicanism, almost completely ignored Dixie's promising literary harvest.[65] *Lippincott's* was as receptive as Holland's monthly to the themes and authors of the former Confederacy, but the greater influence and resources of *Scribner's* made it the real "Maecenas of Southern literature."[66] The relationship was mutually profitable, for while Cable, Thomas Nelson Page, Joel Chandler Harris, Lanier, and many other lesser writers reached a wide northern audience through *Scribner's*, its editors found in the work of these authors full justification of their policy of reliance on American literature.

This new generation of southern writers accepted national reunion. If they wrote fondly of the old regime, it was not to revive sectional controversy but to memorialize the traditions of the South they loved. Northern readers, long insulated by the slavery dispute from this mellower aspect of the antebellum South, responded warmly to the romanticized picture of a civilization that they had fought to destroy. In its selection of fiction, as in its editorials, *Scribner's* tended to strengthen the ties between North and South.[67]

The focal character in the southern literature of the 1870s was most often the black. Cable dared to break a regional taboo by writing realistically of black men and women as characters frequently more worthy of respect than the proud Creoles who despised them. Both "The Grandissimes" and "Madame Delphine" dealt with the problems of quadroons in a hostile society, and for thus recording the pathetic results of miscegenation, Cable won the undying enmity of the Creoles.[68]

Typically, however, southern writers used blacks to dramatize the accepted theory of race relations, painting them either as faithful family retainers or as confused freedmen and women under the friendly wardship of white people. More than any other magazine, *Scribner's* carried these portraits into northern homes, and the repetitive inanity of the plots in these stories did not seem to diminish their appeal.

The sentimentalized interpretation of the blacks' role originated in balladry. As early as 1871, Thomas Dunn English contributed the first dialect verse to *Scribner's*. In his "Caesar Rowan," a freedman told how his "Young Mas' Randolph" had died in saving him from drowning, and how he repaid the debt by caring for Randolph's dazed father. In "Mama Phoebe," another dialect poem by English published in the same year, an old plantation nurse recalled how she had reared her son and his young master as playmates and had found them side by side in death on a Civil War battlefield.[69]

Page, a Virginian, gained his fame in the 1880s through the short story, but his "Uncle Gabe's White Folks," a dialect poem in *Scribner's* of April 1877, contained the essence of his later romances, notably the type of the idealized household slave bound by mutual affection to his equally idealized master.

In the work of Sidney Lanier and his brother Clifford, the sterotype of the black took on more life. In the mid-1870s they collaborated on two ballads that were widely quoted after they appeared in *Scribner's*.[70] "The Power of Prayer" (June 1875) portrayed the terror of an old black man who mistook the first steamer up the Alabama River for the devil. "Uncle Jim's Baptist Revival Hymn" (May 1876) was a vivid rendering of the religious feeling among the untutored blacks.

The acknowledged pioneer in the realistic treatment of the blacks, however, was Irwin Russell, a gifted but dissipated young Mississippian who died when his promising career had only begun. Such writers as Page, Harris, and others recorded their debt to Russell's use of dialect, but what gave vitality to his ballads was his insight into the minds of illiterate blacks, with their superstitions, their interpretation of the cosmos in local and contemporary terms, and their humor. Had Russell lived, said Harris, "all the rest of us would have taken back seats so far as representation of life in the South was concerned."[71] Unlike English and Page, he did not dwell on the glory of prewar days, but dealt with the freedmen at work on the farm—as in "Nebuchadnezzar," concerning a black plowman's difficulties with a balky mule—or at home in the cabin, as in his most famous ballad, "Christmas Night in the Quarters." Russell was almost exclusively a *Scribner's* author. His verse was first published in the magazine in January 1876; until his death three years later at twenty-six, he wrote regularly for "Etchings" and "Bric-à-Brac." When he came to New York, Gilder and Johnson, along with Bunner, became virtually his guardians, trying to keep him away from alcohol and nursing him in his illnesses and hangovers.[72]

Harris was not a discovery of *Scribner's*, but Holland's monthly gave his work its earliest periodical publication. "A Rainy Day with Uncle Remus," in June 1881, introduced readers to one of the most famous and lovable characters in American folklore. Harris was an important contributor to the *Century* for many years.

In the 1880s writers of local color peopled the magazines with variegated types of southern whites as well as blacks. Richard Malcolm Johnston foreshadowed this trend in the 1870s. Johnston's career provides an excellent instance of the crucial importance of the northern periodical to the southern writer. A planter ruined by the Civil War, he had published his stories of middle Georgia in the South as early as 1864 without attracting the least notice. He was fifty-seven when he submitted "Mr. Neelus Peeler's Conditions" to Holland, who ran it in June 1879, yet it was the first story for which he had ever been paid. His association with *Scribner's Monthly* launched him on a profitable career as magazinist and lecturer.[73]

In 1881 Holland noted that a recent issue of the magazine had seven contributions by southern writers.[74] But Dixie's local-color heyday was still to come. In the decade that followed, a wide assortment of provincials trooped across the pages of the *Century*, fascinating its readers with their outlandish colloquialisms and unique folkways.

In contrast to this fresh infusion of local color in fiction and balladry, the magazine's serious verse ran in a thin, pale stream through well-worn channels of meter and sentiment. An army of female bards filled every spare half page with pious songs and tributes to nature. In the issue of November 1872, every line of verse was written by a woman. So incessant was the outpouring of these writers that the editors in one instance (December 1879) pooled the contributions of twenty authors under the single heading, "Poems by American Women." This flood of verse was so undistinguished that "magazine poetry" became a term of contempt.

On a higher level of craftsmanship was the work of the group of New Yorkers—Stedman, Stoddard, and Taylor among them— for whom Gilder made *Scribner's* a stronghold. To these writers, poetry was an idealization of beauty and right feeling to be handed down from old to new generations in traditional forms. They patterned their creations after past masters, especially the English Romantics and Victorians, and did not suffer the turbulence of contemporary American life to enter into their delicate verse structures. Preoccupation with traditional prosody was carried to its extreme by Brander Matthews and Bunner, who, fascinated by a British revival of French metrical forms, introduced the rondeau, the ballade, and the triolet into the United States through the pages of *Scribner's* (June 1878).[75]

Among the nation's poets in this period, only Whitman shattered the old patterns completely, and for this, as much as for his frank treatment of sex, he was excluded from the magazine during Holland's reign. Holland was a warm friend of another important experimenter in verse, Emily Dickinson, but, although he privately praised her work, he apparently never asked her to write for his monthly.[76] The third poetic genius of the 1870s, Sidney Lanier, contributed a number of pieces to *Scribner's*. His "A Song of the Future" in the August 1876 number struck the centennial note with considerable eloquence. His important poem, "Corn," appeared in *Lippincott's* after Holland rejected it as too long for his monthly. *Scribner's* was a big help to this poet in his struggle against ill health and poverty. On one occasion, Lanier told his father that Holland had paid him a $200 retainer "just in time to save me from I know not what extent of mortification and suffering."[77]

Two distinguished additions to the magazine's list of contributors were the nature essayists, John Burroughs and John Muir. Burroughs, born in upstate New York, wrote of the trees and woodnotes of his native haunts with such literary charm that several periodicals sought his work, but throughout the 1870s he moved increasingly closer to *Scribner's*, sending in manuscripts frequently and sometimes serving as a literary adviser. In "Nature and the Poets" (June 1879) he took to task a number of authors, past and present, for careless and inexact references to nature— a scientific approach to poetry which provoked T. W. Higginson to a counterattack in the *Atlantic*.[78]

Far different in temper and experience from "John of Birds" was "John of Mountains." Muir had tramped the continent from Alaska to Florida before finding his special habitat in the wilderness of the Yosemite. There he roamed and wrote for forty years, conveying to eastern readers a feeling for the splendor of the Sierra country. From 1878, when "The Humming-Bird of the California Waterfalls" appeared in *Scribner's*, the editors begged him for every product of his pen. His friendship with Johnson not only brought his best work to the *Century* but led to a partnership of influence in conservation, which helped to save some of the most picturesque California forests.[79]

Within ten years of its founding, *Scribner's Monthly* could pick and choose from a growing number of American writers. Where the editors in the early years had to hunt hard for talent, by 1880 Gilder joked that most people he met carried concealed manuscripts. A class of professional writers had arisen, dependent mainly on the magazines for their living. Even the most famous literary figures got their income more from serial publication than from books, while persons of lesser genius who tried to live off their pens relied almost entirely on the periodicals.[80]

Holland warned these magazinists not to depend on writing for subsistence. "Probably there are not ten persons in America, out of a salaried position," he said in an editorial of August 1873, "who get their living by literature." The *Literary World*, taking issue with him, placed the number of authors who earned their keep at nearly 1,000 and observed: "Perhaps Dr. Holland's idea of a 'living' is more extravagant than that of the majority."[81]

Yet Holland's cautionary note was warranted. While rates of payment to authors advanced from about $3 or $5 to about $10 a printed page as a result of the postwar magazine boom, it took a prolific as well as an able writer to make ends meet. *Scribner's* paid $10 a printed page for articles by the travel writer, S. G. W. Benjamin, and the well-known meteorologist, T. B. Maury, but in both instances the authors had to provide the illustrations.

Although her "Saxe Holm" stories were her most lucrative, Jackson got only $400 for "My Tourmaline," which ran in four installments under that pseudonym. So gifted a writer as Cable, who got $50 for his first contribution to *Scribner's*, was paid only $80 for "Café des Exilés" three years later, and not until 1879–80, when the serialization of "The Grandissimes" brought him $1,500, did his annual income from fiction rise above the subsistence level.[82]

In spite of the precarious nature of authorship, the experience of *Scribner's* during the depression years of the 1870s indicated that ever-increasing numbers of persons were trying to gain at least part of their livelihood by writing. The magazine received just over 1,700 manuscripts in 1873, over 2,000 in 1874, more than 2,400 in 1875, and 3,200 in 1876. This upward trend was no doubt due in part to the monthly's rising prestige, but, as the editors pointed out, the "piteous letters" accompanying some of these contributions showed that "hard times" were instrumental in stimulating authorship for pay.[83]

The influx of new writers, together with the broadening circulation of the magazines that took their work, signified a democratization of American letters. In this process Holland's magazine played a dual role, bringing good literature—as well as some not so good—to thousands of homes beyond the orbit of the book stores and creating a wider field for native authorship. *Scribner's* was not unique in this effort, but as the one major new periodical of the decade, it played a peculiarly catalytic role. One midwestern author observed that *Scribner's* "gave such an impetus to art and letters in the country, that for a time it looked as if everybody meant to be an artist or a writer." To the masses who had neither money nor leisure for books, Holland declared, the periodical had become "the democratic form of literature." And while some critics saw in this popularizing trend a downgrading of taste and standards, it was, in fact, a move toward the creation and appreciation of a vital American literature.[84]

NOTES

1. Writing to Gilder from Milwaukee, Wis., on Jan. 21, 1872, for example, Holland gave directions for changing various articles and sto-

ries and told his assistant to have the "articles set at once and forwarded to *Chicago* so that I can see them one week from today." From Springfield, Ill., on Feb. 8, 1872, Holland returned an article in which he deleted passages, saying, "All these I take the responsibility of wiping out." GP. There were very many such letters in the magazine's early years.

2. Holland to Gilder, Dec. 25, 1874. GP.

3. I am indebted to Herbert F. Smith for pointing out a number of factors that increased Gilder's influence compared to Holland's. See his *Richard Watson Gilder*, Twayne U.S. Authors Series no. 166 (New York, 1970), 21–23.

4. Bryant to Holland, Apr. 17, 1877, Theodora V. W. Ward Collection.

5. T. S. Perry, "American Novels," *North American Review*, 65 (1872):366–78; Carl Van Doren, *The American Novel* (New York, 1922), 109–24; W. D. Howells, *Literary Friends and Acquaintances* (New York, 1911), 117; Frank Luther Mott, *A History of American Magazines*, 5 vols. (Cambridge, Mass., 1930–68), 3:255.

6. Burnett to Gilder, n.d., 1878, GP.

7. Vivian Burnett, *The Romantick Lady (Frances Hodgson Burnett): The Life Story of an Imagination* (New York, 1927), 44–64, and Maurice F. Egan, *Recollections of a Happy Life* (New York, 1924), 107.

8. Ruth Odell, *Helen Hunt Jackson ("H. H.")* (New York, 1939), 112–13, 135–49.

9. Publishers' department, Apr. 1873, p. 5.

10. H. H. Peckham, *Josiah Gilbert Holland in Relation to His Times* (Philadelphia, 1940), 156–57.

11. Editorial, Mar. 1878.

12. "The Old Cabinet," Nov. 1875.

13. Taylor to Holland, Apr. 2, 1872, Ward Collection.

14. Editorial, Oct. 1882.

15. Editorial, Jan. 1872.

16. Editorial, June 1876.

17. Laura Stedman and George M. Gould, eds., *Life and Letters of Edmund Clarence Stedman*, 2 vols. (New York, 1910), 1:449–50, 460–61.

18. Stedman to Holland, Oct. 13, 1872, and Oct. 15, 1874, Ward Collection.

19. Stedman to Holland, Dec. 28, 1874, Ward Collection.

20. M. R. Murray, "The 1870's in American Literature," *American Speech*, 1 (Mar. 1926):325.

21. Horace Traubel, *With Walt Whitman in Camden*, 3 vols. (New York, 1961), 1:184.

22. Stedman and Gould, eds., *Stedman*, 2:106. Stedman's "Walt Whitman" ran in the Nov. 1880 issue.

23. Portia Baker, "Walt Whitman's Relations with Some New York Magazines," *American Literature*, 7 (Nov. 1935):282–301; Stedman and Gould, eds., *Stedman*, 2:109; L. Frank Tooker, *The Joys and Tribulations of an Editor* (New York, 1924), 38.

24. Holland to Gilder, Sept. 19, 1880, quoted in Robert Underwood Johnson, *Remembered Yesterdays* (Boston, 1923), 337–38.

25. Gilder to Holland, Dec. 5, 1872, Ward Collection, and Rosamond Gilder, ed., *Letters of Richard Watson Gilder* (Boston, 1916), 54, hereafter cited as Gilder, *Gilder.*

26. Stedman and Gould, eds., *Stedman*, 2:335.

27. Stedman to [Holland], Dec. 26, 1876, in Stedman and Gould, eds., *Stedman*, 2:20–21.

28. Gilder to R. R. Bowker, Nov. 16, 1871, Bowker Collection, New York Public Library.

29. Mott, *Magazines*, 3:20, and Roger Burlingame, *Of Making Many Books: A Hundred Years of Reading, Writing, and Publishing, MDCCCXLVI-MDCCCCXLVI* (New York, 1946), 199.

30. Davis stories: Sept. and Nov. 1874 and Mar. 1875.

31. Smith, *R. W. Gilder*, 68, and Johnson, *Remembered Yesterdays*, 123.

32. William Peirce Randel, *Edward Eggleston: Author of "The Hoosier Schoolmaster"* (New York, 1946), 148.

33. Henry James, Sr., to Holland, Feb. 16, 1874, copy in Ward Collection.

34. "Adina," June and July 1874; "Crawford's Consistency," Aug. 1876; "The Ghostly Rental," Sept. 1876; "Four Meetings," Nov. 1877; "Longstaff's Marriage," Aug. 1878.

35. Leon Edel, *Henry James: The Conquest of London, 1870–1881* (Philadelphia, 1962), 386.

36. Turgenev, "The Living Mummy," Aug. 1876, and "The Nobleman of the Steppe," July 1877; Boyeson, "Ivan Tourgeneff," June 1877.

37. Tooker, *Joys and Tribulations*, 244, and Smith, *R. W. Gilder*, 87.

38. Warner to Holland, Feb. 10, 1871, Davis to Holland, May 26, 1870, Parton to Holland, Aug. 21, 1870, Terry to Holland, July 1870, Trowbridge to Holland, Aug. 22, 1870, Godwin to Holland, Sept. 21, 1870, Phelps to Holland, July 4, 1870, Harte to Holland, Nov. 17, 1870, Ward Collection.

39. Johnson, *Remembered Yesterdays*, 90, and Holland to anon., n.d., Josiah G. Holland Papers, New York Public Library.

40. Harte to Osgood, May 26, 1875, in Geoffrey Bret Harte, ed., *Letters of Bret Harte* (Boston, 1926), 51–52; George H. Stewart, Jr., *Bret Harte: Argonaut and Exile . . . .* (Boston, 1931), 226–27; Harte, ed., *Letters*, 110–12. At some point in his career, Smith adopted "Roswell-Smith" as his surname. The hyphen was transitory, but Smith's employees invariably addressed him as "Mr. Roswell Smith."

41. Odell, *Jackson*, 110–11.

42. Stedman to Bayard Taylor, Jan. 8, 1871, and to Taylor, May 2, 1872, in Stedman and Gould, eds., *Stedman*, 1:449–50, 459.

43. Stedman to Taylor, Dec. 25, 1873, ibid., 488–89.

44. Howells to James, Dec. 5, 1873, to Warner, Sept. 4, 1876, to

Stedman, Dec. 8, 1874, to William Cooper Howells, Apr. 14, 1878, all in Mildred Howells, ed., *Life in Letters of William Dean Howells*, 2 vols. (Garden City, N.Y., 1928), 1:181, 210, 197, 273, and Gilder to Aldrich, n.d. [1874], Aldrich Papers, Harvard University, Cambridge, Mass.

45. Gilder to Howells, Sept. 15, 1881, Howells Papers, Harvard University.

46. Martha Dickinson Bianchi, *The Life and Letters of Emily Dickinson* (Boston, 1924), 82–83.

47. Samuel G. W. Benjamin, *The Life and Adventures of a Free Lance* . . . . (Burlington, Vt., 1914), 251–52.

48. Noble to Holland, Apr. 4 [1871?], Davis to Holland, May 26, [1870?], Ward Collection; Lanier to Mary Day Lanier, Oct. 23, 1874, in Charles R. Anderson, ed., *The Centennial Edition of the Works of Sidney Lanier*, 10 vols. (Baltimore, Md., 1945), 9:106; Bunner to Learned, Nov. 24, 1880, in Gerard E. Jensen, *The Life and Letters of Henry Cuyler Bunner* (Durham, N.C., 1939), 59; Johnson, *Remembered Yesterdays*, 90.

49. Lanier to John B. Tabb, Aug. 25, 1877, in Anderson, ed., *Works of Lanier*, 9:465–66; Johnson, *Remembered Yesterdays*, 113; Tooker, *Joys and Tribulations*, 118–19.

50. Lanier to Bayard Taylor, Oct. 6, 1876, in Anderson, ed., *Works of Lanier*, 9:401.

51. *Literary World*, 4 (Jan. 1874):125–26.

52. J. Henry Harper, *The House of Harper: A Century of Publishing in Franklin Square* (New York, 1912), 253.

53. Editorial, Nov. 1878.

54. G. H. Lewes to Holland, Aug. 21 [1870?], Ward Collection; Burlingame, *Of Making Many Books*, 162; Harper, *House of Harper*, 358, 384; William James Stillman, *The Autobiography of a Journalist*, 2 vols. (Boston, 1901), 2:488–89.

55. An unhappy experience with Jules Verne, the French author, may have helped to disillusion Holland about foreign works. Verne's "The Mysterious Island" was serialized in *Scribner's*, beginning in 1874, but the installments became shorter and shorter—dwindling, in one instance, to two and one-half pages—and the novel dragged on for twenty months, more than twice as long as was planned for it. Johnson, *Remembered Yesterdays*, 124.

56. *Critic*, 3 (Jan. 13, 1883):8.

57. Longfellow to Holland, Sept. 7, 1870, Mrs. Moulton to Holland, Mar. 18, 1871, Ward Collection, and "The Old Cabinet," May 1872.

58. Editorials, Aug. 1873 and Apr. 1877.

59. Gilder to Helena Gilder, Oct. 12, 1877, in Gilder, *Gilder*, 147–48.

60. Johnson, *Remembered Yesterdays*, 335–36.

61. C. C. Buel, "The Author of 'The Lady, or the Tiger?'" July 1886. 1886.

62. Harte to [Holland], Nov. 17, 1870, Ward Collection, and Stewart,

Harte, 223. Harte's "Luke," a dialect poem, appeared in Dec. 1873; the short stories, "A Monte Flat Pastoral" and "Wan Lee, the Pagan," in Jan. and Sept. 1874, respectively.

63. Randel, *Eggleston*, 107–53 passim, and Tooker, *Joys and Tribulations*, 249. "Ben" appeared in May 1871, "Priscilla" in Nov. 1871.

64. Lucy L. C. Biklé, *George W. Cable, His Life and Letters* (New York, 1928), 45–48, and Louis D. Rubin, *George W. Cable: The Life and Times of a Southern Heretic* (New York, 1969), 13–18.

65. Paul H. Buck, *The Road to Reunion, 1865–1900* (Boston, 1937), 224–25.

66. Ibid., 221–24; Mott, *Magazines*, 3:397; John H. Nelson, *The Negro Character in American Literature* (Lawrence, Kans., 1926), 96.

67. Buck, *Road to Reunion*, 196–200, 235.

68. E. L. Tinker, "Cable and the Creoles," *American Literature*, 5 (Jan. 1934):317–26.

69. "Caesar Rowan," July 1871; "Mama Phoebe," Nov. 1871.

70. Introduction to Lanier, in Anderson, ed., *Works of Lanier*.

71. Julia Collier Harris, *The Life and Letters of Joel Chandler Harris* (New York, 1918), 164.

72. John S. Kendall, "Irwin Russell in New Orleans," *Louisiana Historical Quarterly*, 14 (July 1931):321–29; Jay B. Hubbell, *Southern Life in Fiction* (Athens, Ga., 1960), 80; Nelson, *Negro Character*, 97. "Nebuchadnezzar" appeared in June 1876, "Christmas Night" in Jan. 1878.

73. *Autobiography of Col. Richard Malcolm Johnston* (Washington, D.C., 1900), 89–90; Sophie Bledsoe Herrick, "Richard Malcolm Johnston," June 1888; Buck, *Road to Reunion*, 199.

74. Editorial, Sept. 1881.

75. Norman Foerster, "Later Poets," in *The Cambridge History of American Literature*, 3 vols. in 1 (New York, 1946), 3:31–52; Jensen, *Bunner*, 36–39; Brander Matthews, *These Many Years* (New York, 1917), 259.

76. Bianci, *Dickinson*, 79–80. Dickinson's warm friendship with Holland, and even more with his wife, is revealed in Theodora Van Wagenen Ward, ed., *Emily Dickinson's Letters to Dr. and Mrs. Josiah Gilbert Holland* (Cambridge, Mass., 1951).

77. Anderson, ed., *Works of Lanier*, 9:445n, 1:131n, 9:77.

78. Clara Barrus, *The Life and Letters of John Burroughs*, 2 vols. (Boston, 1925), 201–2, and *Atlantic Monthly*, 45 (Mar. 1880):417–18.

79. Robert E. Spiller et al., *Literary History of the United States*, 3 vols. (New York, 1948), 2:873–74, and Linnie Marsh Wolfe, *Son of the Wilderness: The Life of John Muir* (New York, 1947), 198.

80. Gilder to Charles G. Leland, Jan. 5, 1880, GP, and William Dean Howells, *Literature and Life: Studies by W. D. Howells* (New York, 1902), 7–8.

81. *Literary World*, 6 (June 1875);4.

82. Mott, *Magazines*, 3:13–16; Benjamin to Holland, July 13, 1871,

and editorial note thereon, Ward Collection; Odell, *Jackson*, 131; Biklé, *Cable*, 50n. Gilder helped Cable by introducing him to President Daniel Coit Gilman of Johns Hopkins Unversity, who hired Cable to give a series of lectures for which he was paid $1,000. Rubin, *Cable*, 120.

83. "Scribner's Miscellany," Sept. 1877, p. 10.

84. Maurice Thompson, quoted *Newsdealer*, 1 (Dec. 15, 1890):309; editorial, Mar. 1873; Charles Eliot Norton, "The Launching of the Magazine," *Atlantic Monthly*, 100 (Nov. 1907):579–81; *Literary World*, 2 (Nov. 1871):88.

5

The Alliance of Art and Morality

In its forceful social commentary and its cultivation of American literature, *Scribner's Monthly* made distinctive contributions to the development of the American periodical, but it was through its leadership in illustration that Josiah Gilbert Holland's magazine swept to popular success. Doubting the value of pictures at the outset, Holland by 1878 saluted the art department as the leading factor in the magazine's striking gains.[1] The fame of the wood engravings in *Scribner's* was by then international. Roswell Smith, touring Europe in 1879, was "astonished to find the estimation in which Scribner's art work is held [and] the desire of everybody to contribute to it."[2]

A surge of public interest in the graphic representation of events helped carry the new monthly to this height of recognition. The newspapers of the postwar period markedly increased their pictorial features, and illustrations in books, once exceptional, became the rule. Such illustrated weeklies as *Appleton's Journal* and *Every Saturday* gained large circulations, and *Harper's Weekly* headed the field. Among the monthlies, *Harper's* featured woodcuts that were an improvement over the steel engravings of the ladies' books and, although generally feeble as art and often irrelevant as illustration, helped win its national readership. Frank Leslie's various publications required the services of sixty-eight wood engravers in 1870, and in that year there were about 400 engravers in the United States; there were only a score a generation earlier.[3]

The contrasting fates of *Scribner's* and the *Galaxy* indicate the importance of catering to this demand for pictures. Established two years before Holland's magazine, the *Galaxy*, despite the excellence of its text, was outdistanced by its younger New York rival. It lacked the pulling power of a "Timothy Titcomb" and the business resourcefulness of a Smith, but probably the more fundamental cause of its failure was the inadequacy of its illustrations, which were so poor that Mark Twain satirized them in its own pages. But the public evidently preferred bad illustration to none at all, for the *Galaxy* reached its peak circulation of 23,000 in 1871 and, after dropping engravings a year later, sold less than 6,000 copies an issue at the end of 1877—just as *Scribner's* was preparing a midwinter issue of 100,000 copies.[4]

Having chosen to feature engravings, *Scribner's* staff exploited the decision with characteristic thoroughness, printing more than 2,700 woodcuts in its first five years at a cost of nearly $100,000.[5] Critical praise for the art work in the early numbers was nearly unanimous, and within a few years the press saluted the monthly's illustrations as unrivaled in the magazine field, while London observers called them the equal of the best work in Europe.[6] Yet these early pictures were crude in comparison with what was to come, for in the late 1870s *Scribner's* art department developed techniques that opened a golden age of magazine illustration.

For this achievement the monthly owed much to Alexander W. Drake, its art superintendent for more than forty years. A blonde, wiry man with thick blond beard and mustache, Drake had a simplicity of character and a deceptive vagueness of manner that he could dispel with a twinkle of his shrewd eyes. He had been trained as an artist and had been a professional wood engraver. His most distinctive trait was an exquisite taste that he sought to gratify at whatever cost in time and energy. Pursuing beauty in many inexpensive forms, he ransacked the tenements of New York and the ghettoes of Europe to build a fabulous collection of objets d'art and bric-a-brac, ranging from wrought brasses, tapestries, and paintings to bird cages, ship models, band-boxes, and oddly shaped bottles.[7]

Drake prodded and encouraged his retinue of artists and engravers to high standards of excellence. He schooled them also in a special technique. Under the system of engraving prevalent in 1870 the artist drew, in reverse, directly on the wooden block, a cramped medium requiring a skill at which few first-rate draftsmen were willing to try their hands. Drake perfected a method by which the block was sensitized—like a photographic plate—and the drawing or painting transferred to it by means of a camera. The engraver, with the original picture to guide and inspire him, then cut away with his burin. The new process could re-create not merely the line but the shades and textures of brush or crayon work of originals, regardless of size. This technique opened the way for the best artists of the time to contribute to the magazine without the risk of having their work misrepresented in reproduction.[8]

The new method called forth a special school of engravers, of whom Timothy Cole was the leading figure. A crusty, wry-humored little man, only five feet two in height, Cole came to *Scribner's* on Drake's invitation in 1875 and soon attracted attention by his ability to capture on wood the tone and the essential spirit of even the richest paintings. His engraving of James Edward Kelly's *The Gillie Boy* in the August 1877 issue was a milestone in magazine illustration that led to wide imitation of Cole's technique. In the following year he began a series of frontispiece reproductions from Wyatt Eaton's crayon portraits of famous American literary figures—William Cullen Bryant, Henry Wadsworth Longfellow, Ralph Waldo Emerson, Oliver Wendell Holmes, John Greenleaf Whittier—which, framed and hung in readers' homes, added greatly to the reputation of the craftsman and of the monthly that employed him. The issue of February 1878 carried two of Cole's most famous early wood engravings: the portrait of Abraham Lincoln, from Eaton's drawing, run as frontispiece to this number, and a detailed engraving of the fine bas-relief executed by Augustus Saint-Gaudens for the chancel of St. Thomas' Church in New York, a reproduction that the sculptor himself called "stunning."[9]

Almost equally notable in these years was the work of Frederick Juengling, whose engravings in several numbers of *Scribner's*, taken from drawings by Kelly, "made the first obvious, continued assertion of the new point of view." Meanwhile, *Harper's Monthly*, through its able art editor, Charles Parsons, also encouraged the new school, and the rival publications entered into a healthy competition for excellence in illustration.[10]

To exploit its new engraving method, *Scribner's* enlisted many of the country's foremost artists. New York in the late 1870s was teeming with young painters whose return from the ateliers of Europe promised a renaissance in American art. In spite of a broader public interest in art than ever before, however, these artists of the new school could not find a ready market for their canvases. The rising potentates of industry and finance, and the dealers who catered to them, preferred to invest in the real or supposed masterpieces of Europe, while the older patrons of native painting, through inertia or timidity of taste, continued to favor the conventional landscapes and portraits of an earlier day. The new generation of painters were forced to seek their income from teaching or illustration.[11] In 1878 Holland, recalling that leading painters had formerly refused to draw for the magazines, observed, "Within the past twelve months, some of the best artists in this country have been more than willing to furnish their exquisite work for the *Monthly*, and it will soon be impossible for any but the best artists to get magazine work to do."[12] In the past year to which he referred, serial novels in *Scribner's* had been illustrated by Walter Shirlaw and Charles S. Reinhart, poems by Will H. Low and John La Farge, and a single article on New England farm life by Winslow Homer, Shirlaw, Kelly, and Louis C. Tiffany. This was the year also in which the frontispieces by Eaton and Cole were attracting enthusiastic attention. With understandable pride, *Scribner's* issued its two handsomely bound volumes for 1877–78 with the names of illustrators and engravers listed for the first time in the table of contents.

In the next three years Thomas Eakins, W. M. Chase, Douglas Volk, A. B. Frost, Robert Blum, Edwin Austin Abbey, F. S. Church, Roger Riordan, Francis Lathrop, and Joseph Pennell were added to the list of American artists who drew for *Scribner's*. The editors even reached across the Atlantic Ocean for art work, hiring the famous, Spanish-born Daniel Vierge of the Parisian *Vie Moderne* to portray scenes from Eugene Schuyler's serialized biography of Peter the Great. "He's a ripper, and we'll have to look out for squalls," wrote a *Harper's* artist to his employer.[13] "Peter the Great" was first in a succession of lengthy biographies featured in *Scribner's* and the *Century* that depended for their appeal as much on the engravings as on the text. Articles of travel and description also lent themselves to lavish pictorial embellishment. William H. Rideing's "The French Quarter of New York" (November 1879), for example, was illustrated by Low, J. Alden Weir, J. H. Twachtman, Volk, and Blum. Essays on artists and

their work also offered opportunities for the magazine to parade
its corps of illustrators and engravers.

Celebrating this preeminence in illustration, Scribner and Company in 1879 offered *A Portfolio of Proof-Impressions from Scribner's
Monthly and St. Nicholas*, three-fourths of the plates taken from
Holland's magazine, and all produced under Drake's direction.
When a second portfolio appeared in the following year, 500
copies were exported to Britain, where critics extolled the skills
of its makers. "It is impossible for an Englishman to look through
this collection . . . without a deep feeling of humiliation," said
a writer in the London *Standard*. "English artists and engravers
do not produce such work." As the self-conscious champion of
American engraving, *Scribner's* in 1880 inaugurated an annual
prize competition for students of the craft. Thirty-two contestants
offered nearly 100 blocks for the first judging.[14] Holland boasted
that "American engraving has achieved its eminence in the world
simply because *Scribner's Monthly* has demanded, guided and stimulated it."[15]

An indispensable factor in the monthly's pictorial ascendancy
was the expert printing of its engravings. Holland's determination
to make *Scribner's* "as handsome a magazine as America produces"
was reflected in a typographical excellence that won high praise
for the earliest issues.[16] Yet three different printing houses were
tried before Drake's exacting standards for reproduction were
satisfied; he was happy only after the assignment was given, in
1876, to a devoted craftsman, Theodore Low De Vinne. As the
active partner of Francis Hart and Company, De Vinne had supervised the press work for *St. Nicholas* since 1873, and now he
joined Drake and Gilder to form the long-standing team that
produced the best looking publication in the United States. Thick-
set and bearded, deliberate in manner, De Vinne had schooled
himself in French, German, Italian, and Latin in order to master
the literature of his craft. Technically and artistically, he was
probably the foremost printer of his time in the United States.[17]

In printing engravings, De Vinne employed paper overlays,
cut in varying shapes, to stress certain areas of the electrotype
made from the woodcut and to bring out the tones of the original
art work. The initial press run of each number found the two
perfectionists, Drake and De Vinne, hovering anxiously over the

first warm sheets, and an issue of *Scribner's* might wait for days while the master printer laboriously padded some sunken section of the press bed in order to achieve a true reproduction. The ubiquitous Smith added his bit to the improvement of press work by suggesting a dry printing process, which was adopted successfully.[18]

While the work of Drake and De Vinne lent style and dignity to the magazine, Richard Watson Gilder was the guiding spirit in making *Scribner's* a spokesman for the arts and an exemplar of good taste. He aspired to make its pages, like his poetry, an expression of the ideal beauty to which he was devoted. Gilder's home was a rallying point for the younger artists of the country, to some of whom, just back from Europe, it seemed an oasis in a desert of materialism. Returning to America, Munich-trained painters like Frank Duveneck, Chase, and Shirlaw, and former Paris students like Weir and the Canadian-born Eaton were soon involved in a conflict with the established artists who dominated the National Academy of Design, which had been founded in 1826. Excelling in technique and individuality, the new men won so much attention in the Academy's exhibition of 1877 that the older painters, in self-defense, voted to relegate the work of this new school to obscure positions in the gallery. The inevitable revolt was touched off by the anger of Saint-Gaudens over the Academy's rejection of one of his sculptural sketches. The fiery sculptor met with Shirlaw, Eaton, and Mrs. Gilder at The Studio one evening in November 1877, and they formed the Society of American Artists, a rebel group, which most of the new school soon joined. Gilder became their editorial champion and amply exploited in *Scribner's* the new spirit of American art that their movement represented.[19]

Gilder took full advantage of the improvement in engraving technique to convey to readers his own eager interest in the fine and decorative arts. As early as 1871 *Scribner's* had given 6 percent of its total space to articles on these subjects; by 1880 it was 10 percent (Tables 1 and 2). The growing editorial enthusiasm for art was strikingly displayed in the space given to art and artists, too. Coverage in the early years was limited to departmental reviews of current exhibits, along with occasional articles, such as D. O'C. Townley's brief essays on "Living American Artists," illustrated with conventional portraits of the painters and sculptors he discussed. The marriage of art and engraving in the late 1870s produced a succession of major features richly illustrated with the best creations of brush, crayon, pencil, or pen. With the authoritative Russell Sturgis providing the descriptive text, *Scribner's* acquainted its readers with the line drawings and caricatures of Britain's John Leech, William Makepeace Thackeray, and George Cruikshank. A more romantic English genius was represented in nine illustrations accompanying Horace E. Scudder's "William Blake—Painter and Poet" (June 1880). William C. Brownell's article on expatriate James McNeill Whistler (August 1879) and Philip Gilbert Hamerton's essay on "Mr. Seymour Haden's Etchings" (August 1880) were other features designed to interest the magazine's new readers abroad as well as those at home. In three "Glimpses of Parisian Art" (December 1880, and January and March 1881), the editors provided samples of distinctive work in contemporary France. Helena de Kay Gilder translated Alfred Sensier's life of Jean François Millet, and this first full-scale treatment of the French peasant-painter, illustrated by his own distinctive landscapes and figures, was serialized over a five-month period in 1880. Gilder himself contributed an essay on Bastien LePage, the Parisian painter who had trained so many Americans. Ranging far in time as well as space to find masterworks for reproduction, *Scribner's* presented Clarence Cook's lengthy analysis of Leonardo da Vinci and the recent creations of American artists like Elihu Vedder and the versatile La Farge.[20]

The amplest pictorial spreads were those that reflected the renaissance in American art and aimed to gratify the awakened public curiosity about things artistic. In this category were Brownell's descriptions of New York and Philadelphia art schools, with reproductions of canvases by teachers and students. Brownell also wrote three articles on "The Younger Painters of America," with engraved examples of their work to support his critique. In William H. Bishop's "Young Artists' Life in New York" (January 1880), Holland's distant religious readers could learn that the atmosphere of the metropolitan studios, if esoteric, was earnest and moral.[21]

Readers were given a more informal look behind the easels in three articles that showed to what degree Gilder had made the monthly a semiofficial organ for the country's younger painters. These features followed the adventures of a group of new-school men who met once a week for companionship and mutual criticism, and rather jestingly contributed to the decorative craze of the period by daubing at tiles, often with pleasing results. Members of the fraternity were given whimsical nicknames—"The Gaul," "The Griffin," "The Grasshopper," "The Owl," "The Saint," or "The Pagan." In a humorously casual style that captured the *esprit* of the new movement, William Mackay Laffan ("Polyphemus" to his fellows) described a typical meeting in "The Tile Club at Work" (January 1879) and, with Earl Shinn, the highlights of a painters' picnic ("The Tile Club at Play," February 1879) and of a canal boat frolic ("The Tile Club Afloat," March 1880). *Scribner's* even followed American artists abroad, reporting on their life and work in the fields of Normandy (March 1878) and amid the scenic pleasures of Fontainebleau (May 1878).

Gilder hoped that noble monuments, planted amid the symbols of urban materialism, could inform the daily lives of Americans with beauty. In this spirit *Scribner's* published comments by Cook on recent church decoration (February 1878). Discussing La Farge's murals and stained glass windows for Trinity Church, Boston, and his design for the chancel of St. Thomas, New York, Cook noted that these were the first instances in which artists had been asked to enhance the splendor of churches in the United States. Gilder paid great attention to public monuments that he thought provided aesthetic education as well as inspiration to their beholders. Praising Saint-Gaudens's statue of Admiral David Farragut in Madison Square, he saw in this addition to the city's relatively few first-rate monuments a sign that popular appreciation of their value was on the rise (June 1881).[22] A similar faith in the educative force of culture was implicit in James Jackson Jarvis's "American Museums of Art" (July 1879), which suggested how smaller cities could support such institutions.

Thus *Scribner's Monthly*, first emphasizing art for illustration's sake, came to stress its broader significance in the life of the nation. Its editors thought of themselves as patrons of artists and exponents of their aims. In 1880, with the combined purposes of guiding public taste and encouraging native talent, they set up "The Scribner Art Agency," a nonprofit service to prospective purchasers of paintings and objets d'art. To its clients the magazine offered free advice on values, sent photographs on request, and stood ready to arrange transactions. In spite of a hearty endorsement by the newspaper press, the scheme evidently brought a disappointing response, for after announcing that orders were "slowly" coming in, the editors ceased to mention the agency.[23]

Holland, who attributed his monthly's leadership in art to Gilder and Drake, was genuinely proud of their achievement. "This magazine is buying invention and good composition constantly," he said in an editorial in August 1878, "and we do not hesitate to say that the two volumes which contain in any year the issues of *Scribner's Monthly*, can show more of both than any single exhibition of our National Academy . . . since the magazine began its existence." In the same year, a publishers' advertisement noted that while *Scribner's* was "a magazine for the people" with no single specialty, it could claim to have "become in reality a MAGAZINE OF ART."[24]

This was an anomalous development for a magazine founded on religious principles and directed by an editor who had won fame and fortune as champion of the plain Puritan virtues. While Gilder was the dynamic agent in the monthly's transformation, it is again worth noting how Holland's broadening view of life, resulting from his travels in Europe and his residence in New York, permitted him to welcome these changes in tone and content. To the Yankee who had struggled for an education, the cultural wealth of the Old World was a revelation. It was worth twenty years of work, he wrote Charles Scribner in 1868, to "roam over these old fields of art and civilization." He also brought back from his two years on the Continent an appreciation for gracious living, including the enjoyment of good food. In a September 1875 editorial, he defended transatlantic voyagers. The American who spent a year in Europe, he said, "got more pleasure for his money, more priceless memories, more useful knowledge, more culture in language, and manners, and art, than it would be possible for him to get at home in fifty years." What his adopted New York needed, said Holland (June 1877), was "to be made interesting, as London and Paris and Rome and

Florence and Munich are interesting." The European paintings that hung in Holland's spacious house on lower Park Avenue were the outward sign of his new delight in the world's aesthetic treasures.[25]

The New York in which Holland started his magazine was just awakening to its possibilities as a cultural metropolis. Much of the swiftly mounting wealth of the nation funneled into Manhattan. It was headquarters for the new captains of industry and finance who became patrons of the arts, and if their Midas touch brought forth much gilt, it also stimulated a genuine aesthetic efflorescence. New York was at once the magnet for native genius and the focal point at which European influence in arts and letters was drawn into the New World. It was, in short, an excellent vantage point from which to dispense information about the nation's accumulating cultural resources to the middle-class readers who, like Holland himself, were beginning to feel the need for an enrichment of American life.

"Timothy Titcomb" soon made himself at home in the metropolis. Eminently social by nature, he kept good horses and a carriage and entered joyfully into the pursuits of the urbanite. He found the city's lights and shops and companionship especially delightful in the winter months, in contrast to the remembered austerities of rural Massachusetts.[26] Combining his Yankee sense of civic duty with his newly whetted zeal for culture, Holland called on his fellow New Yorkers to make their community worthy of its size. He envisioned "village improvement" on a grand scale.

> The rich and well-to-do people, of all parts of the country, should be able to find in New York that which will make it a delightful home to them. The opera, the theater, the picture gallery, the museum, the library, the literary and scientific lecture, the choicest eloquence of pulpit and platform, bright and stimulating society in multiplied and multiform organization—all these should combine to make a winter residence in New York so desirable that all who have money and leisure, wherever they may live, will indulge in the luxury.[27]

One wonders how many of Holland's readers noted that religion was represented in this exciting image of the city only by the single word "pulpit."

Scribner's alternatively hailed civic and cultural progress—the creation of Central Park (September and October 1873) and the establishment of the Metropolitan Museum of Art (August 1871)—and deplored the city's shortcomings. "We have no libraries, no galleries of pictures and statues, worthy even of a large town, much less of a city that writes herself 'Metropolitan.'" These words appeared in the department, "Culture and Progress," in November 1873, and Gilder's authorship, or at least influence, can be suspected. But Holland seems to have accepted fully Gilder's belief in the tonic effect of art. Calling on New York's millionaires to endow an adequate gallery of art (the Metropolitan Museum was only a nucleus of what it was to become), Holland listed the obvious advantages—more art students, more visitors, more stimulus for genius—and then made a more sweeping claim. Such a gallery "would greatly change for the better the tone of society, and powerfully modify the civilization of the country."[28]

Scribner's also encouraged progress in private architecture. The process of converting wealth into "noon-day hideousness" was still going on in New York, Gilder observed (December 1877), but there were signs of improvement, with more trained architects at work than ever before. Looking to practical problems as well as aesthetic considerations, the monthly published James Richardson's argument for multistoried apartment buildings as the solution of the city's housing difficulties (May 1874). Urging the middle class to shed their prejudice against living in flats, the author presented finely illustrated plans for multiple dwellings.

Musical events in the city were reviewed each season as a part of "Culture and Progress." The magazine rejoiced in the triumphs of the American soprano, Clara Louise Kellogg, and, while paying tribute to the captivating Swedish singer, Christine Nilsson, observed that the taste of audiences in the United States had reached the point where concert managers could no longer deliver second-rate European artists to the public. *Scribner's* was especially appreciative of Theodore Thomas, the German-born conductor who was doing much to popularize symphonic music in America. An article in praise of Thomas (February 1875) urged New York to give him a permanent position, and when Thomas chose to lodge his orchestra in Cincinnati, Holland scolded his fellow-citizens for letting this talent get away. At the editor's request, Thomas, in March 1881, discussed "Music Possibilities in America," advocating the development of singing societies and more musical education in the schools.[29]

It was in his attitude toward the theater that Holland exhibited most strikingly his growing sophistication. It was he who had been responsible for the *Springfield Republican*'s reprobation of the stage, but in New York he shifted from antagonism to tolerance and finally to staunch defense of the theater. He had discovered that he himself could enjoy a good comedy or drama without endangering his soul; later, noting with satisfaction that refined and religious people were increasingly attending stage plays, he felt "no fears of a bad moral result of the theater upon the public."[30]

The magazine's coverage of the theater followed the ascending curve of Holland's approbation. Beginning with brief reviews of each season's outstanding events, *Scribner's* was soon printing feature articles on players and companies. One of these (June 1876) hailed Charlotte Cushman as a brilliant exemplar of American genius who stood for a wholesome trend in the theater. As leading European actors came to tread the New York boards, *Scribner's* acclaimed them as reinforcements in the struggle to purify and elevate the stage. Tommaso Salvini, the Italian tragedian, was "a revelation from another world" (December 1873); Helen Modjeska, the Polish actress who, like Salvini, was a frequent guest at The Studio, was praised in an essay by Gilder's brother-in-law, Charles de Kay (March 1879) and apostrophized in verse by Gilder himself (January 1879).

For its dramatic criticism and features, *Scribner's* relied principally on the versatile magazinist, Brander Matthews. Beginning in 1874, sometimes under the pseudonym "Arthur Penn," he wrote for "Home and Society" about suitable vehicles and staging techniques for amateur theatricals. His "Actors and Actresses of New York" (April 1879), for which Abbey and Reinhart drew Lester Wallack's performers in costume, was the first of several features in which the finest artists and engravers helped bring the contemporary theater to the pages of *Scribner's*. In "The American on the Stage" (July 1879), Matthews described the stage recreation of indigenous types like Colonel Mulberry Sellers, Rip

Van Winkle, and Davy Crockett. In "The London Theaters" (January 1881) and "Foreign Actors on the American Stage" (February 1881), both anonymously written, *Scribner's* continued to capitalize on the pictorial interest of the dramatic art.

So the Muses surrounded Holland's pulpit, and the good doctor smiled at their presence. At times, it is true, he was impelled to warn his readers against the "monstrosity" of art for art's sake or to remind them that "culture has not one purifying, or ennobling quality when unaccompanied by religion." Yet he heartily acclaimed his magazine's gathering reputation as champion of the arts. He recognized Gilder's lofty motives and accepted his assurance that the monthly's cultural function had moral ends. In Gilder's view, good art, like good poetry, was an expression of ideality that edified as well as enriched its beholder. "While there should be a purpose in every work of art," yet "it seems to be in the nature of things that each work of genius, though lacking the original and informing purpose, should have its beneficent lesson. . . . The painter brings you a bit of landscape; though he may have set about its painting with no special motive, still if he is a genius—master of method and lord of the aim— it is a piece of nature; the spirit of the woods and of the hills is in it, and that is the Spirit Eternal."[31] Although this equation of beauty with infinite truth was not explicitly Christian, Holland could easily agree with its moral purport. Both men aimed to improve American society, and Holland accepted Gilder's conviction that the inculcation of good taste would serve that end.

The crusader for good taste in the Gilded Age hardly knew in which direction to tilt his lance. With the onrush of material progress, Americans displayed an urge to add color and ornament to the increasingly urbanized environment. While the new millionaires spent fortunes on the art treasures of Europe, middle-class Americans shook off their Puritan heritage of austerity and began to litter their parlors with ornaments commensurate with their income. Books on pottery and home furnishing sold widely, and companies specializing in household decoration—Cottier's, Marcotte's, Herter's—sprang up to meet the demand of those with enough money and discrimination to patronize them. In one early manifestation of this art craze, *Scribner's* noted, one million painted Japanese fans were unloaded from a single ship at San Francisco. By the middle of the decade, one writer in the monthly remarked, old clocks, chairs, and china commanded nearly their weight in money. Holland noted that art had become "a sort of new gospel." Multitudes were "'decorating' porcelain, learning the 'Kensington stitch' in embroidery, painting on satin, illuminating panels, designing and putting together curtains, making lace, drawing from the antique, sketching, daubing, etc. etc."[32] Satirizing the overexuberance of the new devotees, a *Scribner's* cartoon in May 1877, showing an interior crammed with vases, china, Japanese fans, and bric-a-brac, was captioned: "This is not a museum, nor a crockery store, but simply Arabella's reception room."

The monthly's major effort to guide this popular fervor came in the mid-1870s when Cook wrote a series of eleven profusely illustrated articles on home furnishing under the title, "Beds and Tables, Stools and Candlesticks." Advice and suggestions were spooned out so liberally in these essays that Holland thought it right to warn his readers against overdecoration. Old washstands might be picturesque, he observed, but "we believe in plumbing."[33] This was common sense, but there was a moral point to be made, too, and there was a hint of editorial pressure in Cook's preface to his concluding article (May 1877). He had taken it for granted, he said, that his readers "knew how little furniture, and decorations, and equipage, have to do with happiness or with true largeness of life." All the same, *Scribner's* continued to encourage interest in household fineries with articles on ceramics, china, macrame lace, antiques, and embroidery. Such features were often chiefly displays of engraving talent, and they decreased in number as the magazine used its illustrative skills more seriously in descriptive views of art and the artists' life.

The wave of popular interest in things artistic reached its crest at the Centennial Exhibition in Philadelphia, where the picture galleries were continuously thronged. To Holland, this eager appreciation of culture marked "an era in the national life and development. To us it is the most hopeful and promising of all the possible results of the Great Exhibition." Gilder was less impressed, noting that admiration was greatest for the showiest rather than the best paintings and remarking that the education of taste was a long and subtle process. "It takes a strong stomach to stand all this modern babble about 'Art,'" Gilder lamented, "—to see people of 'culture' paying a thousand dollars for an imitation Japanese vase who would not pay ten cents for a photograph from Leonardo, or five dollars for a cast of one of Barye's lions."[34]

Gilder sought to improve taste less by preaching than by example. Using the magazine's expertise in engraving to spread before its readers the finest representations of plastic and graphic art, he aimed to make each number of *Scribner's* a silent sermon on beauty. He even turned its cover into a work of art in 1880, getting Stanford White to create a classic scroll design that, on tasteful tan paper, replaced the lilac-hued period-piece which the magazine had used during its first ten years.[35] Summarizing the aesthetic mission of their periodical, the editors declared: "In a country like ours, where galleries are few and worthy paintings rarely to be seen by people of culture out of the great cities, the educational service to be rendered by such art-work as that of *Scribner's* . . . is incalculable."[36]

Readers did not always take kindly to this tutelage. Some protested that the monthly's illustrations were not sufficiently pictorial, but to these dissidents Holland offered only a paternal pat. Most of them, he explained, had a love of the beautiful but "no knowledge whatever" of the principles of art. "Our people have seen so much less of fine art than those of France and Italy, that it has taken them longer to get inside of its meaning, and to understand its better methods; but they are rapidly acquiring knowledge in the right direction. We trust the time may soon come when they will have a hearty interest in the various experiments we make for their benefit, and understand the meaning of those essays in art which they have been wont to regard as fragmentary and imperfect." Those readers who demanded "finished" pictures, said the editor, had not yet learned to appreciate the "artistic suggestion" that *Scribner's* emphasized in its sketches. They had not yet come to realize that the "value of art—as even the value of nature—must be in what it reveals of spiritual truth, and not in its representation of external form and texture."[37]

The moralist thus embraced the arts not as indulgences but as allies in his purpose of improving American society. True, this partnership had wrought notable changes in the magazine. The sober format of 1870 had given way to richly illustrated pages. In content as in tone the transformation was apparent—only half as much space was devoted to religion at the end of the decade as at its beginning, and twice as many columns were given to literature and the arts (Tables 1 and 2). These changes reflected a subtle change in editorial emphasis. The note of evangelical Christianity sounded ever fainter in the late 1870s; as Gilder increasingly shaped the monthly's character, his ideality replaced revealed religion as the philosophical base of editorial policy.

Yet Gilder's essential purpose marked a revision rather than a rejection of Holland's original aim. The heritage of social criticism and concern for public affairs was retained, as a corps of earnest reformers took up the task that Holland had carried on with the help, chiefly, of a few clerical friends; their critique of society often invoked the ethics and spirit of Christianity. As Gilder took command, an ideal standard—for art, for literature, for public and private conduct—still gave cohesion to the magazine's policies.

NOTES

1. Editorial, Nov. 1878.

2. Smith to Holland, June 24, 1879, SC.

3. Frank Luther Mott, *American Journalism: A History, 1690–1960*, 3rd ed. (New York, 1962), 501–3; *Literary World*, 1 (Oct. 1870):72; *American Newspaper Reporter*, 5 (July 31, 1871):799; *American Literary Gazette and Publishers' Circular*, 16 (Nov. 15, 1870):35.

4. Frank Luther Mott, *A History of American Magazines*, 5 vols. (Cambridge, Mass., 1930–68), 3:379–81, and Sheldon and Company's statement in Galaxy Correspondence, New York Public Library; "Scribner's Miscellany," Mar. 1878, p. 7.

5. *Index to Scribner's Monthly, Volumes I to X* (New York, 1876), preface.

6. Gilder to R. R. Bowker, Dec. 15, 1870, Bowker Collection, New York Public Library, and publishers' department, Dec. 1872, p. 6.

7. Robert Underwood Johnson, *Remembered Yesterdays* (Boston, 1923), 99–102; William Webster Ellsworth, *A Golden Age of Authors: A Publisher's Recollection* (New York, 1919), 69–70; A. B. Paine, "A Memory," introduction to Alexander W. Drake, *Three Midnight Stories* (New York, 1916), xi–xiii; undated note [1950] from Rodman Gilder to the author.

8. Charles H. Caffin, "Timothy Cole and American Wood Engraving," *Printing Age*, 4 (Feb. 1905):339–43; Johnson, *Remembered Yesterdays*, 99–100; editorial, July 1879.

9. Augustus Saint-Gaudens, *Reminiscences*, ed. Homer Saint-Gaudens, 2 vols. (New York, 1913), 1:256; Caffin, "Timothy Cole," 339–41; Alpheus P. Cole and Margaret Ward Cole, *Timothy Cole: Wood-Engraver* (New York, 1935), 20–23.

10. Frank Weitenkampf, *American Graphic Art* (New York, 1924), 126; Caffin, "Timothy Cole," 339–41; J. Henry Harper, *The House of Harper: A Century of Publishing in Franklin Square* (New York, 1912), 202; Elizabeth Robins Pennell, *The Life and Letters of Joseph Pennell*, 2 vols. (Boston, 1929), 1:39.

11. Samuel Isham, *The History of American Painting* (New York, 1936), 359–60, 374.

12. Editorial, Nov. 1878.

13. E. V. Lucas, *Edwin Austin Abbey: Royal Academician. . . .*, 2 vols. (New York, 1921), 1:95. After some early work for *Scribner's*, Abbey became closely associated with *Harper's*.

14. London *Standard* quoted in "The Rise and Work of a Magazine," supplement to Nov. 1881 issue, 27–28; editorials, Apr. 1880 and Apr. 1881; advertisement, Dec. 1879, p. 309.

15. Editorial, Nov. 1880.

16. See quotes in publishers' department, Oct. 1871.

17. Mott, *Magazines*, 3:467; Johnson, *Remembered Yesterdays*, 108–12; Pennell, *Pennell*, 1:39; Ira H. Brainerd, "Theodore Low De Vinne: The Printer, the Author, the Man," *Printing Art*, 35 (May 1920):201–7.

18. Ellsworth, *Golden Age*, 199–203, and L. Frank Tooker, *The Joys and Tribulations of an Editor* (New York, 1924), 43.

19. Isham, *American Painting*, ch. 19; Will H. Low, *A Chronicle of Friendships, 1873–1900* (New York, 1908), 238–39; Rosamond Gilder, ed., *Letters of Richard Watson Gilder* (Boston, 1916), 81–82; Saint-Gaudens, *Reminiscences,* ed., Saint-Gaudens, 1:186–87; "The Old Cabinet," May 1878.

20. Cruikshank, June 1878; Leech, Feb. 1879; Thackeray, June 1880; LePage, June 1881; da Vinci, Jan. 1879; Vedder, Nov. 1880; La Farge, Feb. 1881.

21. Brownell on art schools, Oct. 1878 and Sept. 1879; on "The Younger Painters of America," May and July 1880 and July 1881.

22. This is a good example of how Gilder's personal ties and admirations were reflected in the magazine. On the evening of the *Farragut* unveiling, the Saint-Gaudenses celebrated with dinner at the Gilders. Gilder liked to brag that his legs were the model for Farragut's. Louise Hall Tharp, *Saint-Gaudens and the Gilded Era* (Boston, 1969), 157.

23. Editorial, Mar. 1880, and advertising section, May 1880, p. 11.

24. Editorial, Aug. 1878, and advertising section, Dec. 1878, p. 16.

25. Holland to Scribner, Aug. 16, 1868, SC, and author's conversation with Mrs. Theodora V. W. Ward, Holland's granddaughter, June 2, 1949.

26. Author's conversation with Mrs. Ward, June 2, 1949, and Mrs. H. M. Plunkett, *Josiah Gilbert Holland* (New York, 1894),197–99.

27. Editorial, June 1877.

28. Editorial, July 1874.

29. Nilsson, "Culture and Progress," May 1871; Kellogg, Apr. 1873; editorial, Aug. 1875.

30. Editorials, June 1872, Feb. 1875, May 1879, Feb. 1881; Richard Hooker, *The Story of an Independent Newspaper* (New York, 1924), 52; H. H. Peckham, *Josiah Gilbert Holland in Relation to His Times* (Philadelphia, 1940), 198.

31. Editorials, Apr. 1872 and July 1878, and "The Old Cabinet," May 1872.

32. Editorial, Jan. 1879; "Culture and Progress," Feb. 1873 and Aug. 1875; Noah Brooks, "A Fan Study," Sept. 1873; Oliver W. Larkin, *Art and Life in America*, rev. ed. (New York, 1960), 249–57.

33. Editorial, June 1877.

34. Editorial, Nov. 1876, and "The Old Cabinet," July 1878.

35. Ellsworth, *Golden Age*, 158–59, evidently errs in naming Saint-Gaudens as a collaborator on this cover. Rodman Gilder showed the author a copy of a letter from Drake, dated Sept. 1, 1913, in which Drake said: "I consider Stanford White's original cover design the finest magazine cover that I have ever known." A *Century* editorial of Mar. 1908, recalling the story of this cover, said that "an architect of genius" made "a new design in which the lettering was concentrated at the top of the page, in monumental fashion, and the color was changed." It added that the new design "was received with much ridicule" but eventually revolutionized magazine covers.

36. "The Rise and Work of a Magazine," Nov. 1881.

37. Editorial, Nov. 1880.

CHAPTER

6

Roswell Smith at Business

By 1880 *Scribner's Monthly* had passed the 100,000 mark in circulation and was gaining rapidly in popularity and prestige. Of
the three key figures in its rise to success, Josiah Gilbert Holland
and Richard Watson Gilder made clearly recognizable contributions—the one through his established ties with a national readership, the other by guiding the magazine into broader paths of
culture. Roswell Smith's part in the monthly's triumph, although
performed largely behind the scenes, was equally important.
Without him, as Holland and his associates knew and testified,
Scribner's could never have prospered.[1]

The austere business manager lacked the winning social warmth
of the editors with whom he worked. He seldom sought the
world's company, and although a few close friends understood
and loved him, many of his acquaintances, including his employees, stood in awe of his tall, bulky figure and bearded, pa-
triarchal presence.[2] Unlike Holland, the best-selling novelist and
eagerly read editorialist, he was virtually unknown to the public.
Compared with Gilder, the dynamic representative of a great
city's aesthetic interests, he was in the 1870s an obscure member
of New York's literary and publishing circle. But Smith, tending
to his own and the Lord's business with equal diligence, had by
1880 laid the firm groundwork for a great magazine and a new
and important book-publishing house.

He was a shrewd financial manager, possessed of natural acu-
men bolstered by legal training. Beyond this, he was a pervasive
influence in every phase of the magazine's operation, from its
editorial planning to its mechanical reproduction. He was an early
advocate of bulk mailing and prepaid postage for magazines,
although his friends may have claimed too much in citing him
as "largely responsible" for the adoption of this scheme into law

in 1874. He foresaw clearly that abolition of the practice by which the subscriber paid for stamps on his periodical would bring circulation gains that would more than compensate the publisher for absorbing the mailing costs.[3]

As a pioneer in magazine advertising, Smith tapped a rich source of revenue with a systematic thoroughness that introduced a new era in the economics of periodical publication. His fathering of successful new publishing enterprises added further to the funds on which the editors could draw in expanding the scope and appeal of their monthly. He conceived as well as financed the most famous of the magazine's early features, the "Great South" series, and carried it through on the dramatic scale that made it as much a promotional as an editorial triumph—for it gave *Scribner's* a "permanent and extensive circulation throughout the West and North-west" as well as the South.[4]

His brain continually teemed with such projects, some excellent but many of them appalling to his associates. "I never knew a more active or fertile mind," said Robert Underwood Johnson, the assistant editor, "nor one less capable of judging of its own products." Although his anxious partners and subordinates felt it necessary to curb his inventiveness, his busy imagination gave a progressive cast to editorial policy even as his business skill enlarged its range. He brought suggestion rather than dictation to the editorial office, accepting graciously when Holland vetoed one of his pet editorial notions.[5]

Meanwhile, he was an invaluable aide to the editor in the negotiations with high-priced writers and in the execution of plans for expensive serials. At times, as in the case of Bret Harte, it was his initiative that secured prized contributors for the magazine. Although no one had a sharper eye for the saving of pennies, he would spend boldly to put the stamp of authority on a special feature. Thus, he offered $7,200 for the text of Eugene Schuyler's "Peter the Great" and personally directed a search of European cities for its illustrations at a cost of about $25,000. He had "no relish for success by detail," Edward Eggleston observed, but "a passion for undertakings of the cosmical sort."[6]

Although Smith sometimes doubted the outcome of his own schemes, he was satisfied to accept the Lord's decision, and from this trust in Providence stemmed his calm propensity for moving forward in times of crisis. He showed this trait to advantage in the magazine's first year, when circulation charts indicated a dangerously static situation. *Scribner's Monthly* had been priced at $3 a year, one dollar less than *Harper's Monthly*, and its owners hoped that this rate would win them 100,000 purchasers by the end of 1871. The advance from the initial edition of 40,000 was dishearteningly slow, however, and Smith, faced with rising manufacturing costs and determined to put more money into advertising, decided that the price of the monthly must be raised and its size and scope increased. "The truth is that we have failed to get the $3 crowd," he told his partners. "We are on the other tack—and we must fight it out on that line." Holland agreed that this change was "the only thing that promises very brilliantly for the magazine."[7]

Accordingly, *Scribner's* raised its subscription fee to $4 in May 1872, explaining to its readers that it would otherwise "fall short of the ideal of excellence and power which had inspired the undertaking." At the same time a new and condensed type was adopted, which added "the equivalent" of thirty-two pages to each number. (Beginning with 112 editorial pages, the magazine was extended to 128 pages with its third volume, to 136 with the tenth volume, to 144 with volume eleven, and with the sixteenth volume, in 1878, to 160 pages.) The gamble was successful. A temporary loss in readership was repaired within three months, and *Scribner's* had edged up to a circulation of 47,000 in 1873 when financial panic gripped the nation.[8]

The hard times that followed posed another critical test for the management. As hard-pressed readers began to cancel their subscriptions, the publishers pointed their promotional arguments against this "mistaken economy," declaring that the magazine was more than ever needed by those sacrificing costlier amusements. But *Scribner's* fought for readers with more than pleas. Instead of retrenching, the editors, with Smith's support, raised their payments for contributions to bring into the periodical the best names in contemporary American literature. The purchase of Edward Everett Hale's magazine *Old and New* in 1875 added several thousand names to the subscription list, and in the same year Holland reported that his monthly, in spite of the depression, was "rising to a great success." The *Boston Transcript* pointed out that the publishers' "lavish spending" had been an indispensable factor in bringing *Scribner's* to its "exalted position" among magazines.[9] The average edition of 75,000 in 1878 showed that the young periodical had weathered the crisis.[10]

Nor did the tight money conditions at the close of 1873 stop Smith from proceeding with two new ventures that he had planned earlier that year. One of these schemes was to buy up the existing periodicals for young people and consolidate them into a single unrivaled publication. Accordingly, Scribner and Company (the magazine firm, not the book-publishing house) took over *Our Young Folks* from its Boston publishers and absorbed other juvenile periodicals, including the *School-Day Magazine* and the *Children's Hour* of Philadelphia and the *Little Corporal* of Chicago. The first printing of the new monthly was set for November 1873, and despite the panic, *St. Nicholas* appeared on schedule and grew rapidly in circulation and achieved fame never equaled by any other juvenile magazine. Mary Mapes Dodge was its editor for thirty years, a sane and practical woman with a gift for persuading the world's best authors to write stories for children without obviously writing down to them. To its publishers, *St. Nicholas* was a double bonanza, profitable both in itself and as the magnet for serialized tales that subsequently sold widely as books. When Smith broke with Charles Scribner's Sons in 1881, the corps of *St. Nicholas* writers was one of the most valuable assets he took into his new publishing house.[11]

In the same year Smith broke new ground by bringing out an English edition of *Scribner's Monthly*. Efforts to establish periodicals that would appeal to both Britons and Americans antedated the Civil War, but such ventures had originated in London and had made small appeal to readers in the United States. Smith's decision to take *Scribner's* abroad rested on a growing subscription list in England and a confident judgment that American magazines were outstripping their foreign counterparts in general excellence. In 1873 Smith sent advance sheets of the October issue to Frederick Warne and Company, with instructions that they be reprinted and bound with the advertising pages. Two thousand copies appeared on the Strand.[12]

Coincident with this invasion, such articles as Edmund C. Stedman's "Victorian Poets" and J. A. Froude's "Annals of an

English Abbey" were run in an obvious attempt to attract British readers; yet it was as a "characteristically American monthly" that Holland presented his magazine overseas. The transatlantic subscription list, as we have seen, did not deter *Scribner's* from featuring American fiction, and "The Great South" won as much attention in England as any article in the early issues. The advertisements were adapted to the British market, but the editorial content was identical in both countries, and the editors observed that their monthly's foreign readers were "all the kindlier toward it for its essential American quality."[13]

The press gave the newcomer a cordial reception, its comments growing increasingly enthusiastic as *Scribner's* began to exhibit its pictorial supremacy. The *New York World*'s London correspondent reported in 1880 that the illustrations in *Scribner's* "made its way easy" in England, and British critics agreed that its art work was incomparably better than that of any magazine published in their own land. The *London Times* hailed the invader as "a really magnificent triumph of American pictorial art and literary genius." More important, readers returned the same verdict. Aided by a price of one shilling—considerably lower than the thirty-five cents charged in the United States—circulation rose at an accelerating rate. The 15,000 copies of the November 1880 London edition reached a readership greater than any British monthly could boast in its own country. By 1881 an issue in England sold 18,000 copies. Meanwhile, Smith sent *St. Nicholas* abroad in 1876, where its success was proportionately as great as that of its sister publication. The years of uncontested triumph for *Scribner's* ended in 1880, when *Harper's Monthly* began its London edition and immediately became a strong rival for British patronage.[14]

The biggest single factor in the financial success of *Scribner's* was Smith's active solicitation of advertising. The *Atlantic Monthly* had carried advertisements as early as 1860, but no monthly with a large circulation had systematically cultivated the field of advertising before *Scribner's*. *Harper's* actually discouraged advertisements until the 1880s; its owners preferred merely to promote the books of the publishing house to which it was long regarded as an appendage. The pioneer advertising agent, G. P. Rowell, stood by in amazement as Fletcher Harper refused $18,000 from the Home Sewing Machine Company for the use of his monthly's last page for a single year. National advertisements in the religious and illustrated weeklies evidently suggested to Smith the adaptation of such business to his own publication, but he had to combat a persistent belief that any displays other than book notices lowered the dignity of a literary monthly. By breaking with this view, Smith not only insured the success of *Scribner's Monthly* but gave the first impetus to periodical advertising on a scale that led to the modern magazine of mass circulation.[15]

In 1870 Smith let it be known that *Scribner's* would run advertisements

> of a character likely to interest magazine readers. These will not increase the postage, while they will add materially to the ability of the publishers to render their magazine readable and attractive. . . . It is now well understood that a first-class popular magazine furnishes to all men who seek a national market the very best medium for advertising that exists. It is both widely distributed to the prosperous and intelligent classes of society, and carefully read and preserved.[16]

Following this announcement, Smith appointed Henry F. Taylor as the first full-time advertising manager in periodical history and began an earnest campaign for business. He set moderate rates—$100 for an ordinary page, $200 for a page adjacent to reading matter—emphasizing that *Scribner's* was seeking permanent patrons rather than large immediate returns.[17]

The amount of space sold mounted swiftly through the 1870s (Table 3). The magazine's fifth volume (November 1872 through April 1873) contained 88½ pages of paid advertisements. A drop to 81⅓ in the same months of 1873–74 marked the inroads of the depression, but the figure rose to 120 pages in the comparable period of 1875–76 and soared to 163 pages in volume twenty (November 1880 to April 1881). In the Christmas issue alone for 1880 *Scribner's* carried 42 pages of paid advertising.[18]

The character of these advertisements indicates as plainly as Holland's editorials that the monthly's readers were preponderantly from the substantial middle class. A breakdown of advertising contents for six months of 1880–81 shows that books, periodicals, and newspapers occupied 34 percent of all paid ad-

TABLE 3. Volume of Paid Advertising in *Scribner's Monthly*, 1872–81

Volume No.	Months	No. of Pages
4	May–October 1872	88½
5	November 1872–April 1873	101
6	May–October 1873	. . .
7	November 1873–April 1874	81⅓
8	May–October 1874	95½
9	November 1874–April 1875	97
10	May–October 1875	108
11	November 1875–April 1876	120
12	May–October 1876	. . .
13	November 1876–April 1877	. . .
14	May–October 1877	85
15	November 1877–April 1878	118
16	May–October 1878	82
17	November 1878–April 1879	116
18	May–October 1879	96½
19	November 1879–April 1880	138½
20	May–October 1880	118
21	November 1880–April 1881	163
22	May–October 1881	143

NOTE. Data are given as the number of pages sold, exclusive of cover pages, in each volume. The figures are based on page count of bound volumes of the magazine. Scribner and Company advertisements are not included in the totals. Three dots = not available.

vertising space and made up the largest single category of articles offered for sale (Table 4). Another index to the cultural level of subscribers was provided by the regular display advertising of the John Rogers statuary groups that enlivened so many parlors in this period. The staples of well-to-do family life—seeds and plants, home furnishings, clothing, musical instruments, clocks and watches, sewing machines—gave a dominant domestic tone to the advertising pages. Offers of wagons and farm journals on the one hand, and the buyers' guide to the shops of Manhattan on the other, were evidence that *Scribner's* spanned the distance between rural and urban America.

Striking changes in the nation's way of life were registered as the typewriter, the telephone, the fountain pen, and the bicycle made their way into the commercial displays. The rapid expansion

TABLE 4. Analysis of the Advertising Contents of *Scribner's Monthly*, Volume 21 (November 1880–April 1881)

Category of Article	Percent of Total Space
Publications	34
Patent medicines	15
Seeds and plants	6
Home furnishings	6
Music and musical instruments	6
Clothing	4
Educational	4
Pens and pencils	3
Machines and tools	2
Jewelry and watches	2
Bicycles	1
Sewing machines	1
Food	1
Miscellaneous	15
Total	100

NOTE. Data show the various categories of commodities advertised and the percentage of advertising space occupied by each category. The data are based on a page count and classification of advertisements in the bound volume. Scribner and Company advertisements have been subtracted from the total, so that the percentages are based on the 163 pages of paid advertising.

of the West was reflected in the Union Pacific Railroad's regular offer of free transportation and homesteads for settlers. A grimmer topical note was struck in July 1877 when the Western Gun Works of Chicago featured a new revolver called the "Tramps' Terror," with the observation: "Tramps, Burglars and Thieves infest all parts of the Country. Every One Should Go Armed."

Neither Smith nor Holland would have countenanced a liquor advertisement, but there were few such taboos. Patent medicines—many of them alcohol-based, one may be sure—occupied 15 percent of all display space in 1880, more than any class of goods except publications. To a physician who protested, Holland retorted that patented remedies were no more all frauds than medical men were all quacks. "The advertisements for the cure of disgusting and disgraceful diseases, involving immorality, will be published by no respectable man," said Holland, but the editors must be the judges of whether medical articles were good and useful, as many undoubtedly were.[19]

Some of the nostrums advertised in Holland's magazine must have taxed his credulity, however, particularly the "magnetic" cure-alls that a London firm began to promote in 1880. "Dr. Scott's Electric Hair Brush," with a handle that was supposed to produce an electric current, was "warranted" to end nervous headaches or neuralgia and to prevent baldness. The company next featured an "Electric Flesh Brush," advertised as a cure for lumbago, rheumatism, toothache, impure blood and impaired circulation. "By a happy thought," readers learned a short time later, the miraculous new principle was adapted to ladies' corsets. These "should be tried at once by those suffering from any bodily ailment," for they not only molded the figure but prevented any "tendency to extreme fatness or leanness." In a final extension of his magic, the redoubtable Dr. Scott put most remaining human ills to flight with a curative clothing which, if worn as directed, would "positively cure" asthma, rheumatism, constipation, impotence, paralysis, kidney disease, and seasickness.[20]

Toward an advertising abuse of a different sort, *Scribner's* took a more enlightened stand because of Gilder. It was common journalistic practice in the 1870s to carry concealed advertisements in the form of subsidized editorial features, and Holland, perhaps because of his newspaper background, could see no great wrong in accepting payment for such articles, as long as they were "squarely based on the merits of the thing praised." When Holland opened the monthly's pages to a thinly disguised publicity piece in 1878, Gilder made a strong remonstrance and immediately won his point. Holland's response showed his essential decency. "I don't think I would do wrong quicker than you if I could see it. I am inclined to think that your eye for a cracked thing is better than mine. One thing is certain: No money can come to me through arrangements of the character you criticize that will pay me for hurting your feelings, or the lowering of the moral standard of the smallest man in my employ. I shall certainly do as you ask me to do." Gilder's marginal note on this letter was: "There were no more paid-for or assisted articles in the magazine after this."[21]

Gains in advertising revenues in the late 1870s were even greater than the gains in volume of advertising, for mounting circulation enabled Smith to raise his rates. He had asked $100 for an ordinary page in the early years but had at times accepted half that amount to encourage business. By 1878 an advertising agency paid Scribner's $112.50 per page, and Smith could sell the first inside page for $150. By 1880 the standard rate for a regular page was $270.[22]

Meanwhile, *St. Nicholas* was also prospering, and Smith had developed a big business in the publication and sale of hymn books. From these various enterprises Scribner and Comany drew so much income that its stockholders divided $30,000 in profits for 1878. At the same time, indebtedness was virtually eliminated. By 1880 the amount for dividends had reached $50,000 with the expectation of continuing profits so strong that stock in the partnership sold at $1,000 a share. (Holland sold most of his shares in that year to his magazine associates at this price.) Capitalized in 1870 at $12,000, ten years later the magazine company was worth half a million dollars.[23]

In the very process of scoring this dramatic success, Smith and his associates brought about the break up of Scribner and Company, for in building up the magazine firm's activities and resources, they had virtually created a general publishing house of their own. Smith's ambitious schemes brought into the open a conflict of views as to the proper scope of the magazine company's operations—a conflict hard to resolve, in part, because of the uncertain terms of the partnership formed in 1870.

Scribner and Company had been organized in that year, with Holland and Smith owning 60 percent of the stock and the remaining 40 percent in the possession of Charles Scribner's publishing house. Scribner had been troubled by Holland's insistence on complete editorial independence, but this and other differences between these two Christian friends were soon adjusted. However, Scribner died in 1871, in his fifty-first year, and his book firm was reorganized as Scribner, Armstrong and Company, the partners including two of the founder's associates, Andrew C. Armstrong and Edward Seymour, and his eldest son, John Blair Scribner. When Seymour died and Armstrong retired, in 1878, the second Charles Scribner joined his older brother in the business, and their concern, now known as Charles Scribner's Sons, retained intact the two-fifths interest in Scribner and Company.[24]

It was with these two sons of his old friend that Holland and his colleagues differed, eventually irreconcilably, over the status and policies of the magazine company.

The key figure in the dispute was Smith, and the central point at issue was his determination to operate Scribner and Company independently of the book firm and on his own terms. It is not surprising that the Scribners objected to this attitude, for the leading American magazines had traditionally been adjuncts of publishing houses, and *Scribner's Monthly* had been in a sense an outgrowth of Scribner's *Hours at Home*. Just as understandably, Holland and Smith resented any suggestion that their magazine was a mere stepchild of the book company. Not only did they own a majority interest, but they had brought their magazine through the depression and had made it one of the most popular and profitable monthlies in the United States. Both were men who craved recognition for their accomplishments. "I know it to be simply right," Holland told J. Blair Scribner in 1878, "that we two men who have wrought out the brilliant success of these two magazines should . . . be treated differently from a clerk and a hired editor." Smith, especially, had labored in comparative obscurity, Holland said, and he thought the business manager deserved both more credit and more salary. "Your house is richer by $200,000, and I am richer by the same sum, for this work of Mr. Smith," Holland told Charles Scribner in 1880, "yet through all these ten years he has had no public recognition. . . . For five years, at least, he has labored under a constant sense of wrong." (Eventually Holland halved his own salary to double Smith's.)[25]

Blair Scribner's view—that the "remarkable success of the two magazines is in a *very great* measure due to the time and attention which you have both given to them"—seemed to reserve some credit for success to the Scribner connection. As late as 1881 Holland still complained of the "persistent reiteration by the press of the idea that the magazine house is only a department of the book house and the outgrowth of a business policy originated outside of these rooms—than which nothing could be more provokingly untrue."[26]

What Smith wanted most, however, was not mere recognition of past achievements but a free hand to expand his company's business in whatever direction his inventive mind might wish it to go. It was evidently with the book firm's approval that he started and built up the children's magazine. Even when the magazine company in 1877 published its first book, a collection of poems and stories from *St. Nicholas* called *Baby Days*, the house of Scribner was not perturbed. But when Smith branched out from this special project into the regular publication of books, a sharp dispute was in the making.

Smith's entry into the book field was, he believed, another instance of his fruitful working alliance with Providence. His Presbyterian pastor, the Reverend Charles S. Robinson, had compiled a hymn book that, through Smith, he offered to the Scribners for publication. When they declined it, Smith decided that Scribner and Company should print and market the volume. By 1879 the magazine firm had scored a great success with Dr. Robinson's *Spiritual Songs* and with a second collection of hymns for Baptists compiled by Robinson in collaboration with another minister. In that year Smith purchased the plates, copyright, and stock of Robinson's remaining works and prepared to extend this profitable sideline.[27]

Young Charles Scribner, barely twenty-five, and left in command of the family business by the death of his brother in January 1879, was alarmed at these events. He accused Smith and Holland of usurping the good will of his concern by publishing books under the Scribner name. The magazine partners countered with an offer to change the name of their organization to Roswell Smith and Company. They insisted that their articles of incorporation gave them the right to issue "magazines, *books* and pamphlets," and pointed out that Scribner had earlier conceded this prerogative. When Scribner asked his attorney to look into this claim, the lawyer reported, "There is as you expected an ugly clause." He expressed the fear that Smith was "pushing" to build up a great rival concern.[28]

How far Smith and his associates would have gone in book production had they remained on friendly terms with Scribner is problematical. Until 1880 they always gave him first chance at book material. By that time, however, both sides were embittered by misunderstandings and accusations, and the magazine people were prone to press their "rights."[29] In 1880 Gilder notified such contributors as John Hay and Frances Hodgson Burnett that the monthly might "one of these days" find it possible to publish its serials in book form also. A short time later Gilder told Scribner that the magazine firm would "not be driven" into general publishing unless "driven away" from the house of Scribner altogether, but if there were some books "out of our own pages—or suggested by our connections—that we think we can handle more advantageously—we want you to join in the enterprise of letting our house run them."[30]

If Scribner felt wronged by his magazine partners, they in turn cited grievances against his company. By established practice, Charles Scribner's Sons enjoyed special rates for its advertisements in *Scribner's Monthly*. Although willing to continue this concession, Smith complained that the book firm preempted the most desirable space, which he could otherwise sell at premium rates. The public's confusion of Scribner and Company with Charles Scribner's Sons meant that correspondence, subscriptions, and orders intended for the magazine concern frequently went to the book house. On at least one occasion, a Scribner representative demanded that his firm's books receive special consideration in the monthly's editorial columns, to which the editors retorted that their reviews must be free from prejudice or obligation.[31]

Smith's eagerness to be rid of these entanglements and restrictions was made clear as early as 1878, when he undoubtedly foresaw the forthcoming rapid expansion of business. In March of that year he and Holland surprised the Scribners with an offer to buy their 40 percent interest in the magazine company. "This affair quite knocked me at first," J. Blair Scribner admitted, but he was soon "ready for a fight all around if necessary." He believed Smith and Holland would offer $500 a share for his firm's 200 shares. This would have assured the Scribners of a tidy profit, since the shares were valued at only $24 when the company was founded; however, Scribner observed, "We cannot afford . . . to part with the stock at any price if we go on in the Book business."[32]

As business and profits for Scribner and Company reached new high levels in the next two years, Smith determined to end the ties with the book company. In November 1880, he submitted three succinct questions to Charles Scribner: Would he sell his interest in Scribner and Company? If not, would he buy out Smith and Holland? If neither, would he consent to changes which would make the magazine company independent in fact and name?[33]

Young Scribner faced a serious dilemma. He was inexperienced in the production of a magazine and felt that purchase of complete ownership would place too great a drain on his energies and finances. He knew, too, that Smith would use the capital derived from the sale to set up a competitive publishing house.[34] Yet Scribner was equally reluctant to sell. His investment in Scribner and Company brought him increasingly larger dividends. More important, as long as he held his shares, he exercised at least a partial control of an organization that, if turned over entirely to Smith, would be an even more powerful competitor.[35] So he rejected Smith's new offer of $200,000. He would not sell for less than $300,000, he declared, nor would he promise not to start a magazine of his own. Declining these terms, Smith persisted in his efforts to get full ownership, offering to refer the price and conditions of sale to arbitration.[36]

Holland, meanwhile, was in poor health, weary of the conflict, and ready to retire. At the end of 1880 he sold enough of his stock to Smith to insure the latter's majority interest and disposed of most of his remaining shares—at $1,000 a share—to the "younger men" of the magazine: Gilder and Johnson of the editorial staff; Alexander W. Drake of the art department; and Frank H. Scott, Charles F. Chichester, and W. W. Ellsworth (a cousin of Smith's) of the business office.[37] The struggle was now directly between Scribner and Smith, and it was, in Scribner's own view, "irrepressible." The prospect of a last-ditch fight with the man whom even the charitable Gilder called "inexorable" in business matters was not a pleasant one. As one of Scribner's associates reminded him, Smith, although "an honorable man and a good Christian I doubt not," was "a man of a very different calibre to Dr. Holland who was a fast friend of your Father and of his family."[38]

Holland summed up for Scribner the futility of his further resistance:

The magazine house will never again be managed with the slight-est reference to the business interests of Charles Scribner's Sons. . . .
if you claim that they are publishing books in a name resembling
that of the bookhouse, they will, I believe, petition to have the
name of the company changed. That they are determined to have
a free and independent publishing house, I am certain, and you
cannot possibly prevent it. They have the right by charter and
practice, and by the majority interest.[39]

Confronted with these realities, Scribner decided that selling
his interest would be the lesser evil. On April 4, 1881, Smith
purchased, in the name of his wife and himself, the 200 Scribner
shares for $200,000. The contract stipulated that the name of
Scribner and Company was to be changed as soon as practicable
and that the name *Scribner's Monthly* was also to be altered, be-ginning with the November 1881 issue. Scribner agreed not to
start a competing periodical within five years—an injunction that
he took quite literally, for he launched *Scribner's Magazine*, much
to Smith's chagrin, almost immediately on the expiration of this
grace period.[40]

The contract provided that $120,000 of the purchase price be
paid in notes at 6 percent, to be retired in one to six years. Smith
doubtless expected to meet this obligation out of the magazine's
profits, but when a railroad was built through some coal prop-erties he had retained in Indiana, he was able to sell his land for
nearly the whole amount of the debt—a fortuitous development
for which he duly once more gave the credit to Providence. Thus
his publishing house began its course on a solid financial footing.[41]

At Gilder's suggestion the new firm was called the Century
Company—after the well-known Century Club—and *Scribner's
Monthly* became the *Century Illustrated Monthly Magazine*. The
renamed monthly resumed its career as a swift-going concern.
Its management, with increasing resources at its disposal, had
confidence born of experience and a new freedom to be as ven-turesome as it wished to be. The subscription list of *Scribner's*,
its connections with the worlds of literature and art, and its
tradition of social and political criticism were all carried over
intact to the *Century*. With veteran editorial and art departments,
headed by men who were themselves proprietors, the magazine
set out upon a fresh and brilliant phase of its history.

NOTES

1. Holland to Charles Scribner, Nov. 17, 1880, SC, and Robert Underwood Johnson, *Remembered Yesterdays* (Boston, 1923), 97.

2. George W. Cable, *A Memory of Roswell Smith* . . . . (New York, 1892), 11–12, 42, and L. Frank Tooker, *The Joys and Tribulations of an Editor* (New York, 1924), 59, 95–96.

3. William Webster Ellsworth, *A Golden Age of Authors: A Publisher's Recollection* (New York, 1919), 11, and Washington Gladden, "Roswell Smith," June 1892. Smith no doubt helped win acceptance of the prepaid plan, but Postmaster-General John A. J. Cresswell had proposed it in his report for 1869, before Smith entered the magazine field.

4. Quoted from the *Boston Transcript* in Mar. 1876 issue, inside back cover.

5. Johnson, *Remembered Yesterdays,* 96, and Gladden, "Roswell Smith."

6. Edward Eggleston, "Roswell Smith," *Harper's Weekly,* 36 (Apr. 30, 1892): 416; Smith to Charles Scribner, Sept. 23 and Oct. 26, 1880, SC; advertising section, Mar. 1880, p. 8.

7. Smith to Andrew C. Armstrong and Edward Seymour, n.d. [1871], and Holland to Smith, July 21, 1871, SC.

8. Publishers' department, May 1872, p. 7, and *George P. Rowell and Company's American Newspaper Directory* (New York, 1873), 158.

9. *Boston Transcript* quoted Mar. 1876, advertisement inside back cover; advertising section, Jan 1874, pp. 6–7; editorials, May and July 1875.

10. Smith to J. Blair Scribner, n.d., SC. Prior to the establishment of the Audit Bureau of Circulation in 1914, published circulation figures were generally based on publishers' claims or estimates. Based on checks that can occasionally be made on such claims in the editors' or publishers' private correspondence or memoranda, I have found the figures given by *Scribner's Monthly* and the *Century* to be generally reliable.

11. Editorial, June 1881; *New York Tribune,* Apr. 20, 1892 (Smith's obituary); J. C. Derby, *Fifty Years among Authors, Books and Publishers* (New York, 1884), 706–7; Frank Luther Mott, *A History of American Magazines,* 5 vols. (Cambridge, Mass., 1930–68), 3:501. For retrospective impressions of a generation's delight in *St. Nicholas,* see the preface and introduction to Henry Steele Commager, ed., *The St. Nicholas Anthology* (New York, 1948), xv–xvii, xix–xxi.

12. "A Greeting to Our English Readers," editorial, Nov. 1873; advertising section, Nov. 1875, p. 11; Mott, *Magazines,* 4:229; Clarence Gohdes, *American Literature in Nineteenth Century England* (New York, 1944), 59–63.

13. Advertising section, July 1874, p. 5, and "The Rise and Work of a Magazine," Nov. 1881.

14. *London Times,* quoted in Scribner and Company advertisement, *Critic,* 1 (Jan. 29, 1881):14; advertising sections, July 1874, p. 5; Nov.

1875, p. 11; Apr. 1880, p. 12; Feb. 1881, p. 6; May 1881, pp. 145–46; Gohdes, *American Literature in Nineteenth Century England*, 59–63; Mott, *Magazines*, 3:467.

15. Frank S. Presbrey, *The History and Development of Advertising* (Garden City, N.Y., 1929), 457, 466, 470; George P. Rowell, *Forty Years an Advertising Agent, 1865–1905* (New York, 1906), 23, 444; Mott, *Magazines*, 3:9; *Literary World*, 4 (Jan. 1874):120. From 1874 to 1880 inclusive, *Harper's* carried no paid advertising; S. A. Sherman, "Advertising in the United States," American Statistical Association *Publications*, n.s., 7 (Dec. 1900):122.

16. Quoted in Presbrey, *Advertising*, 468.

17. Advertisement inside back cover, June 1872, and Scribner and Company advertisement in publishers' department, same issue, p. 3; Presbrey, *Advertising*, 469; Ellsworth, *Golden Age*, 121.

18. Author's count from bound volumes in Library of Congress. See also Mott, *Magazines*, 3:9.

19. Editorial, June 1881. Tobacco advertisements were accepted.

20. These Scott advertisements carried over into the magazine's years as the *Century*.

21. Rosamond Gilder, ed., *Letters of Richard Watson Gilder* (Boston, 1916), 87–88. The objectionable article was evidently one called "How Pencils are Made," Apr. 1878, which fulsomely praised the products of the Dixon plant.

22. Memorandum, Scribner and Company to Charles Scribner's Sons, Apr. 17, 1881, Smith to Scribner, Mar. 10, 1880, SC; *N. W. Ayer and Son's Directory of Newspapers and Periodicals* (New York, 1880), 56. The rate was actually quoted at $12.50 per 10 agate lines.

23. Smith to Holland and Charles Scribner, Mar. 10, 1880; J. Blair Scribner to John I. Blair, Jan. 1, 1881; Holland to Charles Scribner, Jan. 1, 1881, SC.

24. *New York Tribune*, June 14, 1878, and advertising section, Aug. 1878, p. 7.

25. Holland to J. Blair Scribner, Aug. 17, 1878, to Charles Scribner, Nov. 17, 1880, SC; Johnson, *Remembered Yesterdays*, 83.

26. J. Blair Scribner to Holland, Aug. 22, 1878, and Holland to Charles Scribner, Jan. 10, 1881, SC.

27. Advertising section, July 1879, p. 6, and Johnson, *Remembered Yesterdays*, 83.

28. Holland to Charles Scribner, Dec. 24, 1880, and A. B. Crane to Charles Scribner, Oct. 15 and Dec. 17, 1880, SC.

29. Holland to Charles Scribner, Oct. 26, 1880, SC. Smith declared that if the *right* of the magazine partners to publish books were granted, they would be willing to make concessions to the Scribner book firm out of courtesy. Smith to Charles Scribner, Mar. 30, 1879, SC.

30. Gilder to Charles Scribner, Jan. 15, 1881, SC; Gilder to Hay, Nov. 26, 1880, and to Mrs. Burnett, Dec. 31, 1880, GP.

31. Smith to Charles Scribner's Son's, June 20, 1878, Scribner and Company to Charles Scribner's Sons, Jan. 31, 1881, Smith to Charles Scribner, Mar. 30, 1879, Holland to Charles Scribner, Nov. 3, 1880, R. U. Johnson to Charles Scribner, July 19, 1879, SC.

32. J. Blair Scribner to John I. Blair, Mar. 20, 1878, SC.

33. Smith to Charles Scribner, Nov. 13, 1880, SC.

34. Charles Scribner to Holland, Nov. 1, 1880, SC. None of the parties doubted Smith's intention of remaining in the publishing business. In making what appears to be his final bid to sell to Scribner in March 1881, Smith reserved for himself the right to acquire the hymn book business by compensating the other stockholders for their interest in it. This would give him the nucleus for a publishing house. He agreed not to ask for any Scribner and Company employees. Smith offered 260 shares owned by himself and his wife for $260,000; he evidently had acquired sixty shares from Holland. Smith to Charles Scribner, Mar. 1, 1881, SC.

35. Several memoranda and letters in the Scribner archives refer to a "two-thirds rule," suggesting that the Scribner interest could technically block or influence major policy decisions of the magazine company.

36. Smith to John I. Blair, Dec. 13, 1880, copy in SC.

37. Holland to Charles Scribner, Jan. 1 and Jan. 3, 1881, SC; *New York Tribune*, Apr. 6, 1881.

38. Charles Welford to Charles Scribner, June 17, 1879, Smith to John I. Blair, Dec. 13, 1880 (copy), SC; Gilder to Sidney [de Kay], Apr. 29, 1884, GP.

39. Holland to Charles Scribner, Jan. 1, 1881, SC.

40. Copy of contract, SC; Rowell, *Forty Years*, 415; Roger Burlingame, *Of Making Many Books: A Hundred Years of Reading, Writing, and Publishing, MDCCCXLVI-MDCCCCXLVI* (New York, 1946), 200–2.

41. Ellsworth, *Golden Age*, 110.

7

Gilder in Command

Josiah Gilbert Holland died at sixty-two on October 12, 1881, a few days after a copy of the first number of the *Century* was placed in his hands. He had known for several years that his heart ailment was incurable, but had worked calmly on, enjoying "the privilege of this precious relation to a million interested and affectionate readers." To the end, his admirers remained devoted to him. Many made vacation pilgrimages to "Bonnie Castle," his summer cottage on one of the Thousand Islands, and carried off pebbles from his driveway as cherished mementoes of "Timothy Titcomb." Representative of small-town sentiments were the tributes read at the teachers' institute of St. Joseph, Illinois, to "the two great Americans who have recently passed away—President James A. Garfield and Dr. J. G. Holland." As the *New York Tribune* remarked, perhaps no other American author's death would have touched so large a number of people with a sense of personal loss.[1]

In the metropolis, too, where many of his erstwhile critics had come to respect his sincerity and tolerance, Holland was warmly remembered. The staff of his magazine recalled his unfailing gentleness and his numerous acts of kindness, as well as his forbearance of faults. As Richard Watson Gilder wrote to William Dean Howells, "We all had an affection for him which has grown deeper to the last—and which was returned by him with large interest. A gentler and tenderer heart there never was."[2]

While Holland was sincerely mourned as friend and counselor, his death was not a serious blow to the monthly he had helped to establish. As the moralizing author of "Topics" he was, to some readers, irreplaceable—and Gilder, as we shall see, did not try to supplant him as sole editorialist. But the publication that bore Holland's imprint at its birth had grown into a national institution independent of any personal following. Gilder had already assumed a large share of the editorial direction and infused the magazine with his ideas and tastes. When he formally replaced Holland, he already possessed the experience, the talent, and the will to be one of the great editors of his time. Within a year after Gilder took command, the *Nation* called his monthly "perhaps the most judiciously edited magazine in the world."[3]

Gilder, at thirty-seven, had already been moving and working for ten years at the prodigious pace that periodically brought him to the verge of nervous exhaustion. Ceaselessly active as poet and editor, he got caught up also in civic and cultural causes, his sympathies leading to engagements that his conscience magnified into duties. His absent-mindedness and lack of punctuality were symptoms, not of daydreaming, but of his complete absorption in every task or conversation. He was not a deep or original thinker, but he had a remarkable capacity for enthusiasm about people, music, works of art, and the United States. Augustus Saint-Gaudens, searching for a phrase to express his own admiration for Robert Louis Stevenson, said, "I now understand the condition of mind Gilder gets into about people." He drew out the best in his contributors by his intense sympathy with their efforts. He did not simply critique a piece of fiction, Frances Hodgson Burnett recalled; he entered into it, identified with the characters, exclaimed about them and the plot. "His notes about one's work," Burnett said, "were the most wonderful notes in the world."[4]

Since every waking hour represented a missionary opportunity for Gilder, he was a tremendous and cheerful worker. Good editors usually work long hours and dig into details, but Gilder exceeded the norm in both respects. The French artist André Castaigne, commissioned to re-create the Seven Wonders of the World in a series of paintings for the *Century*, was astounded at Gilder's detailed suggestions for obtaining information on the vanished monuments; he thought it was "quite wonderful that a man like you, with a head full of so many big enterprises, should give attention to these trifles. This is another proof that a poet can be . . . a clever and cunning administrator."[5]

Although his standards of conduct were severe, for others as for himself, Gilder was too humane to be self-righteous, and he had none of the zealot's vindictiveness. His good will and boyish good humor endeared him to a host of friends, from impecunious poets and artists to presidents of the United States and millionaires. Andrew Carnegie told Henry Holt, the publisher, that he had never loved any other man as he loved Gilder. Walt Whitman, who marched to a far different drummer than Gilder, nevertheless declared that Gilder "has my admiration for some things he has done . . . and my personal love surely, always, always." Men tended to regard Gilder as an earnest but not censorious keeper of their consciences.[6]

Energy, enthusiasm, an enormous bank of good will among those who knew and dealt with him—these, then, were some of Gilder's assets as an editor. To these one must add another attribute—courage. If Gilder's poetry ran—in Whitman's phrase—to "delicatesse," and his literary taste to gentility, if his editorial crusades often transcended the meaner areas of political and social conflict, it was not timidity but aspiration that led him to shun the earthier plane. When conscience told him it was necessary, he could get down in the dirt and fight, as he did in his battles for municipal reform and the improvement of tenements. And however much he scattered his energies, his efforts were powered by a central purpose: to realize the ideals in which he had a missionary faith.

Gilder's editorial staff enthusiastically supported his high aspirations, maintaining for thirty years an esprit de corps that thrived on purposeful striving toward ideal ends. Gilder's chief lieutenant during all of this time was Robert Underwood Johnson, a loyal adherent to the banner of ideality. A stickler for order and form, whether in literature or in the social amenities, Johnson as he matured became the academician par excellence. Erect, trim, neatly bearded, he was vain and stiff-mannered but kindly. "I do not think there is a truer or more loyal man living," said Maurice Francis Egan. He had the conservative's respect for responsibility, executing thoroughly every task assigned him while conscientiously suggesting ways to improve the magazine.[7]

Born in 1853—nine years after Gilder—Johnson was the son of a prominent Indiana lawyer and judge. He was graduated from Earlham College, a Quaker school in his native state, at the age of eighteen. With no more than a "vague predilection" for literature, he accepted a clerkship in Scribner's educational book agency in Chicago. Two years later, at his employer's suggestion, he went to the East to fill the editorial vacancy left on *Scribner's Monthly* when Frank R. Stockton moved over to *St. Nicholas*.[8]

He soon proved to be an invaluable member of the staff, especially as a proof reader. He had an unerring eye for misspellings, grammatical lapses, and bad literary form, and a deadly hatred of inaccurate quotations. Working in a methodical, leisurely manner, he was usually at his desk long after his associates had departed. Himself a successful poet, he was a sensitive critic of creative writing within the rigidly conventional limits he recognized. Gilder came to feel "the very highest respect" for his judgment.[9]

His trustworthiness soon brought him an assistant editorship; in 1879–80, when Gilder was abroad to recover his health, Johnson was Holland's managing editor. On Holland's death he became associate editor and Gilder's heir-apparent; but he had to wait more than a quarter of a century for his chance to direct the monthly, and when the call came, his magazine's star had set. But in the 1880s and 1890s, the glory years for the *Century*, Johnson was a power in his own right, a profound and conservative influence on the periodical literature of his age.[10]

Next in line to Johnson was Clarence Clough Buel, the assistant editor. Although born in New York State, in 1850, Buel was raised in the Midwest and was one of the first students to enroll at the University of Minnesota. After completing his university training at Berlin and Munich, he broke into journalism as assistant editor of the *Minneapolis Tribune*, then moved to the *New York Tribune*. Joining the *Century* staff in 1881, he brought with him a useful knowledge of public affairs and a practical sense of what made an article newsworthy.[11]

Buel, although affable and full of quiet humor, was puritanical, discreet, and retiring. Although slow-spoken, he was always busy and bustling, his desk stacked high with manuscripts and correspondence. A stocky, bearded man of robust integrity, he was at his best in attacking political chicanery. In addition to his editorials in this vein, he wrote an exposé of the Louisiana lottery in 1892 that Johnson thought "the most important single article ever published" by the magazine. Despite an undramatic manner, he was capable of very striking editorial suggestions. It was he who originated the plan for the Civil War articles that collectively were the *Century*'s greatest triumph.[12]

Gilder, Johnson, and Buel formed the policy-making inner circle. They were aided by a staff which was as remarkable for its continuity as for its smooth efficiency. One of the important additions was Sophie Bledsoe Herrick, who joined *Scribner's* in 1878 after impressing the editors favorably with her scientific articles and her contributions to the department "Home and Society." As a young girl she had assisted her father in editing the *Southern Review*, then a Methodist quarterly. For Gilder's magazine she served as first reader of manuscripts, scanning all prose articles and stories and passing up the chain of command those that she felt merited further consideration. As the flow of contributions increased, Harriet Bliss, a Smith College graduate, and Douglas Z. Doty, who was editor-in-chief in the magazine's declining years, joined the staff to help Herrick with these initial readings. Still another staff addition in later years was William Rose Benét.[13]

One of the most valuable among the assistants, as well as the most colorful, was William Carey, a stout, lovable young Irish-American whose wit was admired not only by his colleagues but by such connoisseurs as Mark Twain. Starting as an office boy, he became the liaison between editors and production men, checking forms, helping in makeup, shuttling proofs from author to printer and back. In addition he performed chores for the editors' wives, amused their children, and piloted visiting writers about the city. During the years when Johnson and Buel were preoccupied with the Civil War articles, he was Gilder's right-hand man, useful not only in emergencies but "in all matters of taste and judgment."[14]

Carey was responsible for a famous office joke. Gilder, scheduled to read a poem at a Smith College commencement, sent the school authorities a proof of the verse as a matter of courtesy. Carey and Buel, with the aid of a friend in the Western Union office, concocted a telegram to their chief from Northampton that read: "Faculty doubt morality of fourth stanza. Can it be changed?" The puzzled editor agonized over the question for fifteen minutes before he learned of the hoax.[15]

Carey's immense popularity with visiting celebrities aroused mild resentment among the senior editors. Such writers as Thomas Nelson Page, F. Hopkinson Smith, James Whitcomb Riley, and George W. Cable were his affectionate friends. Rudyard Kipling when in New York hailed him as a long-lost brother. On one occasion a famous general, dropping into the office, stopped at Carey's desk near the door, and after a brief chat proposed lunch at Delmonico's; not until late afternoon was he ready to do business with the editors. It was to put Carey in his place that, in 1891, the management for the first time imprinted the names and titles of Gilder, Johnson, and Buel on the editorial department letterhead. (Holland was the only editor whose name had been carried regularly in the magazine itself.) This symbolic distinction of the titled from the untitled hurt the pride of some subordinates, especially Herrick's, in spite of Gilder's explanation that it merely designated the "responsible" editors.[16]

More serious grievances among the assistants were mentioned by L. Frank Tooker in his published reminiscences, which suggested that the general atmosphere of sweetness and light in the editorial offices did not suffuse all the staff at all times. A Yale graduate with a love of literature and the sea, Tooker contributed two poems to the magazine in the 1870s and joined its expanding staff in 1885. An intermediate manuscript reader, he winnowed the crop already sifted by Herrick and gave a first judgment on special articles sent personally to the top editors. An "admirable arbiter of style," in Johnson's words, he made a specialty of tailoring copy to a uniform standard of punctuation, spelling, and grammar. His special interest and knowledge also brought him general supervision of stories and articles about the sea. The *Century* published a number of his poems, short stories, and novels, nearly all about ships and the sea, of which "Under Rocking Skies," serialized in 1905, was perhaps his best effort.[17]

In spite of these varied services, Tooker—seriously insulated from his office mates by deafness—in forty years with the *Century* never broke into the inner circle. In his first years, he recalled, he suggested some "big ideas" to his superiors, but, getting no response, resigned himself to his role as an underling. His problem was that Gilder, Johnson, and Buel were relatively young men when they succeeded to the top positions, and their long reign was assured not only by the magazine's success under their direction but by the far-sighted policy of the management in making them proprietors. Tooker complained because the editors favored by Roswell Smith in this way did not extend this policy to himself and other junior staff members. The analogy was not entirely apropos, however, for while Gilder and Johnson had helped to establish a difficult venture, the *Century* when Tooker joined it had reached its zenith.[18]

However, on the whole the *Century* office was a remarkably happy one, characterized by easy camaraderie, a certain gaiety, a minimum of fault-finding, and pride in the magazine's excellence. The ranking editors seldom came to work before ten o'clock, but they did not balk at taking loads of manuscripts home in the evening. Gilder, in spite of his rigid standards, was kind and tactful in his criticisms of his staff, thus redoubling the loyalty of his subordinates.[19]

On the other hand, Gilder gave and demanded a passionate attention to the details of magazine-making that added to the *Century*'s dignity, accuracy, and authority, and he laid down rules that were scrupulously observed. Johnson circulated yellow memorandum slips to emphasize the need for uniformity. All quotations, names, and dates were minutely verified. Proofreading was a deadly serious ritual. Once Gilder, rushing into the office, opened the new issue of the magazine and, pointing to a typographical error, cried, "We ought all to resign!" This was, Tooker recalled, "the only case approaching open reproof with the office that I can remember of Mr. Gilder." Although Gilder did not routinely proofread, he went over every important line in the magazine, either in manuscript or proof, and had an especially watchful eye out for slang, coarse expressions, and statements likely to offend readers. Equal precautions were taken against making errors of fact. Articles were often sent in proof form to be scanned by experts.[20]

Such painstaking work laid a solid foundation for the flawless magazine Gilder sought to construct and, along with Alexander W. Drake's superb illustrations and Theodore Low De Vinne's unsurpassed typography and printing, served to make the *Century* a production that perfectly embodied its editor's ideals. "Sometimes I get mad at it," Whitman said of Gilder's monthly; "it seems so sort of fussy, extra nice, pouting; but then . . . those very limitations were designed—maybe rightly designed." Granting its purpose, Whitman conceded, the magazine could hardly have been better.[21]

An important factor in the excellence of the *Century* was the continuity of its leadership, due not only to longevity but to Smith's foresight. In 1880, when the proprietors were exulting over the prosperity of *Scribner's,* Smith warned his partners that they faced a critical period of higher production costs and more vigorous competition. To cement the loyalties and encourage the energies of employees, he proposed that 10 percent of all cash dividends up to $50,000 a year be "applied on salaries, in some equitable division." This would not only be a matter of "justice and fair dealing" to those who had helped establish a valuable property, but also a "simple measure of precaution, or self preservation, so far as we are concerned." There was such a vexatious amount of detail about the publishing business, Smith pointed out, so many chances to save and gain if employee interest were stimulated, that this profit-sharing scheme would pay for itself. This argument apparently convinced Smith's colleagues, for there is evidence that his suggestion was adopted: Gilder in 1881, for example, referred to Drake's "interest in the 'ten per cent.'"[22]

Equally liberal and equally shrewd was Smith's policy of bringing his most valuable employees into the ownership of his company. When Smith bought nine-tenths of Holland's stock, the remaining tenth was sold to the "young men" of importance in the editorial, art, and business departments. The key figures who were made proprietors by this transaction—Frank H. Scott, W. W. Ellsworth, and Charles F. Chichester of the business office along with Gilder, Johnson, and Drake—guided the destinies of the magazine for many years. The *Century* thus entered an era of competition operated by a strong team bound together in a community of interest. Gilder in 1881 noted the significance of this in the case of Drake, the nearly indispensable presiding genius of the art department. Although Drake had offers from competitors willing to pay him more, he was "now anchored here forever," Gilder pointed out, by the prospect of participating in future profits. Throughout his life Smith carried on this policy of making shareholders out of useful workers, and he provided in his will for its continuance after his death.[23]

Aiming at making his magazine reflect his own ideals, Gilder had too sound an editorial instinct to neglect the interests of his readers. Even as Holland's aide, he had impressed Smith with his "fine sense of what the public likes, and what the newspapers will take to."[24] His problem was, as he saw it: "How to button-hole a couple of million readers! If you don't get them by the button-hole they slip past and you have only a special audience instead of the audience that one naturally aims at when publishing the 'Century.'"[25] At one time he compiled a list of diverse acquaintances—a young man, an old doctor, a widow, a soldier, a teacher, a housewife, and others—and consciously tried to include in every issue something for each. He knew the *Century's* serious essays reached a great audience only because they were surrounded by lighter articles and fiction. "We are . . . so much interested in serious subjects that we are apt to err editorially, in the direction of 'heaviness.'" Asking the economist Edward Atkinson to clarify and condense an article he had submitted on the single tax, the editor explained that his "constant temptation" was to "make the Magazine really a review, which would at once restrict its circulation and spoil the audience which we should like to have for just such papers as this one of yours." It was this sensitive instinct for the intellectual saturation point of his readers that made Gilder's monthly, for a time at least, the most powerful educative force among periodicals.[26]

As Gilder took over, he promised his readers renewed emphasis on history and on "the best of all magazine material, the elaborate discussion of living practical questions." To make his monthly's essays authoritative, he called as often as possible on experts to write them, while the work of professional magazine writers was submitted to specialists for revision or criticism.[27]

As the *Century* became a rallying point for conservatives seeking to stabilize and guide American society in a period of stress and change, Gilder enlisted their spokesmen not only for signed articles but also for editorials. To keep the "Topics of the Time" as homogeneous as possible, he carefully picked writers in sympathy with his general editorial view. This view was well summed up by a writer who submitted a sheaf of "Topics" composed in "what I understand to be the vein you want to work—the philosophical study of our national development, with criticism for faults, praise for good tendencies, and a generally hopeful rather than pessimistic tone."[28]

One of these contributing editorialists was Alexander Johnston, professor of jurisprudence and political economy at Princeton University, whose anonymous commentary on such subjects as labor, marriage and divorce, socialism, ballot reform, and postal savings banks appeared as "Topics" for several years before his death in 1889. He represented the right wing of the magazine's editorial corps, regarded profit-sharing as socialistic, and dismissed Henry George and Terence V. Powderley as "frauds." Gilder valued him as a sturdy exponent of "the old-fashioned idea of personal freedom with its corollary of personal initiative and responsibility." That Gilder did not surrender his editorial prerogatives in accepting these contributions is indicated by Johnston's acknowledgment that "I have never seen any emendations in my Topics that were not improvements."[29]

The principal contributor to this department in the 1890s was Joseph Bucklin Bishop, regularly an editorial writer for the *New York Evening Post*. He wrote frequently on political corruption and reform, but perhaps his most notable columns were those attacking the silverite "heresy." These, collected into a pamphlet called *Cheap Money*, were employed as sound-money propaganda for a number of years. It was probably at Bishop's suggestion that his colleague on the *Post*, Edward P. Clark, was assigned "Topics" on public affairs, for which Clark collected fees ranging from $25 to $50.[30]

Other occasional editorialists were Mariana Griswold (Mrs. Schuyler) Van Rensselaer, author, art critic, and close friend of the Gilders (they were living temporarily in her home at the time of his death); Walter Hines Page, who discussed the liquor problem; and two clerical leaders in the social gospel movement, Theodore T. Munger and Washington Gladden. Gladden, whose signed articles also appeared in the magazine for a whole generation, began contributing to "Topics" in 1884 and continued doing so until 1910.[31]

Sometimes editorials were constructed in the *Century* office from material assembled and submitted by experts. In other instances, documents and statistics provided by specialists were turned over to professional writers to be worked into finished editorials. Still another practice was to condense material submitted as full-length essays into departmental copy. Gilder's own editorials averaged less than one per number of the magazine, but in the variety of ways shown above he marshalled the talents of what amounted to an unofficial staff and directed a drumfire of small shot at the multiform abuses of American life.[32]

In 1883 all the old departments except "Topics" and the humor column were swept away to make room for the great series of articles on the Civil War. Gilder explained that the *Century* no longer wished to "encumber its pages with departmental records, such as may be elsewhere and earlier obtained, namely in our weekly and daily periodicals." Instead of "Literature" (which had replaced "Culture and Progress" in 1881), "The World's Work," and "Home and Society," an abbreviated section of "Open Letters" was inserted to provide "brief and pithy signed essays on all subjects." This correspondence was solicited and paid for, and hence played its part in Gilder's grand design.[33]

Like Holland before him, Gilder aimed to make his magazine count in the national life, but he could draw on infinitely greater resources of capital, talent, and experience than his predecessor. The *Century* began with 125,000 subscribers.[34] Gilder's list of contributors in his first volume included Twain, Howells, James Bryce, Stockton, and John Burroughs. Symbolic of the magazine's new prestige was its headquarters. From its beginning, *Scribner's Monthly* had shared office space with the Scribner book house in two locations on lower Broadway. In the fall of 1881 the Century Company celebrated its debut as an independent publisher by moving into its own home on the fifth floor of a new building on Union Square. It was a handsome establishment, much favored by sightseers. Gilder jokingly called it "the wonder of the world." Within a few years, critics, in all seriousness, were applying similar superlatives to the *Century*.[35]

NOTES

1. Editorial, Dec. 1881; Edward Eggleston, "Josiah Gilbert Holland," Dec. 1881; *New York Tribune*, Oct. 23, 1881; H. H. Peckham, *Josiah Gilbert Holland in Relation to His Times* (Philadelphia, 1940), 199–207.

2. Gilder to Howells, Oct. 19, 1881, Howells Papers, Harvard University, Cambridge, Mass.

3. *Nation*, 35 (Sept. 28, 1882):265.

4. Augustus Saint-Gaudens, *Reminiscenses,* ed. Homer Saint-Gaudens, 2 vols. (New York, 1913), 1:384; Burnett tribute, Feb. 1910; Mrs. Schuyler Van Rensselaer, "Richard Watson Gilder—Personal Memories," *Outlook*, 130 (Mar. 8, 1922):376–79.

5. Castaigne to Gilder, May 31, 1896, GP.

6. Horace Traubel, *With Walt Whitman in Camden,* 3 vols. (New York, 1961), 2:241, and Henry Holt, *Garrulities of an Octagenarian Editor . . .* (Boston, 1923), 245.

7. Egan to Gilder, Nov. 9, 1891, CC; L. Frank Tooker, *The Joys and Tribulations of an Editor* (New York, 1924), 61–62; author's conversation with Rodman Gilder, May 16, 1950.

8. Robert Underwood Johnson, *Remembered Yesterdays* (Boston, 1923), 3–78 passim.

9. Gilder to Edward L. Burlingame, Aug. 28, 1883, SC, and Tooker, *Joys and Tribulations,* 61–62, 70–71.

10. Johnson, *Remembered Yesterdays*, 133, and Hamlin Garland's tribute in *New York Herald Tribune*, Oct. 24, 1937. James L. Ford, a literary rebel of the 1890s, called Johnson "unquestionably the one dominant figure in American literature" of his time, but I have seen no evidence to support his implication that Johnson controlled the *Century's* fiction policy in this period. *The Literary Shop and Other Tales* (New York, 1894), 62–64.

11. *New York Times*, May 23, 1933, and Johnson, *Remembered Yesterdays,* 121.

12. Tooker, *Joys and Tribulations,* 57, and Johnson, *Remembered Yesterdays,* 121–23, 189–90.

13. *New York Tribune*, Jan. 18, 1878; R. U. Johnson memorandum, n.d., "H. & S. Subjects," CC; Johnson, *Remembered Yesterdays*, 121. See written opinions of Doty and Herrick on manuscripts in CC.

14. Gilder to F. H. Scott, Jan. 16, 1889, copy in GP; William Webster Ellsworth, *A Golden Age of Authors: A Publisher's Recollection* (New York, 1919), 31–33; Johnson, *Remembered Yesterdays*, 114–15, 418.

15. Johnson, *Remembered Yesterdays*, 93–94.

16. Gilder to Herrick, Jan. 31, 1891, GP; Ellsworth, *Golden Age*, 31–33; Tooker, *Joys and Tribulations,* 337–38.

17. Johnson, *Remembered Yesterdays*, 139, and Tooker, *Joys and Tribulations,* 48–55, 60–62, 136–39, 290–97, 344–45.

18. Rodman Gilder to the author, n.d. [1950], and Tooker, *Joys and Tribulations*, 340–41. Tooker was also aggrieved because the senior editors, who took long weekends, saved up vacations and took trips to Europe on the accumulated time, whereas he was not similarly rewarded when he sacrificed vacation time. Ibid., 351–53.

19. Tooker, *Joys and Tribulations,* 54–57, 74, and Johnson, *Remembered Yesterdays,* 39, 93–94.

20. Tooker, *Joys and Tribulations*, 54–57, 69–70, 74–76, and Johnson, *Remembered Yesterdays*, 127–28.The magazine's correspondence provides many examples of reading by outside experts. E. V. Smalley's article on the U.S. Patent Office, for example, was submitted for correction to the patent commissioner himself; C. H. Duell to Johnson, Nov. 3, 1900, CC. Prof. Henry A. Beers of Yale perused Amelia Barr's historical novel, "Friend Olivia," for anachronisms; Beers to Johnson, Aug. 23, Sept. 2, and Sept. 18, 1889, CC.

21. Traubel, *With Walt Whitman*, 2:483, 3:241.

22. Smith to Holland and Charles Scribner, Mar. 10, 1880, and Gilder to Scribner, Jan. 15, 1881, SC.

23. Gilder to Scribner, Jan. 15, 1881, SC; author's conversation with Rodman Gilder, May 16, 1950; *New York Tribune*, Apr. 6, 1881. In 1881, Gilder owned ten of the company's 500 shares, while Scott and his wife owned eight shares, Johnson and Drake five each, and Chichester four; memorandum by Charles Scribner, n.d. [Jan. 1881], SC.

24. Rosamond Gilder, ed., *Letters of Richard Watson Gilder* (Boston, 1916), 98.

25. Ibid., 389.

26. Gilder to Richard T. Ely, Dec. 10, 1889, GP; Gilder to Atkinson, May 29, 1889, Atkinson Papers, Massachusetts Historical Society, Boston; author's conversation with Rodman Gilder, May 16, 1950. William Roscoe Thayer thought the *Century* led all magazines in the 1880s in "cultivating 'the masses'"; Thayer to Gilder, June 1, 1889, CC.

27. Editorial, Nov. 1881.

28. Gilder to O. B. Bunce, Dec. 29, 1881, GP, and Edward P. Clark to Gilder, Jan. 28, 1889, CC.

29. Johnston to Gilder, May 6, July 30, Aug. 28, Sept. 28, and Dec. 3, 1886, May 14 and July 25, 1887, Feb. 8, May 8, Aug. 3, and Sept. 21, 1888, CC; editorial, Oct. 1889.

30. Bishop to Gilder, Jan. 21, Sept. 21, and Dec. 11 [1891], and Mar. 23 [1892], Bishop to William Carey, July 13 [1893], Clark to Gilder, Mar. 22 and Apr. 30, 1887, Jan. 29, 1889, May 5, Aug. 10, and Aug. 26, 1890, CC.

31. *New York Times*, Nov. 20, 1909; Gilder to William T. Baker, Aug. 12, 1892, GP; Page to Gilder, Dec. 19 and Dec. 24, 1896, Munger to Johnson, Mar. 4 and Mar. 8, 1896, Gladden to Gilder, Apr. 3, 1884, and to Johnson, May 8, 1900, CC.

32. W. O. Atwater to Buel, Apr. 14, 1897, and George F. Parker to Gilder, Oct. 6, 1890, CC. J. B. Bishop's series on foreign labor and the apprentice system was "inspired" by Col. Richard T. Auchmuty; editorial, Oct. 1893, and Bishop to Gilder, Jan. 5, 1894, CC.

33. Editorial, May 1883, and Gilder to William Dean Howells, June 2, 1884, asking Howells to send a bill for the "Open Letter" he had written, Howells Papers.

34. Editorial, Nov. 1881.

35. Gilder to T. B. Aldrich, Jan. 6, 1884, Aldrich Collection, Harvard University, and advertising section, Nov. 1882, pp. 24–25.

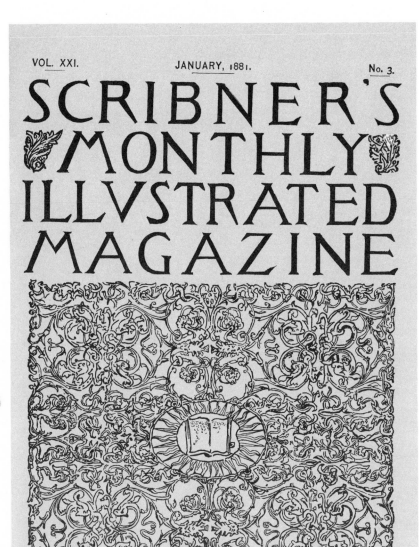

VOL. XXI. JANUARY, 1881. No. 3.

SCRIBNER'S MONTHLY ILLVSTRATED MAGAZINE

CONDVCTED·BY·J.G.HOLLAND
SCRIBNER·AND·CO.743·BROADWAY·NEW·YORK
F.WARNE&CO.BEDFORD·ST·STRAND·LONDON

This scroll design by Stanford White, which replaced a lilac-hued "period-piece," marked a distinct departure in the style of the *Scribner's Monthly* cover.

Richard Watson Gilder, shown here in his office in 1894, made the *Century* an editorial projection of his own ideals.

Helena de Kay Gilder sits with her son Rodman in "The Studio," at 103 East 15th Street.

Roswell Smith, one of the co-founders of *Scribner's Monthly*, bought out the Scribner interest and launched his own publishing house, The Century Company.

Josiah Gilbert Holland, one of the most popular authors of his time, was the first editor of *Scribner's Monthly*.

Frank R. Stockton, a junior editor with Scribner and Company, later contributed humorous short stories to *Scribner's Monthly* and the *Century*.

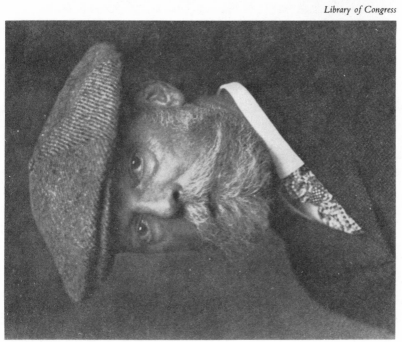

Alexander W. Drake, art superintendent of the *Century*, along with Gilder and the printer Theodore L. De Vinne, was responsible for the fame of the *Century's* wood engravings.

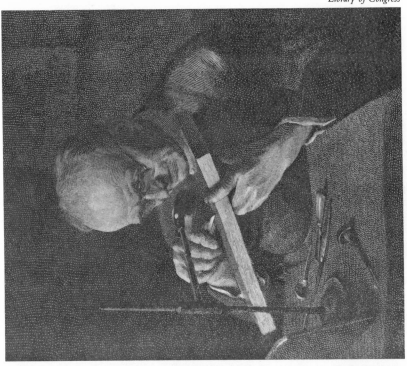

Timothy Cole, shown here at work in an engraving of a portrait by his son, Alpheus P. Cole, was a leading light in the *Century*'s group of brilliant wood engravers.

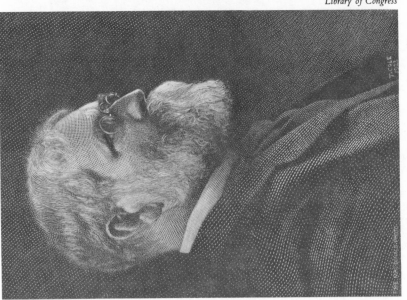

Robert Underwood Johnson, associate editor—and later editor—of the *Century* is shown here in later life in an engraving by Timothy Cole.

Charles Dana Gibson was one of the *Century*'s best known illustrators; this sketch appeared with "The Anglomaniacs" (August 1890).

These illustrations by Frederic Remington enhanced John G. Bourke's "General Crook in the Indian Country" (March 1890).

Joseph Pennell's famous etchings of New York skyscrapers appeared in March 1905.

This detail from Rembrandt's *The Night Watch* was engraved by
Timothy Cole for the Old Masters Series (December 1893).

The north end of Notre Dame was drawn by Joseph Pennell for the series on French cathedrals (August 1906).

The cover of the April 1885 issue of the *Century* proclaimed a first edition of 225,000. The Civil War Series later sent circulation up to 250,000, unprecedented for a magazine of the *Century*'s class.

8

The *Century* at Its Peak

Richard Watson Gilder and his young associates won the attention and admiration of the nation's periodical readers with several striking projects in the *Century*'s first decade. Their experience with "Peter the Great" in the last year of *Scribner's* suggested that illustrated history or biography was their forte; with Edward Eggleston's "A History of Life in the Thirteen Colonies," the *Century* made its entry into this field. Since each of the thirteen chronicles was complete in itself, the editors were able to run them episodically from 1882 to 1890. In the intervals Eggleston pursued his investigations, aided by generous grants from Roswell Smith which helped to finance two visits to England. Although this was Eggleston's first historical effort, he proved adept at research. He uncovered in the British Museum important unused material, such as John White's drawings of American Indians. This pioneer work in social history, ultimately published in book form as *The Beginners of a Nation*, was so impressive that Eggleston was made president of the American Historical Association.[1]

The *Century*'s interest in history, combined with its spirit of enterprise, led to its greatest triumph, the story of the Civil War as told by many of its leading participants. The "War Series" began in November 1884 and continued for more than three years, its echoes reverberating for many months afterward. This was the climactic event in the history of the magazine, for it vastly increased the *Century*'s readership, prestige, and prosperity, and added tremendously to its power as a voice for conservative ideals.

As early as February 1877, *Scribner's* had printed an account of "Farragut in Mobile Bay," and in the following year Allen C. Redwood began occasional reminiscences of his experiences in the Confederate army. In July 1883 appeared "Recollections of the John Brown Raid, by a Virginian Who Witnessed the Fight" (former U.S. Senator Alexander R. Boteler), along with a rejoinder by Frank B. Sanborn, the New England radical who had helped finance Brown's desperate scheme. Clarence Buel, the assistant editor who had suggested pairing these contrasting versions of a single episode, was struck by the idea that leaders of the opposing causes might be persuaded to tell the story of the whole war in the same way. Gilder, who as a nineteen-year-old had served briefly in a Pennsylvania battery at Gettysburg and who was proud of his chaplain-father's part in the war, was quick to approve this plan. Smith was less enthusiastic. He thought the *Century* had already reached its maximum circulation—about 125,000—and stood to gain little from the huge outlay of money, time, and energy that such a feature would require. Nevertheless, he deferred to the judgment of his editors and threw the company's resources into the project.[2]

The editorial announcement of the history declared that its aims were

> to clear up cloudy questions with new knowledge and the wisdom of cool reflection; and to soften controversy with that better understanding of each other, which comes to comrades in arms when personal feeling has dissipated. . . .
>
> No time could be fitter, we think, for a publication of this kind . . . when the passions and prejudices of the Civil War have nearly faded out of politics, and its heroic events are passings into our common history where motives will be weighed without malice, and valor praised without distinction of uniform.[3]

It was a timely story, too, from the magazine's point of view, in that most of the war's aging heroes were around to recount it.[4]

Anticipating that the series would attract more attention than any of their earlier undertakings, the editors were nonetheless suprised by its reception. They planned originally to tell the story in twelve months, but when they discovered the strength of its appeal and the importance of the fresh material uncovered, they hastily brought up reinforcements and carried it on to nearly the length of the struggle they were recording. When the series was finished, 230 participants, from generals to privates, had contributed bits to the grand mosaic, and 1,700 engravings had illuminated it.[5]

Gilder put Robert Underwood Johnson in charge of the history, with Buel as assistant, and for months this tireless pair were completely absorbed in the tremendous task. Their first problem was to rally the military leaders, many of them taciturn men who hesitated to criticize their former comrades-in-arms. Johnson set his cap for Ulysses S. Grant, and when he met with a refusal, the whole series seemed imperiled. But when the general's banking house failed, he could no longer turn down the $500 per article that Smith offered—a sum the publisher later voluntarily doubled. Johnson was dismayed when Grant's first article, on Shiloh, turned out to be a virtual copy of the offical records. He visited the old warrior, drew him out on his personal impressions of the battle, and persuaded him to include this more colorful material without weakening the blunt honesty that characterized Grant's narrative style. This first contribution by the nation's greatest living hero, followed by his subsequent accounts of Vicksburg, Chattanooga, and the Wilderness, insured the success of the series.[6]

William Tecumseh Sherman, second among the stalwarts of the Union cause, also refused to participate at first, even though the editors "persecuted" him with telegrams and a personal plea from Grant. He declared that he had told everything about his march to the sea in his published memoirs. When the history had run nearly two years, however, he commended the *Century* for its documentation of the conflict and acknowledged that "in common with millions of our people," he had read every article. He consented finally to write on "The Grand Strategy of the War of the Rebellion" in order to counter any impression that it was "only a scramble of power by mobs, and not a war of high principle."[7]

Meanwhile, lesser military figures, sensing the authority and impartiality of the series, seized the opportunity to set the record straight. General W. S. Rosecrans wrote his account, believing that he had "a duty to the living and to the dead."[8] Admiral David D. Porter and Generals George B. McClellan, Lew Wallace, John Pope, and Don Carlos Buell were among the Union commanders who wrote for the series.

On the Confederate side, Robert E. Lee was dead, and his personal papers were unavailable. The ranking general became Joseph E. Johnston. The editors found him suspicious and irascible, but induced him to submit his version of "Manassas to Seven Pines" and of the resistance to Sherman's march to Atlanta. The southern cause was well represented by James Longstreet, Wade Hampton, D. H. Hill, and the dashing W. T. Beauregard, who started the series with "The Battle of Bull Run."[9]

Finding the military leaders and persuading them to contribute were but the beginnings of the editorial burden. Johnson and Buel, in addition to condensing the narratives, making them readable, and checking them against the official records for accuracy, had virtually to fight the war over again with contributors and correspondents. Nearly every article brought a flurry of emendations and rebuttals. To provide a fair hearing for every viewpoint, the editors not only scheduled additional articles but included in each number of the magazine a supplementary department of "Memoranda on the Civil War." In spite of this impartial attitude, Johnson was twice challenged to a duel, once by a Union general and once by a Confederate colonel. The arbiters of this great debate were themselves caught up in its heated atmosphere—often a weary "Now, R.U.J!" or an excited "Oh, Buel!" would resound through the office as the two friends argued about an old campaign.[10]

For the entire *Century* staff the War Series was a stirring experience. They felt immersed in a dramatic re-creation of epochal events as manuscripts and letters poured in from soldiers and noncombatants. Visits from the commanders lent a martial air to the office. "Grant one day and Beauregard the next!" wrote the fascinated Gilder to his wife.[11] The editor was fired with the spirit of the epic struggle. When Edmond Gosse, the monthly's agent in England, complained that readers there were tired of the war articles, Gilder scolded him: "Is there nothing 'interesting' to you but art and literature? Now let me tell you—I would rather have one article by Grant on a battle won by him . . . than twenty articles by Daudet on Mistral. . . . Heavens! A great world , changing, heroic events told by the hero of it! . . . Yes, you ought to be proud of a magazine that is conducting to unparalleled success the largest enterprise yet undertaken by a periodical. Don't let literature and art make dilettantes of us!"[12]

To authenticate their history the editors toured the battle sites, often with the commanders who described their disputed charges or acts of heroism. Artists accompanied them to get realism into their sketches. "Think of hearing of the death of Stonewall Jackson from the lips of the men who carried him off the field," Joseph Pennell marveled. Pictures from the war years helped add the color of combat to the story. Winslow Homer altered his wartime sketches to provide fifteen illustrations. Many more came from the battlefront photographs of the pioneer camera men, Matthew B. Brady and Alexander Gardner. A profuse display of maps indicated the positions and tactics of the rival forces—and incidentally touched off some of the sharpest controversies among the commanders. Alexander W. Drake, who made the weary round of the battle sites, thought the War Series the most troublesome and aesthetically the least satisfying task of his career, but the illustrations both clarified and enlivened the narrative.[13]

Public response to the War series was immediate and stunning. No sooner was the project announced than letters began to arrive at the magazine's headquarters, many of them offering unpublished documents or pictures. Veterans eagerly volunteered additions and corrections, some of which proved useful to Buel and Johnson when they collected and expanded the war stories into a successful four-volume book.[14] The *Century*'s history became the talk of New York clubs and dinner tables. In St. Louis, sales of the monthly increased 50 percent with the number carrying the first installment of the big feature. Circulation nearly doubled within six months and continued to rise until it had reached 250,000—"the largest audience that was ever gathered about any periodical of its class in the English language." The War Series made $1,000,000 for the Century Company—twice what the firm had been worth a few years earlier—and this profit not only financed new large-scale projects of the company but confirmed the policy of risking heavy expenditures in their execution.[15]

The search for another historical serial of comparable appeal began when the War Series was only a few months old; it ended when Smith and Gilder hit upon the monumental life of Abraham

Lincoln on which Lincoln's former secretaries, John Hay and John G. Nicolay, had been at work for several years. Although Josiah Gilbert Holland in 1880 had pronounced their manuscript too long and detailed for magazine use, Gilder and his publisher viewed it as a logical successor to the War Series. "The Century must have it!" Smith wrote Colonel Hay in March 1885. By November, having dazzled the authors with the record offer of $50,000 for the serial rights alone, he had contracted for both magazine and book publication.[16]

To shorten "Abraham Lincoln: A History" to usable length was a formidable editorial problem. Nicolay objected to Gilder's idea of "skimming the cream" from the work, on the ground that it would hurt the sale of the book. Gilder then proposed to print the whole thing, excepting only "those long and dull documents, if any there be, which add dignity and value to a literary volume, but which the ordinary reader skips." Hay protested that the complete history would "tire out the continent," but when Gilder set to work to trim the manuscript, Hay, weary and short-tempered after his exhausting literary effort, frequently found fault with the editorial excisions. In the end about one half of the "Lincoln" appeared in the magazine, the notable omissions being sections dealing with events already covered in the War Series.[17]

That the text was still too long, or at any rate too dull, was evidently the readers' verdict, for the *Century*'s circulation dipped steadily downward during the three years and four months in which the Lincoln history was serialized. Nevertheless, the history kept the monthly in the public eye and sustained its reputation for important undertakings, and as the last installment went to press, Gilder informed the authors of his "great satisfaction that the 'Century' was permitted to give this work to the contemporaneous world." The Century Company published *Abraham Lincoln* in ten volumes in 1890 and within a short time sold 5,000 sets by subscription. Nicolay and Hay continued for many years as consultants to the editors on the Lincolniana with which they all but surfeited their readers.[18]

The third great illustrated nonfiction serial of the 1880s, "Siberia and the Exile System," was a reportorial rather than a historical narrative, but in its thoroughness and its fascination for press and public, George Kennan's description of conditions among Siberian exiles was a journalistic triumph characteristic of the *Century* at its peak. Kennan in his youth had spent more than two years in Siberia as a representative of the Russian-American Telegraph Company. The abortive revolution of the 1870s and the assassination of Tsar Alexander II in 1881 revived his interest in the tsarist government and its radical opposition. When Gilder in the summer of 1884 learned that Kennan was contemplating a return to Siberia, this time as a journalist, he proposed that the *Century* finance his trip and publish his findings. After Kennan in a hasty trip to Moscow and St. Petersburg had gained permission to visit the Siberian mines and prisons, Gilder commissioned him as the magazine's representative.[19]

With Kennan when he sailed from New York in May 1885 was George A. Frost, a Boston artist who had also traveled in Siberia and who, like his colleague, spoke Russian. The two Americans disembarked at St. Petersburg, picked up maps, photographic equipment, and letters of introduction to government officials, teachers, and mining engineers, and headed into the frozen darkness of Siberia. They emerged eighteen months later, ghostly thin and worn from the hardships of cold, poor food, rough transportation, and sleepless nights.[20]

They brought back a story that sent a thrill of horror through hundreds of thousands of readers. After six prefatory articles had described the tsarist prison administration and sketched the background of Russian political protest, Kennan's eye-witness reports began to appear in May 1888 and dominated American magazine literature for many months. Inclined at first to defend the imperial regime, Kennan was convinced by what he saw and heard—from officials as well as prisoners—that the political exiles were for the most part worthy people suffering under a blind and corrupt bureaucracy. Henry Sandham's illustrations, made from Frost's pencil sketches or drawn imaginatively with the aid of convict costumes provided by Kennan, were imbued with the author's sympathy for the exiles. Ultimately Kennan wrote twenty-five articles, for which he was paid about $15,000. He earned another $20,000 on the lecture platform and promptly consigned it to the cause of the exiles.[21]

Kennan's work, published as a book in 1891, was translated into several languages. In Russia itself it contributed to revolutionary pressure, for, although the author was banned from the country and his articles ripped from the magazine before it was permitted to circulate there, Russian liberals reprinted his story and favorable reviews of it appeared in leading publications. The tsarist government attempted no refutation until 1893, when the secretary of the Russian legation in Washington, D.C., presented in the *Century* an apologia that Kennan demolished in a rebuttal.[22]

Kennan's exposé and his subsequent lectures established him as the leading American champion of Free Russia. "Everybody both in Europe and in the United States," he told Gilder, "appeals to me when there is any Russian wrong to be righted." The editors were thrilled at being identified with Kennan's fight against injustice, listing it high among the good causes for which they campaigned. Kennan himself told Smith that his articles were "in harmony with the influence which the *Century Magazine* has always exerted in the direction of right thinking and right living."[23]

After reaching 250,000 during the War Series, the *Century*'s circulation settled back by 1890 to about 200,000. This was an unprecedented readership, however, for a thirty-five-cent magazine and still gave it the lead among the monthlies that dominated the periodical field. Edward Weeks, when editor of the *Atlantic Monthly*, pointed out in 1950 that no other "quality magazine" had ever equalled the *Century*'s circulation in the mid-1880s, even though the reading public had tripled since that time.[24]

Meanwhile, striking gains in advertising volume helped keep the *Century* at the top (Table 5). In the six months from November 1882 through April 1883, the *Century* carried 218 pages of paid advertising. In the comparable period of 1887–88 the total had reached 448 pages. The upward sweep continued until 1892–93, when the six-month volume soared to 646 pages—140 pages in the December issue and an average of more than 100 pages in each of five other numbers. One satirist, noting the constantly fattening bulk of the magazine, quipped, "The *Century*, it is said, will insert a page or two of reading matter between the Italian art and the ads."[25]

TABLE 5. Volume of Paid Advertising in the *Century Magazine*,
1881–1900

Volume No.	Months	No. of Pages
23	November 1881–April 1882	161½
24	May–October 1882	153
25	November 1882–April 1883	218
26	May–October 1883	168
27	November 1883–April 1884	. . .
28	May–October 1884	176
29	November 1884–April 1885	269
30	May–October 1885	254
31	November 1885–April 1886	. . .
32	May–October 1886	282½
33	November 1886–April 1887	. . .
34	May–October 1887	355
35	November 1887–April 1888	448
36	May–October 1888	388
37	November 1888–April 1889	479
38	May–October 1889	423
39	November 1889–April 1890	541½
40	May–October 1890	524½
41	November 1890–April 1891	. . .
42	May–October 1891	552½
43	November 1891–April 1892	643
44	May–October 1892	. . .
45	November 1892–April 1893	646
46	May–October 1893	545
47	November 1893–April 1894	508
48	May–October 1894	431
49	November 1894–April 1895	503½
50	May–October 1895	415
51	November 1895–April 1896	486
52	May–October 1896	417½
53	November 1896–April 1897	. . .
54	May–October 1897	395
55	November 1897–April 1898	486½
56	May–October 1898	352
57	November 1898–April 1899	452½
58	May–October 1899	475
59	November 1899–April 1900	642
60	May–October 1900	460

NOTE. Data show the number of pages sold, exclusive of cover pages, in each volume.
These figures are based on page count in the bound volumes of the magazine. Century
Company advertisements are not included in the totals. Three dots = not available.

Since rates advanced along with circulation, gains in advertising revenue were even greater than those in volume. The quoted price rose from $1.25 per agate line in 1880 (about $270 per page) to $1.75 (about $300 per page) in 1885. *Harper's* standard rate in 1885 was $2.00 per agate line.[26] The differential resulted not from circulation, however—*Harper's* had 25,000 fewer purchasers per number in that year than the *Century*—but from Smith's continued policy of attracting volume through lower rates.

This flourishing business stemmed not only from Smith's aggressive sales campaign but also from the rapid development of a field in which he had pioneered. Periodical advertising more than tripled in the decade after 1880 as larger commercial and manufacturing concerns sought to reach a national market. While advertisements for publications and patent medicines continued as bulwarks of revenue, displays from consumer-goods manufacturers whose profits depended on a wide sales appeal also appeared during these years. Such brand names as Sapolio, Royal Baking Powder, Pear's Soap, and Ivory Soap became familiar to the monthly's readers—the first appearance of Ivory's famous slogan, "It Floats," was in July 1891. About seventy-five concerns advertised in national magazines before 1890 with "more or less system." After the invention of the safety bicycle in 1888, its manufacturers were for a time the most prominent of all the advertisers.[27] In May 1896, the *Century* carried twenty-one pages of display advertisements for bicycles and their appliances.[28]

Magazines tended to rely more and more on advertising revenues. *Harper's*, yielding to the trend, began to seek this profitable business in 1882, and by 1890, with seventy-five pages of paid advertisements in a single issue, had caught up with the *Century*. A more serious competitive threat arising from this national advertising boom was the influx of low-priced magazines in the 1890s. The end product of the revolution in the economics of periodical production, they depended almost entirely on advertising for existence, and they tapped a mass market byond the reach of the higher-priced and more elegant *Century* and its older rivals.

The fortunes of the *Century* were linked closely to those of the Century Company. The magazine's immense prosperity assured Smith of ample funds for new publishing ventures, and its serial features offered usable material for book publication. Ironically, the first year of the War Series was marked by the one outstanding reverse in Smith's triumphant publishing career. At the suggestion of Johnson, who had done so much to help Grant develop his lucid prose style, the general had decided to expand his *Century* articles into a complete book of reminiscences, a prize that he was expected to deliver to the Century Company. The general, however, had lost his fortune in the panic of 1884 and was anxious to provide for his family. So when Mark Twain—who had heard from Gilder at The Studio about the Century Company's intended contract with Grant—guaranteed the general a profit far in excess of the royalties to be gained from Smith's offer, the *Memoirs* went to Charles L. Webster Company, the subscription book house financed by Twain. The remark in Twain's notebook that the Century Company was trying to take advantage of Grant is certainly unjust to Smith. Yet the general did give Smith a chance to match Twain's terms and thus obtain the book, and Smith's colleagues were deeply disappointed in his inability to grasp the importance of Grant's name and work.[29]

Smith's success with the *Century Dictionary*, only a few years later, showed that he had lost neither his publishing instinct nor his boldness. Holland had first proposed such a publication, but not until 1882 did Smith purchase the American rights to John Ogilvie's famous *Imperial Dictionary*. At Buel's suggestion, Smith decided against merely revising the British edition and chose to publish a new and comprehensive reference work. Professor William Dwight Whitney of Yale University, the leading American philologist, was made editor-in-chief and given a staff of fifty, a consultative corps of thirty experts, and the assistance of 500 readers. William L. Fraser, who had joined Drake in the art department, supervised the drawing and preparation of the 6,000 illustrations that would be used in the dictionary. Published in six volumes in 1889–91, the *Century Dictionary* surpassed any work of its kind yet produced in America, and even fairly recently some scholars believed that it had not been "superseded in matters of definition."[30]

The dictionary was ultimately a financial success—of three editions, the last in 1911, about 206,000 sets were sold at prices ranging from $60 to $125. In the short term, however, it was a strain on both the Century Company and the magazine. Smith originally planned to spend $300,000 on the dictionary, but in quest of perfection he courageously sank $1,000,000 into the project before the first edition was completed.[31] That he was able to obtain these funds entirely from the magazine's profits is a measure of the *Century*'s fabulous prosperity. What the drain on the monthly's resources meant to its editors may be judged from Gilder's remarks to Whitney:

> The fact is that the exertions of myself and of my editorial associates are looked to as the means whereby this colossal work is to be carried on. The strain, I assure you, is pretty heavy, when you think that the Magazine must be kept up to such a pitch that its returns shall pay all our usual expenses, and profits and over that, $400 or more a day for the Dictionary; a fact which is impressed upon us of the Editorial Department by the publishers, not in any unpleasant way, but as a truth which cannot be overlooked.[32]

The magazine's obligations to the Century Company were, however, balanced by some advantages it derived from the book house. The fact that its serials might subsequently be made into books increased the magazine's bargaining power with authors, while it spread the risk of acquiring expensive material. Smith's business sense was a valuable aid in securing important features, and it was he who took the final responsibility when the purchase of both book and magazine rights was at issue. In such cases, however, the publisher showed an unfailing trust in his editor's judgment. When the *Century* after long and difficult negotiations bought the autobiography of the actor Joe Jefferson, Gilder thanked Smith not only for his "generous confidence" but for his "spirit of sympathy which means everything."[33]

Gilder, on the other hand, retained full freedom to mold editorial policy. He refused Smith's request to see advance proofs of his editorials, and the publisher with his usual equanimity acceded to this assertion of independence. Gilder zealously guarded his columns against disguised advertisements, advising one correspondent that he wished to avoid "not only evil but the appearance of evil."[34]

As important as Smith's liberal management was the confidence he inspired in his organization. He was the veteran commander who had led his officers and staff to victorious heights, a legend and a symbol of success. There seemed to be truth in his quiet conviction that the Lord was on his side. Throughout these years of triumph he opened every stockholders' meeting with a prayer and never failed to thank Providence for his good fortune. His chief preoccupations were business and religion, and he was irked by any suggestion that the two were incompatible. He found time to engage in such earnest causes as befitted a Christian. He tried to rejuvenate the American Tract Society. He served as president of the Congregational Club of New York, which he made into one of the city's best forums on current topics. He was a benefactor of Berea College in Kentucky, an experiment in interracial education. Toward his associates and employees he displayed an austere magnanimity—a "cordial wish to please by stealth," as Gosse phrased it. One Hoosier reported that Smith sent a free copy of the *Century* into the house of every miner on his Indiana coal properties.[35]

Smith died, at sixty-three, on April 19, 1892, after a two-year illness, of Bright's disease and paralysis. He had lived to see the great dictionary completed and the *Century* the most esteemed of American magazines. Although he had provided for continuity in his company's ownership and direction, he took with him an uninheritable combination of shrewdness, imperturbability, and luck. No wonder that, as the publisher lay dying, Gilder begged Johnson to stay close at hand "when the new and unknown comes upon us." Providence seemed even to attend Smith's passing, for it came on the eve of a revolution in magazine economics that would undermine the *Century*'s supremacy. It is not certain that he could have altered the course of events, but it is significant that the editors and officers he left behind asked each other when the crisis came, "What would Roswell Smith have done?"[36]

In the decade after 1885 the *Century* reached a pinnacle of prestige and influence unprecedented in American magazine history. It had ridden to this height on the buoyant currents of national growth and national consciousness. In its War Series the *Century* touched the wellsprings of this national sentiment, but its steady rise in the years before that climactic triumph reflected as definitely, if less dramatically, the material and intellectual

expansion of the United States. A growing and increasingly lit-
erate middle class in quest of education and entertainment created
a widening demand for the monthly magazine, while the opening
of a market continental in extent promoted magazine circulation
and brought in new revenues from advertising. In the period
1880–90 the number of monthlies increased by 93 percent—a far
greater increase than dailies or weeklies could show—and their
average readership rose from less than 8,000 to more than
11,000.[37] The cumulative popularity of *Harper's* and the immediate success of *Scribner's Magazine*, begun in 1887, showed that
much of the *Century*'s growth was due to a favorable environment.

But the *Century* had earned its leading position by its conscientious efforts to awaken and direct the forces that were bringing
into being a larger national life. If it had profited the most from
advertising, it had done the most to bring forth that manna for
magazines. If it made a lucky strike in its Civil War Series, it
must be remembered that Holland and Gilder had appealed from
the first to a broad patriotism. They had won the acclaim of
earnest Americans, too, by their purposive part in the formation
of the nation's literature and art and in the reformation of its
political and social life. "The increasing excellence and wonderful
prosperity of the *Century* are things of which all lovers of American literature should be proud," a contemporary journal remarked. "And it is not the least among the magazine's merits
that it is intensely American."[38]

Such tributes to the *Century*'s preeminence filled the press of
this period and appeared in the letters and memoirs of its literary
figures. "To the man or woman who moves among cultured
people," said the *Journalist* in 1890, "the reading of the *Century*
has practically become compulsory. Its articles form the subject
of conversation, it is a reflex of the literary and social life of the
world." The magazine's correspondence, preserved in the New
York Public Library, records the high proportion of ministers,
teachers, newspaper editors, and public officials among its fol-
lowers. Educators, reformers, and pleaders of special causes were
eager to spread their messages through its pages, agreeing with
Edward A. Atkinson's judgment that there was "no such circle
of readers as that which can be reached by the *Century*." William
J. Stillman's essays in Gilder's monthly gave him "a Ruskinian

conception of my exalted function of educator of the American public."[39]

The editors in these years took much of the world for their province. They sent Timothy Cole to engrave the art masterpieces of Europe and Pennell to etch the Continent's historic monuments and ancient beauties. They dealt in terms of mutual respect with prime ministers and literary idols of the Old World. The *Century's* fame and circulation were global. In London it outsold any English magazine of its class. To Paul Blouët, the keen French observer of American life, it was "the best magazine in the world." In Rome in 1890, Stillman met people ("women of course") going about with copies of the *Century.* Herbert B. Ames, a Montreal municipal reformer, sent his articles to Gilder because he could thus "reach the greatest number of Canadian readers." One writer found the monthly in Spain, Gibraltar, Morocco, Algiers, Egypt, Palestine, Syria, and Italy, and learned that his essays in it were a "passport to consideration" everywhere.[40]

At home the *Century,* along with *Harper's* and *Scribner's Magazine,* commanded the main highway to literary reputation and fortune. Aspiring authors regarded the editors of these monthlies with awe and noted that even their assistants had "the Olympian look and tone." Gilder and his chief aides were known to writers as the "Satraps of the *Century,*" and the phrase was not mouthed in derision. "It was a sober recognition of rank and authority."[41]

Gilder's personal prestige rose with that of his magazine. He had evolved from aspirant to arbiter in literature and the arts, while gaining new dimensions as one of New York City's most prominent and public-spirited citizens. He became the intimate friend and something approaching the intellectual mentor of Grover Cleveland, visiting and sleeping in the White House on occasion and attending at least one important cabinet meeting. By the mid-1890s the editor who had regretfully missed college had received honorary degrees from Dickinson College and Harvard and Princeton universities.[42] The broadening of his interests and influence could be noted in the increasing variety of people who came to his door. Scholars and reformers joined the poets, painters, actors, and musicians who liked to drop in on the Gilders at The Studio or, in later years, at their more conventional home on Clinton Place.

The *Century* office was the visible symbol if its power and opulence. No other publication in the world was so magnificently housed. The visitor to its fifth-floor home on Union Square entered a world of polished floors, rich Turkish carpets, broad windows, stained-glass doors, and walls hung with the originals of the monthly's most famous drawings. Only Twain dared keep his hat on and smoke cigars in this atmosphere of elegance and dignity. "You never saw anything like those lovely rooms. And aesthetic furniture," wrote Mrs. S. S. McClure to her sister. "Oh, you Americans are all so rich" was Matthew Arnold's outburst as he gazed about him; but another British caller thought the contrast between the *Century*'s headquarters and the shabby editorial rooms of London publications accurately reflected the difference in quality of their respective products.[43]

The business office, designed by Stanford White, was impressive for its tasteful furnishings, and the art department for its size, but the panorama that struck the casual visitor was that of the three editorial rooms, opening one into another in "fascinating and splendid succession." In the first of these, where manuscripts were filed, sat a young woman clerk who acted as receptionist. She escorted eligible callers through the second chamber, where Johnson and Buel, L. Frank Tooker and William Carey sat back to back on swivel chairs, and into the farthest office. At a table in this inner sanctum sat Gilder, before a wide fireplace surmounted by a high-relief profile head, carved in wood, of Holland. In spite of the rich decor and orderly arrangement of this suite, it was full of stir and bustle. Typewriters clicked constantly. The wives and families of the editors often stopped in, Gilder's children—after tiptoeing through the outer office—clattering through the rest of the suite to greet their father.[44]

The *Century*'s home was a rendezvous for the city's litterateurs and even more for out-of-town writers. Genial William Dean Howells came in frequently to see "The Rise of Silas Lapham" through the press. Rustic John Burroughs would wander in casually every spring and fall, lingering in town for days. Taciturn John Muir, who knew every trail in the wild Yosemite, would invariably get lost in Manhattan and turn to Union Square as to home. Twain could halt all business for half an hour, and so could the lovable Joe Jefferson, with his sweet, high-pitched voice and humorous anecdotes. One might see Theodore Roosevelt and his friend, Henry Cabot Lodge, talking to Gilder, or James Russell Lowell and Charles Eliot Norton of an earlier generation. The gaudy Joaquin Miller once appeared in "jack-boots, a Mexican serape, a broad-brim hat, and long hair like a scout," a costume designed, as Gilder remarked, entirely for publicity. More authentic was the garb of the Zuni chiefs whom Frank H. Cushing, the friend and student of the Southwestern Indians, once led into the office.[45]

Humbler and less colorful visitors also came to pay their respects. Cognizant of the public's interest in its operations, the *Century* opened an exhibit at the Chicago World's Fair in 1893, which showed how manuscripts and drawings were prepared for publication. Later, readers were invited to New York to see this same display, as well as the showplace in Union Square that housed it. The *Century* comported itself like the national institution it had become.

Even as the *Century* moved along this plateau of excellence and power, currents of change were beginning to erode its position. But in the 1880s and 1890s it was a matchless medium for the promulgation of Gilder's conservative ideals. The next chapters show these editorial convictions proclaimed and exemplified, then challenged—in literature and the arts, in public life, and in American society.

NOTES

1. Editorial, July 1885, and William Peirce Randel, *Edward Eggleston: Author of "The Hoosier Schoolmaster"* (New York, 1946), 161–62, 214–19, 224.

2. Clarence C. Buel and R. U. Johnson, eds., *Battles and Leaders of the Civil War*, 4 vols. (New York, 1888–89), preface, ix-x; Rosamond Gilder, ed., *Letters of Richard Watson Gilder* (Boston, 1916), 21–26, hereafter cited as Gilder, *Gilder*; Robert Underwood Johnson, *Remembered Yesterdays* (Boston, 1923), 44–45,189; L. Frank Tooker, *The Joys and Tribulations of an Editor* (New York, 1924), 255–57.

3. Editorial, Oct. 1884.

4. Five years earlier, Johnson noted, Civil War wounds were still too fresh, and five years later, many of the commanders who contributed to the series were dead. *Remembered Yesterdays*, 200–1.

5. Editorial, Mar. 1885; Johnson, *Remembered Yesterdays*, 190; Samuel

C. Chew, ed., *Fruit among the Leaves: An Anniversary Anthology* (New York, 1950), 101.

6. Johnson, *Remembered Yesterdays*, 189–94, 213–15. Mark Twain, in his frequently unreliable autobiography, declared that Gilder told him other commanders would not contribute unless Grant wrote for the series: *Mark Twain's Autobiography*, 2 vols. (New York, 1924), 1:31. Grant's articles appeared in issues of Feb., Sept., and Nov. 1885 and Feb. 1886.

7. The Feb. 1888 issue contains Sherman's account of how he refused and then consented to write for the War Series; see also letter from Sherman in July 1887 issue. M. A. DeWolfe Howe, ed., *Home Letters of General Sherman* (New York, 1909), 393, and Johnson, *Remembered Yesterdays*, 202.

8. Opening sentence of Rosecrans, "The Campaign for Chattanooga," May 1887.

9. Chew, *Fruit among the Leaves*, 100, and Johnson, *Remembered Yesterdays*, 199. Gen. Johnston's articles appeared in May 1885 and Aug. 1887. The arrangement of articles corresponded to the chronology of the war, except that Grant's later contributions ran ahead of their sequence to permit their inclusion in his *Memoirs*; editorial, Sept. 1885.

10. Buel and Johnson, eds., *Battles and Leaders*, preface, x; Johnson, *Remembered Yesterdays*, 114, 191–92, 204; Tooker, *Joys and Tribulations*, 81.

11. Gilder, *Gilder*, 126.

12. Gilder to Gosse, July 1, 1885, GP.

13. Elizabeth Robins Pennell, *The Life and Letters of Joseph Pennell*, 2 vols. (Boston, 1929), 1:110–12; Lloyd Goodrich, *Winslow Homer* (New York, 1944), 101–2; Buel and Johnson, eds., *Battles and Leaders*, preface, xi; Drake to Gilder, July 15, 1887, CC; Johnson, *Remembered Yesterdays*, 197, 203–4.

14. Seventy-five thousand copies of *Battles and Leaders* were sold, at $20 and $30 a set, depending on the binding. The publisher announced that at least one-third of the material in the book had not appeared in the magazine. Roy F. Nichols, preface to 1956 edition, iv.

15. Editorial, Nov. 1887; *New York Times*, May 24, 1933 (Buel obituary); Johnson, *Remembered Yesterdays*, 190, 201, 201n; editorial, Mar. 1885; Buel and Johnson, eds., *Battles and Leaders*, preface, x. The rapid rise in circulation caught the *Century* by surprise; it was necessary to print seven editions of the Nov. 1884 number; advertising section, Apr. 1885, p. 1. The cover of the May 1885 number carried the line, "First Edition, 250,000," indicating presumably that that many copies were printed.

16. Helen Nicolay, *Lincoln's Secretary: A Biography of John G. Nicolay* (New York, 1949), 293; William Webster Ellsworth, *A Golden Age of Authors: A Publisher's Recollection* (New York, 1919), 240; Tooker, *Joys and Tribulations*, 307; Johnson, *Remembered Yesterdays*, 98.

17. Gilder, *Gilder*, 173–74, and William Roscoe Thayer, *The Life and Letters of John Hay*, 2 vols. (New York, 1915), 2:37–41. Nicolay, *Nicolay*, 293, said two-thirds of the history ran in the *Century*; Tyler Dennett, *John Hay: From Poetry to Politics* (New York, 1933), 140, said less than one-half was printed in the magazine, and Thayer, *Hay*, 2:37, put the figure at only one-third.

18. Gilder, *Gilder*, 178–79. Nicolay to Gilder, May 30, 1897, and Feb. 1, 1898, CC. For quotations from the press in praise of the history, see the advertising section, Jan. 1887, pp. 6–7.

19. Kennan preface to "Siberia and the Exile System," May 1888. This Kennan was the cousin to the grandfather of George F. Kennan, a present-day expert on the Soviet Union.

20. Kennan preface, May 1888; *Boston Daily Advertiser*, Jan. 25, 1888; Tooker, *Joys and Tribulations*, 314–15.

21. Kennan preface, May 1888; Sandham to William Carey, Apr. 14, 1889, CC; Ellsworth, *Golden Age*, 267.

22. Ellsworth, *Golden Age*, 260-67; Kennan, "Blacked Out," May 1890; Pierre Botkine, "A Voice for Russia," Feb. 1893; Kennan, "A Voice for the People of Russia," July 1893; Kennan to Gilder, Dec. 10, 1887, CC. See also Isabel F. Hapgood, "My Experience with the Russian Censor," *Nation*, 51 (Oct. 23, 1890):318–21.

23. Kennan to Gilder, May 9, 1893, CC, and Kennan to Smith, Jan. 24, 1888, in Ellsworth, *Golden Age*, 265–66.

24. *N. W. Ayer and Son's American Newspaper Annual* (New York, 1890), 501; Edward Weeks, "The Schooling of an Editor," *Bulletin of the New York Public Library*, 54 (June 1950):263–71. The estimated circulation for *Harper's* in 1890 was about 175,000; *Ayer American Newspaper Annual*, 505.

25. *Philistine*, 1 (June 1895):31, and author's page count from bound volumes.

26. *Ayer American Newspaper Annual*, 1885 edition, 63–65.

27. Frank S. Presbrey, *The History and Development of Advertising* (Garden City, N.Y., 1929), 338–40, 371, 412, 469–70.

28. Author's count of pages. See Table 5.

29. Albert Bigelow Paine, *Mark Twain: A Biography. The Personal and Literary Life of Samuel Langhorne Clemens*, 3 vols. (New York, 1912), 2:789–816; Justin Kaplan, *Mr. Clemens and Mark Twain: A Biography* (New York, 1966), 261–62; Gilder, *Gilder*, 123–24; Ellsworth, *Golden Age*, 235; Johnson, *Remembered Yesterdays*, 218–19. Gilder recalled that he was going to get the signature of the general on the morning after his conversation with Twain, but Twain got to Grant a half hour earlier; note to author from Rosamond Gilder, n.d. Whatever hard feelings Gilder had about this breach of hospitality did not last; he and Twain remained good friends. The disappointment was partially offset by everyone's satisfaction that Grant won his race against cancer to finish

the book and leave his family a fortune. The *Century* honored Grant's requests to shorten his Vicksburg article and to run his narratives out of chronological sequence so that they could appear in the *Memoirs*.

30. Chew, *Fruit among the Leaves*, 144–47; *New York Times*, May 23, 1933 (Buel obituary); Robert E. Spiller et al., *Literary History of the United States*, 3 vols. (New York, 1948), 3:143.

31. Chew, *Fruit among the Leaves*, 146.

32. Gilder to Whitney, n.d., GP.

33. Gilder to Smith, Aug. 20, 1888, GP; Johnson, *Remembered Yesterdays*, 97–98. See also Gilder to Howells, Aug. 14, 1883, May 10 and July 31, 1884, Howells Papers, Harvard University, Cambridge, Mass.

34. Gilder to Edward Atkinson, June 29, 1888, Atkinson Papers, Massachusetts Historical Society, Boston, and Ellsworth, *Golden Age*, 148.

35. Poem by Gosse, "Roswell Smith," June 1892; tributes in the same issue by Washington Gladden, Amory H. Bradford, and P. D. Dodge; Edward Eggleston, "Roswell Smith," *Harper's Weekly*, 36 (Apr. 30, 1892):416.

36. Gilder to Johnson, Mar. 4, 1892, GP, and Johnson to Gilder, Aug. 30, 1899, CC.

37. S. A. Sherman, "Advertising in the United States," American Statistical Association *Publications*, n.s., 7 (Dec. 1900):121.

38. *Life*, 5 (May 14, 1885):273.

39. *Journalist*, 12 (Dec. 13, 1890):2; Atkinson to Gilder, Dec. 7, 1889, Stillman to Johnson, Jan. 12, 1890, CC. The *Century*'s advertising pages consistently quoted contemporary tributes. See the advertising section, Feb. 1894, for one sheaf of such comments.

40. Blouët to Buel, Dec. 9, 1895, Stillman to Johnson, Jan. 12, 1890, Ames to Gilder, Mar. 12, 1894, J. M. Buckley to Gilder, Apr. 1, 1889, CC.

41. Irving Bacheller, *Coming Up the Road: Memories of a North Country Boyhood* (Indianapolis, Ind. 1928), 268.

42. To Dickinson's L.L.D. in 1883, Harvard's A.M. in 1890, and Princeton's L.H.D. in 1896 were added before Gilder's death Litt.D.'s from Yale (1901) and Columbia (1907), and an L.L.D. from Wesleyan (1903).

43. Peter Lyon, *Success Story: The Life and Times of S. S. McClure* (New York, 1963), 47; *Spectator* (London), 63 (Aug. 31, 1889):269; *New York Star*, Mar. 16, 1890; *New York Evening Tribune*, Oct. 20, 1889; Tooker, *Joys and Tribulations*, 94; Ellsworth, *Golden Age*, 162–63; Johnson, *Remembered Yesterdays*, 113.

44. *New York Star*, Mar. 16, 1890, which called the Century Company "the best patron of typewriting in New York"; author's conversation with Rodman Gilder, May 16, 1950; Tooker, *Joys and Tribulations*, 90–92. An office fire in 1888 caused $15,000 in damages and destroyed most of the Century Company's correspondence, but the manuscripts

were saved, and there was no delay in publication. The editorial offices were moved to the De Vinne Press on Lafayette Place, but the staff was soon back in its restored quarters on Union Square. Gilder, *Gilder,* 157–59, and *Writer,* 2 (Aug. 1888):212

45. Johnson, *Remembered Yesterdays,* 115, 324, 355, 373, 385–91; Tooker, *Joys and Tribulations,* 156–61; Hamlin Garland, *Roadside Meetings* (New York, 1930), 209.

9

Standards for Readers and Writers

The democratization of reading and writing that *Scribner's Monthly* helped set in motion continued in the 1880s and 1890s. A constantly waxing national appetite for entertainment and information prompted thousands of men and women to take up their pens or—increasingly—bend to their typewriter keys.[1] New organs of criticism, such as the *Dial* (1880) and the *Critic* (1881), marked this upswing in literary interest, and even more indicative of professional self-consciousness were publications like the *Writer* (1887) and the *Author* (1889), which kept magazinists posted on the markets for their writing.

For the new host of storytellers, journalists, and versifiers, the nation's magazines spelled both "bread and fame."[2] Fortunately, a spate of new publications offered fresh outlets for their creations. By the end of the century such magazines as *Cosmopolitan*, *McClure's*, *Munsey's*, and the *Ladies' Home Journal* had opened wide avenues to a reading public, while the rising newspaper syndicates presented an additional source of revenue and repute.

The representative author of 1890, however, dreamed of breaking into one of the three great illustrated monthlies—the *Century*, *Harper's*, or *Scribner's Magazine*. A select few might aim at the *Atlantic*, which was distinguished though poor, but the schemes of the journeyman writer centered about the big three New York rivals that dominated the national magazine scene. The *Century* got more than its share of the literary deluge that descended on this trio. In 1882 about 5,000 manuscripts reached the *Century* office, and by 1890 contributions poured in at nearly twice that number.[3]

Richard Watson Gilder reminded hopeful writers that he could use less than 400 of these offerings each year. He likened his job to picking a bouquet in a flower garden: that he failed to add a particular posey to his collèction, he remarked, did not signify that it was a weed. He was impelled constantly to assure tyros that he welcomed their work, that there was no "favored clique" of contributors. With every budding poet and fiction writer pressing for entry, the editors had to erect safeguards against intrusion and plagiarism. Every unknown writer had to submit character references, and an "Amazon guard" in the outer office protected Gilder and his assistants from bothersome visitors. To the perennial charge of discrimination, however, the best answer was the regular emergence of fresh names in the table of contents. In the issue of August 1898, the *Writer* pointed out, a dozen authors appeared who were absolutely new to ninety-nine out of one hundred readers, while a number of others were only slightly known. Like any good editor, Gilder "lived in the constant hope of discovering genius in every mail."[4]

The *Century* staff not only read each manuscript received, but in many small ways set new standards of courtesy and consideration in dealing with the sender. Alone among major publications it notified writers immediately of the receipt of manuscripts. It paid on acceptance—an uncommon practice in the nineteenth century. It sent back rejected contributions, even to those authors who were too optimistic or forgetful to enclose postage. With rare tact the editors broke the news of rejection in plain envelopes, while using official stationery for acceptances.[5]

To ambitious writers Gilder offered not only private encouragement but public recognition. He was the first editor of a widely circulated magazine to print authors' names with their work. The *North American Review* had made the first break with the traditional anonymity in 1868, and the *Atlantic* two years later had begun to identify authors of contributions, but these precedents identified only a fragment of the writing guild to an equally exclusive audience. A far greater number of unknowns made their debuts in the *Century*, where their names were spread before a million readers. One of the *Century*'s two volumes in 1890 listed 123 different contributors; the *Atlantic* in the same period had only fifty-four. Authors were gratefully impressed, therefore, when Gilder, beginning in 1882, printed their names at the heads of their stories, articles, and poems. *Harper's* followed four years later.[6]

Fortune was an even brighter beacon than fame in drawing talent to the magazine. "During my brief regime," Gilder informed William Dean Howells in 1884, "prices have advanced beyond precedent—largely, I suppose from my desire and ambition to 'get the best.'" He believed he had "a great deal" to do with the generally increased rewards for authorship in the early 1880s. The prosperity resulting from the War Series enabled Gilder to maintain a reputation for liberality throughout the first decade of his editorship. *Harper's* and *Scribner's Magazine* were likewise good paymasters, yet the *Journalist* noted in 1890 that most writers sent their manuscripts first to the *Century*.[7]

Payments by the "Big Three" about 1890 were reported by contemporaries to run from $10 to $100 per magazine page, but it was rare for prices to approach the higher figure. Mark Twain at the height of his fame commanded only $75 a page from the *Century*. Twain, who insisted that the Century Company had underpaid Ulysses S. Grant, had no complaints about his own treatment. "I make no prices with [John Brisben] Walker [of *Cosmopolitan*] and Gilder—I can trust them," he declared. Gilder was willing to give literary reputation its full reward. Thanking him for a generous check, James Russell Lowell exclaimed, "I fear for authorship with these luxurious rates." Later Lowell was reported to have declined a *Century* offer of $1,000 each for as many essays as he would submit. The Century Company agreed to pay Howells for travel articles a sum equal to or greater than the best he could obtain elsewhere. Thomas Bailey Aldrich set his own stipend. Sending Gilder a short story, he quipped, "If you like it, I shall want $250. for it. If the price doesn't suit you, I am willing to take more."[8]

Payments for fiction advanced with the author's reputation. David Gray, who got $50 each for his first sketches of the "horsey set," asked twice as much for the second series of these "Gallops." Chester Bailey Fernald, a regular contributor, raised his price from $175 per story in 1897 (about $23 a printed page) to $200 in 1900.[9]

A sprightly or authoritative article was equal in value to all but the most popular fiction. Thomas A. Janvier averaged about $15 a page for his "Ivory Black" stories in the 1880s, but drew nearly $25 a page in 1893 for a travel feature on Provence. The standard rate for nonfiction in the late 1880s was about $20 a page, although the modest John Burroughs protested that this was too much for his work. The astronomer Samuel P. Langley acknowledged one check that paid him $60 a page.[10]

Prices for verse ranged from a one-year subscription to the magazine—worth $4—for which one tyro sold his creation, to $275 asked by Aldrich on at least one occasion. The typical short poem brought from $5 to $15. Walt Whitman found that the *Century* usually met his asking price. And Edith Thomas once returned a check to Robert Underwood Johnson with the declaration that $15 was "much more" than her twelve-line verse was worth.[11]

The *Century*'s open purse and its fame brought it more good material than it could use. "Oh for room to print in the Magazine all our treasures!" sighed Gilder. The War Series added immensely to the pressures on his columns. The problem of "fitting a quart into a pint" became chronic and, much to Gilder's distress, sometimes caused lengthy delays between acceptance and publication. John Bigelow in 1892 bought back an article he had sold the monthly earlier, declaring testily that he wrote "for readers and not for the sepulchre." At the turn of the century Gilder had "tens of thousands of dollars worth of material waiting to be printed."[12]

This accumulation did not mean that all the writing talent of the country was lined up at Gilder's door awaiting his summons. On the contrary, the backlog resulted in part from the editor's desire to fasten down good copy before the blasts of competition whirled it away. In the 1890s, burgeoning young magazines and newspaper syndicates were challenging the hegemony of the "Big Three," and as these prosperous newcomers bid up the price of periodical literature, it became increasingly difficult for Gilder to keep his writers in the fold. For the first time, contributors began to complain that the *Century* paid less than other publications.

In some cases the *Century*'s prestige or loyalty to its editors effectively countered the pull of the new markets. Marian Manville Pope, remonstrating mildly over the check for $400 she received for a serialized travel article, nevertheless assured Johnson that she would rather have it in the *Century* at that figure than elsewhere at twice the sum. The humorist Charles Battell Loomis got two cents a word from *Life*, but was willing to take less from Gilder, who had guided him at the beginning of his career. Fernald, offering two stories at a combined price of $375, said he could get a better rate in a less famous periodical.[13]

Such loyalty was a diminishing factor in author-editor relationships, however. Literature, once the pastime of the cultivated few, was becoming a business obedient to the law of supply and demand. No longer could an editor find and train a writer with the expectation of enjoying exclusively the rights to his products. George W. Cable and Frank R. Stockton had been faithful to *Scribner's Monthly*, but the *Century*'s discoveries soon ventured into the open market.

One symbol of this commercialization was the literary agent. Josiah Gilbert Holland had dealt with his authors through personal talks or correspondence. As early as 1881, however, Howells turned over his entire output to James R. Osgood for a fixed stipend, Osgood selling the material "wherever he could, mostly to the *Century*." This was unusual procedure in the 1880s, but in the 1890s Gilder bargained with a number of such authors' representatives. They were especially useful in obtaining transatlantic literature. Gilder acquired the rights to Mrs. Humphrey Ward's novel, "Sir George Tressady," through Smith, Elder and Company, negotiated with A. P. Watt and Company for work by Bret Harte and Rudyard Kipling, and at times did business with still another London agency, the Authors' Syndicate. Among the American agents from whom the *Century* purchased material, Paul R. Reynolds was the most prominent.[14]

The mainstream of American literature through the decades of the 1880s and 1890s was marked by the standards that Gilder's *Century* held up for both readers and writers.

"The care of manuscripts is the care of literature" was a Gilder phrase. As caretaker, he had three obligations: to select manuscripts for publication; to revise them when necessary; and to offer suggestions and encouragement to their authors. Of these, the first was the most painful, for choice involved rejection. "It is a miserable business, this sitting in judgment upon other people's writing," Gilder lamented, "but somebody has to keep up the mill-dam or what a wash there would be!" His friendly

personal relations with many contributors made this task all the
harder. To one of them who complained that success had dulled
his understanding of her plight, he replied with grief: "Ah
. . . you little know what 'success' means—getting one's head
and heart . . . up where they can be pierced." Gilder, in fact,
was noted for the kindness with which he softened disappointment. He could reject a manuscript so gently, said the humorist
Bill Nye, as to make its author come 1,000 miles to thank him
and stay for dinner. By the mid-1890s Gilder found "less tear-
shedding and haughtiness" among writers as they came to regard
their dealings with the editor as a business rather than a personal
matter.[15]

The dread of overlooking something good was ever-present.
Gilder long regretted his rejection of Richard Harding Davis's
short story, "Gallegher," which he considered too slangy, but
which *Scribner's Magazine* printed to great acclaim. Such mistakes
were inevitable, but Gilder doubtless was right in thinking that
he was "more in danger of coddling the commonplace than of
neglecting genius."[16]

The *Century*'s hegemony over contributors was asserted in an
unsparing revision of manuscripts. Many of the prescribed changes
were to guarantee purity, but Gilder's editorial pencil worked for
the improvement of style and structure as well as taste. The
magazine's correspondence shows that even veteran contributors
of stories were sometimes asked to amend whole episodes.[17]
Gilder and Johnson were especially scrupulous in perfecting the
verse they scanned. "You two poets are dreadfully hard on my
sonnet," was one writer's rueful comment. "Send back and ask
author to mend faulty line in 4th stanza" ran a typical Gilder
notation.[18]

Sometimes proposals for revision were met with ruffled pride.
H. C. Bunner was insulted when the editors asked him to mod-
ernize the spelling of his dialect poem, "Love in Old Cloathes."
More representative was the attitude of another author who declared, "The appearance of the proof was rather startling, but
after a brief season of meditation I am inclined to believe that
you have used the surgeon's knife to good advantage." Others
were frankly grateful for the editorial pruning. After one of his
pioneer sports surveys had appeared, Walter Camp told Johnson,
"I don't know that I ever received so many compliments upon

an article," but, he added, nine-tenths of the tributes were prompted by "the way the matter is cut up and introduced—something for which the credit is all yours."[19]

It was the editors' observation that established writers were usually amenable to criticism but that the "unknown genius" was apt to regard his work as untouchable. Nevertheless, in their dealings with the ranking literary figures, the *Century* chieftains dropped the mentor's role and became eager, but dignified, solicitors. Howells, although graciously accepting hints and requests for alterations, would not submit more than a sketch of his projected work for editorial appraisal. He sent the outline of his novel, "The Minister's Charge," to *Harper's*, but when Henry Mills Alden, its editor, as much as hesitated, Howells withdrew it and gave it to Gilder.[20]

To great and small alike Gilder and his colleagues offered "editorial anxiety and sympathy" that were "the very life of a literary periodical." Their help took various forms. Richard M. Johnston heeded Gilder's advice to make his stories shorter. Burroughs confided to his journal: "I did not know I had that bank article in me till Gilder told me I had, and commanded me to write." Johnson, returning a story to Joel Chandler Harris for revision, displayed the tact for which the *Century* office was well known: "We like the 'Mocking-Bird,' and in your humility of soul you must remember that it is accepted in good faith. Send it back when you can. If by any chance you should drop below your best standard—why, what are editors for?"[21]

A sampling from abundant testimony, public and private, indicates how conscientiously the *Century* editors performed their most sensitive chore. Mary Hartwell Catherwood felt that in Gilder "for the first time in my life I have an editor who can appreciate the finest ramifications of my work and will unsparingly train me to my best." John Luther Long, author of "Madame Butterfly," wrote the *Century* chief, "If you are as kind to all scribblers as you are to me you certainly cannot escape canonization . . . at their hands." Maurice Francis Egan declared that it was "hard for any young man not to produce his best" under Gilder's influence. Johnson, too, had his admirers. "What kind of Editors there will be in Heaven, I know not," Amelia

E. Barr told him, "but on Earth, I should like just such an editor as yourself—every time."[22]

Along with the responsibility for improving the quality of magazine writing, Gilder accepted the sterner duty of insuring its morality. Like the editors of other family magazines—Howells and later Aldrich of the *Atlantic*, Alden of *Harper's*, and Edward L. Burlingame of *Scribner's Magazine*—he was a guardian of the nineteenth century's accepted moral code. Various strands of the American character and experience were joined in the fabric of gentility: lingering Puritanism and chronic national optimism, awareness of evil and belief in perfectibility paradoxically seem to have contributed to the prevailing modes of conduct and belief. However gentility may be defined, the social base for genteel values lay in the upper middle class to whom the *Century* obviously appealed and among whom the idea of progress, both personal and national, was firmly associated with established morality.

The chief custodian of this orthodoxy was the American woman. Behind the magazine editor, H. H. Boyeson declared, sat "his final judge, the young American girl. She is the Iron Madonna who strangles in her fond embrace the American novelist." Although Gilder denied that the bondage was either so complete or so fatal, he excluded from his family magazine whatever he thought would offend the mothers of the nation or corrupt their daughters. Writers were enjoined to make their stories wholesome, and transgressors either had to amend the proscribed passages or see them struck out by an alert *Century* staff. Gilder demanded a warrant of purity even from Howells, himself an apostle of propriety.[23]

The strongest of taboos barred the frank treatment of sex. Gilder's idealization of all passions reinforced his sense of obligation to shield readers from the naked truth in this respect. His staff was even more vigilantly prudish. Clarence Clough Buel and L. Frank Tooker were the grim Puritans of the office, while Johnson was famous for his sensitivity to offensive passages. Johnson was so wary of the least indelicacy that he even suspected the female proofreaders of maliciously tampering with copy to produce "questionable effects," and Theodore De Vinne had to assure him that they were women of blameless character whose errors were due entirely to negligence. The associate editor ruled out suggestive story situations as well as language. Of a novel by James Lane Allen involving a question of illegitimacy, Johnson wrote, "There is no talk that is objectionable, but the *fact* may be." He concluded that this admittedly "very serious moral work" was "unavailable" for the *Century*, since it would be "impossible to talk about it to young people without reference to the motive."[24]

The cries of wounded readers when a suggestion of immorality slipped past the editorial guard are proof that such prudery was appreciated. Long's charming and eventually famous "Madame Butterfly" drew more than one protest. A North Carolina woman complained that it made Japan out to be "a harlot house of the nations" at a time when Japanese Christians were trying to end licensed prostitution. A Providence, Rhode Island, reader labeled it a "prurient, indecent" story that "degrades womanhood and debases manhood" and declared that nothing in recent American fiction "so shakes faith in family, honor and fidelity and casts so decided a slur on our gallant sailors."[25]

The refusal of Gilder's friend and admirer, Frances Hodgson Burnett, to accept his suggested changes in her novel, "Through One Administration," led to unfortunate results. The story concerned an army officer who fell in love with a girl, was assigned to a frontier post, and returned to find his lady unhappily married. Although technically there was no adultery, the officer's "fatal fascination" with a married woman offended readers, who poured in a stream of protests. The story also brought adverse newspaper publicity. Gilder regarded these criticisms as both "serious" and "correct."[26]

The religious sensibilities of readers also had to be scrupulously considered. Johnson reported wearily to Gilder, "It looks as though to get [James Lane] Allen for the magazine we should have to run the guantlet [*sic*] of either the mothers or the *ministers*." The stiff-necked dogmatism that Holland had fought was, however, diminishing in American life. Even Johnson thought that "the risk of offending the theologians . . . may not be a great risk after all." The imperative was to treat religion, like relations between the sexes, in a genteel fashion.[27]

Often it was the crude speech and undignified procedures of frontier worship, as recounted by the local colorists, that grated on the senses of the refined East. Thus a Pennsylvania Methodist minister protested that "Sister Todhunter's Heart," a short story by Harry Stillwell Edwards, was an insulting caricature of his denomination, although in its own locale, Georgia, the narrative was accepted and enjoyed. Gilder defended his contributor in this instance, but reluctantly turned down another Edwards story because the exclamation, "I'll see you in hell, fust!" would "shock some of our readers, I fear." He asked Mary Hallock Foote to change a passage that referred to the singing of "'Safe in the arms of Jesus' in a monotonous nasal tone." Gilder's verdict was that "the juxtaposition of these tender lines with the words that follow is unpleasant." He detected and banned a similar irreverence in Lucy Furman's phrase, "While some was settin' up on the right-hand of God."[28]

The editors shielded readers from direct contact with the crude phenomena of life in various forms. In scenes of violence, blood might be indicated but not literally spilled. Drunkenness likewise was suggested, not portrayed. Characters might not sweat nor blow their noses. Even the advertisements breathed refinement. "One can be genteel and neat, and still indulge in a love of outdoor sports," an Ivory Soap display proclaimed.[29]

Profanity was outlawed, and there was a rule against slang or "undignified English." A curious exception to this ban was the dialect fiction and verse that glutted the *Century* so regularly as to invite satire. Perhaps Gilder regarded the colloquialisms of blacks and rustics as less likely to inspire emulation than the up-to-date newspaper argot of a Richard Harding Davis. Even so, he was troubled by the realistic dialogue of the local colorists, fearing that "we seem to many persons to be continuing the work of vulgarization" begun by the newspapers. To Hamlin Garland in 1892 he explained that "we value correct pictures of life—of even pretty common life—and the consequence is we are giving an undue proportion, possibly, of dialect fiction. People who are trying to bring up their children with refinement, and to keep their own and their children's language pure and clean, very naturally are jealous of the influence of a magazine—especially of the *Century Magazine*—in this respect." Faced with this predicament, Gilder thought that a dialect story "should very strongly recommend itself before being sent into almost every cultivated household in the United States!"[30]

These various infringements of the *Century*'s code all manifested, in one way or another, the rising tide of realism in American fiction. Writers who dealt consciously with social realities tended to violate simultaneously a number of the rules that defined gentility. Bernard DeVoto has documented the case of Twain, whose "Huckleberry Finn" was blue-penciled not merely for egregiously coarse words or sentences but for whole passages depicting the routine cruelty and viciousness of midwestern villages. Even so, Gilder had to defend the expurgated version. To a western superintendent of schools who found the episodes of "Huckleberry Finn" to be "destitute of a single redeeming quality," the editor replied that Twain's contributions to the *Century* were of "very decided value" and invited his correspondent to compare the book version of the novel with the magazine extracts that had been carefully edited for the *Century*'s audience with the author's full consent.[31]

A more awkward attempt at realism by Robert Grant, a young and proper Bostonian, aroused one of the worst explosions of Gilder's wrath on record. After perusing the proof of Grant's novel, "An Average Man," the editor told the author he would keep his promise to run the story "on condition that you eliminate all the passages marked in red." These passages were objectionable on three grounds: "1st.—*On account of slang running to the point of vulgarity.* 2nd.—*On account of direct and grotesquely inappropriate and repeated references to the generative processes.* 3rd.—*On account of a dogmatic tone with regard to Christianity.*" Gilder concluded his scolding in a fatherly tone. "You may think we are unwisely trying to restrict your liberty of expression; that we are timid and conservative." That was probably true, said the editor, but "we think you will live to thank us." (Nearly half a century later, Grant, who became a well-known Boston judge, acknowledged in his autobiography that he owed Gilder a debt of gratitude for saving him from his own blunders.)[32]

With the new realism as it first appeared, Gilder had no quarrel. Its two chief exponents, Howells and Henry James, had been eagerly sought as contributors for the magazine. They shunned the more sordid aspects of life and, moreover, were deeply concerned with its moral lessons. In his novel, "A Modern Instance," serialized in the *Century* in 1881–82, Howells wrote of an incompatible marriage and divorce with such skill and discretion that Gilder publicly congratulated him on his marriage of art and morality. Even while he argued that the commonplace verities were the novelist's true concern, Howells did not neglect to point out that it was the realist, rather than the romanticist, who could "shame you into at least wishing to be a helpfuler and wholesomer creature than you are."[33]

In the late 1880s, however, Howells, carrying on the fight against romanticism and sentimentalism from his "Editor's Study" in *Harper's*, met with increasing hostility from critics who felt that his school of fiction failed to include inspirational ideals. His example, moreover, seemed to open the door to writers of less impeccable taste. In 1889 an observer in *Current Literature* noted an "avalanche" of books remarkable for their "frank treatment of the passions and of the mental struggles through which thoughtful men are passing." In the newspaper and periodical press, morality in the novel had become a topic of "frantic consideration."[34]

Gilder was both exhilarated and disturbed by this new movement. To his friend Howells he wrote, "I learn this from you— literary frankness; it is to be our salvation!" He added that "I hold out my hand to you as to a voice crying in the wilderness." As an editor, however, Gilder took a more cautious line. Explaining his dilemma to Howells in 1887, he wrote: "I see a great change coming in our fiction;—a greater reality and freedom. I see—a man of Boyesen's talent . . . in danger of rushing into 'realism' in a way which will hurt 'the cause.' I desire, greatly, to help bring about a condition of the public mind which will allow of greater freedom—though editorially it is my duty to go slowly and make as few mistakes as possible."[35] While he aimed at careful promotion of the more genteel realism, Gilder respected the sensibilities of his readers. "There are many who believe that America has the purest society in the world," he declared. "Is not this purity worth paying for with a little prudery?"[36]

But it was not simply to protect his subscribers that Gilder endorsed the rules of gentility. He believed that fiction, if it were to fulfill its highest function, must temper realism with idealism. Along with his *Century* colleagues, he held that the "law of suggestion" was the "surest road to truth." Art, as Johnson defined it, was "a compromise with facts to obtain an effect of truth through beauty and illusion." The realistic method, "if logically adhered to," became mere pathology. Gilder made the same distinction when he said of a story by Mary E. Wilkins that it seemed "like hospital work rather than art work."[37]

The fullest statement of Gilder's considered views on realism appeared in 1887 in the *New Princeton Review*. He held that, since "all art is a selection," there was "no *real* real in literature; and the world will have its own opinion of the taste and art of a writer who is swamped by the commonplace, or who betrays an engrossing love for the unlovely." There was a "reality of the spirit as well as of the flesh," and the great artist of every age united these twin aspects of life; "but it is the ideal side of art and of life that makes the other worth while, and raises mankind ever higher among the beasts. It is the ideal side of our nature that stands in greatest need of culture: and surely none the less in a realistic age like this."[38]

Gilder's theory of literature was a part of his theory of editorship. In some spiritual realm there existed an ideal and absolute Truth. His task, which was also the task of the writers and artists who were his contributors, was to select and arrange the phenomena of life so as to embody that Truth in various forms, or at least to suggest to readers its eternal presence.

In practice, of course, Gilder could not often meet this exalted standard. He could encourage talent, but he could not create genius, and so most of his magazine's stories were of journeyman quality. On the other hand, he and his colleagues were far from dictators, suppressing whatever was vital in American literature, as some critics of both the nineteenth and twentieth centuries have charged. At most they were keepers of a flame cherished not only by their readers but by the best writers of their generation. No family magazine of today is so closely wedded to the finest contemporary fiction as was the *Century* at its peak. The three major American authors of the period were well represented in the magazine—in fact, a conjunction of good literature probably unique in periodical literature occurred in February 1885, when James's "The Bostonians" began its serial run in the same issue that contained episodes from "Huckleberry Finn" and an installment of "The Rise of Silas Lapham."

Howells, in the five-year interval between his resignation as editor of the *Atlantic* and his joining the editorial staff of *Harper's*, was Gilder's most valued contributor. Between December 1881 and February 1886 he gave the *Century*, in addition to literary essays and travel articles, four novels, and two of the novels were among the best of his lengthy career. "A Modern Instance," for all of its moralizing, was a skillful and sound portrayal of New England life and character. Controversial because of the unhappy marriage at the center of its plot, attacked in many quarters as dreary and depressing, it was nonetheless a major achievement in fiction. Gilder pronounced it "a success in every way" and informed Howells that it had an "immense and strongly moved audience." The masterfully wrought "The Rise of Silas Lapham," serialized in 1884–85, had an even greater appeal, and doubtless accelerated the rapid gain in circulation for which the War Series was more obviously responsible. (Out in Indiana, young Booth Tarkington looked forward feverishly to each installment and wept when Silas got drunk and made a fool of himself.) Briefer and less notable novels by Howells appearing in the *Century* were "A Woman's Reason" (1883) and "The Minister's Charge" (1886)—the latter denounced by Bostonians especially for the grim picture it painted of their city and by some readers elsewhere for subjecting them to "low company."[39]

In the single novel he obtained from James, Gilder had no cause for rejoicing. He informed the author of "The Bostonians" that the *Century* had "never published anything that appeared so little to interest" its readers. Still, James's biographer called it "the most considerable American novel of its decade." This novel also stirred up controversy in Boston, where many of the respectable citizens thought they recognized a satire on a well-known lady reformer. James's shorter fictional pieces, such as "The Point of View" (December 1882) and "The Liar" (May and June 1888) were more suited for a magazine. The former, caricaturing international social aspirations, was denounced by reviewers as unfair to the American national character.[40]

In addition to the passages from his masterpiece, "Huckleberry Finn," Twain gave the *Century* excerpts from "A Connecticut Yankee in King Arthur's Court" (1889–90) and a suitably scrubbed portion of his earthy "Pudd'nhead Wilson" (1893). The latter work marked the end of the monthly's association with the best of nineteenth-century realism, although Howells made a brief return in 1896 with his short novel of love in Saratoga, "An Open-Eyed Conspiracy."

Lesser writers, meanwhile, were tending to bear out in a limited way Gilder's contention that magazine fiction represented "with insight and accuracy the various phases of life in the new world." Doubtless they neglected some important aspects of that life, and their insight often lacked depth, and yet compared to their predecessors, they cast a wide look over the fast-changing American panorama. The physical portrait of the nation took shape mainly through the myriad small strokes of short story writers, but the novelists added broad sweeps of local color. In "The Led-Horse Claim" (1882–83) and in "Coeur d'Alene" (1894), for example, Mary Hallock Foote, despite implausible plots in the sentimental tradition, gave authentic pictures of the western mining scene. Edward Eggleston's "The Graysons" (1887–88), about rural people in Illinois, was a still more documentary portrayal of local speech, habits, and customs.[41]

Not only the regions of the nation but its changing manners and social groupings were depicted in the *Century*'s serials. Burnett, once the sentimental mainstay of Holland's contributors' list, brought a firsthand knowledge of Washington society to her story, "Through One Administration" (1881). Of the several novels or novelettes of manners written by Constance Cary Harrison, "The Anglomaniacs" (1890) attracted the most attention. This satire on social climbers was illustrated, appropriately, by young Charles Dana Gibson. In "Characteristics" (1891) and its sequel, "Dr. North and His Friends" (1900), S. Weir Mitchell brought to light the Philadelphia circle of which he was a part.

Some writers turned their attention to the problems germane to an increasingly urban, industrial civilization. Cable's "Dr. Sevier" (1883–84), although its setting was New Orleans, did not, like his earlier tales, evoke the old Creole life but reflected the author's interest in humanitarian reform—to the point where

Gilder rejected Cable's first two drafts as too didactic. John Hay's "The Bread-Winners" (1883–84) was "the first recognition on the part of literature that a class struggle impended in America." It was run anonymously, and speculation as to its authorship combined with heated discussion of its antilabor bias to make it a seasonal sensation.[42]

Another story with a sociological theme was "The Christian League of Connecticut," a four-part fiction beginning in November 1882. Its author was Washington Gladden, and it was written at the suggestion of Roswell Smith, Gladden's "most trusted counselor." The story, which described the organization of an interdenominational league and its beneficial effects on a typical factory town, was a pioneering work in social-gospel fiction. Gladden for three decades was to sound the themes of the social gospel in the *Century* as well as from his Congregational pulpit in Columbus, Ohio.[43]

In the 1890s, however, the *Century*'s writers of fiction, and especially of serial novels, for the most part turned their backs on the turbulent contemporary scene and concerned themselves with the color and adventure of the past. The vogue of the historical novel began, for the *Century*, with Mary Hartwell Catherwood's "The Romance of Dollard" (1888–89), a tale of French Canada for which no less an authority than Francis Parkman wrote an approving introduction. Some years later the Century Company advanced Catherwood funds for research in France, which culminated in her well-documented "The Days of Jeanne d'Arc" (1897). Even more remote in time and place was F. Marion Crawford's "Via Crucis" (1898–99), a story of the Second Crusade.[44]

The monthly's most prized contributor in the historical field was S. Weir Mitchell, the versatile Philadelphian who gained equal fame as physician and fiction writer. Gilder received a synopsis of his "Hugh Wynne, Free Quaker," in the spring of 1896, but, having already engaged a serial for the next year, he merely advised the Century Company to publish it as a book. When William W. Ellsworth, secretary of the company, received the full manuscript, he hailed it as the best novel of the American Revolution ever written, and Gilder, after reading it, rushed the first installment into the November number. Enthusiasm for this serial had barely died down before Mitchell appeared again with "The Adventures of Françoise" (1898), centering in the Paris of the French Revolution.[45]

The dominance of historical fiction in this period reflected a national craze rather than hostility to realism on Gilder's part. The editors would doubtless have welcomed good writers of another school as eagerly as they seized on Mitchell and on the now-forgotten Bertha Runkle, their last discovery of the nineteenth century, whose "The Helmet of Navarre" began its run in August 1900. There was no expression of satisfaction in the editorial of that year which noted that the romantic novel, having supplanted realistic and humorous fiction, was in complete possession of the popular field.[46]

Gilder followed Holland's policy of patronizing American authors. A survey of leading monthlies in 1883 showed that the *Century* was carrying three of the five novels by American writers then being serialized. In that year Gilder featured parts of Robert Louis Stevenson's "The Silverado Squatters," but not until 1891 did he turn again to England for a major piece of fiction. Nor was "The Naulahka," written by Kipling in collaboration with the American-born Wolcott Balestier, of a quality to encourage further imports. In 1895 the editor tried to bolster a fiction list then in the doldrums by paying $18,000 for Mrs. Humphrey Ward's "Sir George Tressady," but this, too, was a disappointment. No other British novel appeared in the monthly before 1900.[47]

Gilder's intense patriotism played a large part in his determination to shun British novels. Writing to Edmund Gosse, the *Century*'s British agent, in 1887, Gilder argued that American writers were being crushed by the lack of international copyright; that it was his duty to think first of them; that printing an English serial would crowd out "some American story which, in our way of thinking, has greater claims upon us." He concluded, "The American policy has always been the policy of the Century but we feel more and more inclined to insist upon it." The unhappy Gosse replied, "I cannot think that an editor has to 'protect' the literature of his country." Gilder and Gosse remained friends, but their business relations worsened to the point where Gosse took an agent's position with McClure's literary syndicate, which was already cutting into the *Century*'s circulation.[48]

The years of Gilder's editorial reign saw the rise of the short story to finished form and wide popularity, a development closely linked to the growth of magazines. As early as 1880 the editors found that novelettes, in place of longer serials, provided "an excellent balance" to weighty features like "Peter the Great," and the next two decades saw a trend to even shorter fiction pieces. Where a typical number of *Scribner's Monthly* had contained one or two brief sketches, the *Century* in the 1880s usually ran three or four short stories each month and in the 1890s sometimes as many as seven. Evidently the accelerating tempo of American life brought less leisurely reading habits, for there was a marked tendency to brevity and crispness during this period in the magazine's nonfiction articles as well as its fiction.[49]

"I regard a good short story," said Gilder, "not only in itself, as a notable work of art, but as . . . a separate scene in the great panorama of contemporary life." It is the latter aspect of the *Century*'s short stories that seems more enduringly significant. Some of them merit attention as examples of craftsmanship apart from their connection with time or place. Such are the shorter pieces of James; several contributions by Twain, especially "The £1,000,000 Bank Note"; the numerous inventions of Stockton; and Kipling's "The Brushwood Boy," which Tooker thought the greatest short story the monthly ever published. But most of the tales and sketches depended for their essential appeal on their delineation of the American milieu and character.[50]

The stream of local-color narration that began in Holland's regime broadened in Gilder's time to take in nearly every section of the United States. The dominant strain, however, was still southern. Gilder acknowledged in 1890 that southern literature had "forced itself upon the attention of the editors" to such a degree that they were "supposed to make a specialty of it, and I had a northern author ask me, not a great while ago, when I was going to give the North a chance."[51]

Cable, the monthly's first discovery, remained a faithful contributor for some years, but his later stories never equaled the first Creole tales that *Scribner's* had gathered from his early work. His sympathy for the freedman increasingly alienated him from his enviroment and tended, moreover, to submerge his art in propaganda. In 1890 Cable sent Gilder the manuscript of what was eventually to become his *John March, Southerner*. Gilder rejected it as too didactic. Two revisions by Cable, the last an extensive one in 1893, did not satisfy the editor, who found in it "an innate disagreeableness." Cable thereupon sold the story to *Scribner's Magazine*, which serialized it in 1894. This disagreement ended Cable's close association with the *Century*, although he and Gilder remained friends. Cable's "Strange, True Stories of Louisiana," which Gilder had published in his monthly in 1888–89, contained more of the flavor of old New Orleans than his later fiction.[52]

The Creoles he had depicted, often critically, were treated more sympathetically by Grace King, who wrote because she felt Cable had "stabbed" her native city "to please the Northern press." Although Gilder rejected her first work, she found a public through *Harper's*, which had followed the *Century*'s lead in accepting southern writers. Subsequently Gilder agreed to take a dozen of her "Balcony Stories," portraying from the inside the Creole society in which she had been reared, the first of these appearing in December 1892. Surpassing King in technique and dramatic power was Kate Chopin, who reached into the bayou country to bring Acadians as well as Creoles into her stories. The *Century* ran four of her short stories in the period 1894–96.[53]

While these writers dealt with an exotic fragment of the southern population, most of Dixie's local colorists exploited the black as a subject. Thomas Nelson Page, who had celebrated the mellower side of the slave-master relationship in verse during the 1870s, now turned the same theme into prose. The *Century* held his "Marse Chan" for nearly four years before publishing it, fearing the public would find its dialect too difficult and tiresome. Its popular success ushered in a virtual reign of dialect in the magazines. Page owed a great deal to the editorial help of Gilder and Johnson. Of Page's later work, the most notable story was "Meh Lady" (1886), which, at Johnson's suggestion, emphasized North-South reconciliation.[54]

The master of speech and character among blacks was Harris,

the shy, round-faced Atlanta journalist whose work combined literary art with folk history. Harris was discovered by northern newspapers, and D. Appleton and Company published a collection of his "Uncle Remus" stories in 1880, but he made his magazine debut in *Scribner's Monthly*, and most of his stories during the 1880s appeared in Gilder's periodical. His "Uncle Remus" was introduced to the readers of *Scribner's* in 1881, and two years later that inimitable plantation narrator spun his shrewd, humorous tales in three successive numbers of the *Century* (July, August, and September). The black in more pathetic guise made his appearance in "Free Joe and the Rest of the World" (November 1884), the story of a manumitted slave at home in neither black nor white society. The authenticity of these characterizations was enhanced by the illustrations of A. B. Frost which, the author said, were "so true to the spirit of the text that they seem to be an echo of my own mind."[55]

After Page and Harris came a deluge of fiction in black dialect; the high-water mark was reached in the years just before and after 1890. The amusing "Two Runaways" (1886) was the first of some twenty tales of the Georgia upland plantations by Harry Stillwell Edwards, and the recession of the vogue may be seen in the relegation of his work in 1893 to the smaller type of "In Lighter Vein." Maurice Thompson's stories also took place in Georgia, while Virginia Frazer Boyle, a *Century* discovery of 1890, pictured the blacks of Tennessee. Other prolific recorders of black lore and dialect were J. A. Macon, whose "Aphorisms from the Quarter" appeared frequently in "Bric-à-Brac," and Ruth McEnery Stuart. Outstanding among these fictional recollections of the Old South was F. Hopkinson Smith's "Colonel Carter of Cartersville" (1890–91), an episodic tale of an impoverished Virginia planter and his faithful black.

The poor whites of the southern back country were also brought to life in the *Century*'s fiction. Harris created a gallery of mountain folk as convincing as his "Uncle Remus." His "Trouble on Lost Mountain" combined tragedy and humor with consummate artistry. Of his numerous other tales in this genre, perhaps the most memorable was "At Teague Poteet's," a whimsical story of Georgia moonshiners much strengthened by Johnson's editorial suggestions, and "Little Compton," which related the troubles of a Yankee living through the Civil War in the South.[56]

Emulating Harris was his protégeé, Matt Crim, an Atlanta woman who sent Gilder several sketches of the Georgia uplanders. Middle Georgia was also the locale for the narrations of Richard Malcom Johnston, an ex-planter who, having won his literary spurs through Holland's magazine, was frequently represented in the *Century* over a span of twenty years. On the far side of the Appalachian Mountains, other local colorists were helping to paint the nation's portrait. "Charles Egbert Craddock" (Mary N. Murfree), although an *Atlantic* discovery, gave Gilder's monthly "The Casting Vote," an atmospheric re-creation of Tennessee mountain life (November and December 1893). The same state provided the backdrop for the tales of Viola Roseboro', more than a dozen of which ran in the *Century* during the decades of dialect. John Fox, Jr.'s "A Mountain Europa" and "A Cumberland Vendetta" were melodramatic episodes of the Kentucky highlands. The stories of "Octave Thanet" (Alice French) were peopled by the poor whites of the Arkansas canebrakes.

Allen was too conscious a stylist and traditionalist to be classified simply as a local-color writer, but his "Two Kentucky Gentlemen of the Old School" was redolent of plantation life in antebellum days. That story was written to complement "Uncle Tom at Home in Kentucky," a descriptive essay that similarly waxed sentimental about the old regime.[57]

In the Midwest the chronicling of rural folkways in short stories proceeded more slowly. Eggleston's fictional contributions in this period were mainly novels. Hoosier manners and spirit were represented best in brief compass by James Whitcomb Riley, whose sentimental dialect was in the vein of local color. Gilder, who printed a quantity of Riley's songs of farm and fireside, compared them to the poems of Robert Burns in their ability to evoke country life. Indianians of a different kind were the Ohio River people of Lucy Furman, who described them so minutely that she would have feared to publish her stories save that these "sanctified people"—her models—shunned the magazines as instruments of Satan.[58]

In 1885 Garland found that, "so far as the pages of the literary magazines of that year were concerned, Wisconsin, Minnesota and Iowa did not exist." Determined to write realistically about the drabness of farm and village life in this region, he made his early stories so documentary that neither *Harper's* nor the *Century* would take them. Gilder, whom Garland thought second only to Howells as a judge of fiction, warned him not to leave beauty out of the picture; thus advised, the young author in the 1890s contrived a blend of romance and realism that proved acceptable to his eastern tutor.[59]

Further West, Anna B. Fuller followed Foote in writing about Colorado, and Margaret Collier Graham used California as a fictional setting. From Britain, Harte sent two stories that evoked the far-off Spanish California of his youth. At the other extreme, the somber colors of New England were caught transiently by several now-forgotten contributors, and more enduringly by Mary E. Wilkins Freeman and Sarah Orne Jewett.[60]

In their careful management of form and effect, Jewett and Freeman were exceptional among local-color writers, most of whom relied more on their material than on their art. Most of them, too, were diffident about their work and looked to New York not only for a market but for editorial tutelage. In most cases their correspondence with the magazine shows that after being discovered, they had to be constantly advised, admonished, and encouraged. In training these authors, and in revealing to readers the fascinating variety of the nation's regions, Gilder's monthly fulfilled its claim to be a genuinely American magazine. Despite their frequent superficiality and sentimentality, the local-color writers collectively made the *Century's* best contribution to the short story.

Meanwhile, a different class of fiction writers had emerged in the cities of the eastern seaboard. Where many of the provincial writers had been women, this new contingent was masculine, urbane, witty, self-assured, seeking editorial acceptance rather than advice. Some, like Aldrich and Bunner, were self-conscious artists who produced skillfully carved cameos. Many more were free-lancers, but wise about the market, like Charles Belmont Davis and "Ivory Black" (Janvier), who relied on style and craft to please their public. Several had journalistic backgrounds, and their stories usually conveyed their familiarity with some special aspect of the urban or suburban scene. David Gray was at home on the hunting course, Brander Matthews in art and theatrical circles, while Richard Harding Davis treated London or Monte Carlo as casually as New York. The slices of life they revealed were thin and unsubstantial, if fashionable. They wrote for their day and, on the whole, their work has not survived.

Special mention should be made of Stockton, who continued to delight his audience with the same whimsical humor that had made his "Rudder Grange" sketches so popular. His "The Lady or the Tiger?" (November, 1882) ended in a riddle that made it probably the most talked-about short story in American history. Readers were left to decide for themselves whether a woman's smile was a signal for the hero's destruction or a blessing on his love. Thousands of solutions poured in to the author, who, however, could never be prevailed upon to give his own answer. Stockton's trademark was a topsy-turvy view of life, manifested, for example, in a ghost who was haunted, and in "A Tale of Negative Gravity."[61]

If Gilder's gentility did not exclude from his magazine the best novelists and short story writers of his time, neither did his idealism inspire a nobler or more vital literature. The editor could insist on minimal requirements for purity and syntax, but he could prescribe no final standard for an art that took meaning and life only from the individual insight, imagination, and style of its creators. The *Century*'s fiction was the least ideal of its major features in terms of its capacity to inspire. Although its authors often pointed the moral, its primary function was entertainment.

The monthly's literary criticism during the 1880s and 1890s was impressive in both volume and quality. The department of "Literature," begun in the first number of the *Century*, was designed for reviews of current books, but it was very shortly dropped in favor of separate essays on important authors, both foreign and American, past and present, or on literary history and theory.

Edmund C. Stedman, who called Gilder and Johnson "my two dearest working colleagues," continued the series he had begun for *Scribner's* on American poets and later brought his "Victorian Poets" up to date by a supplementary essay. His analysis of "The

Nature and Elements of Poetry" (1892) was perhaps the weightiest critical series the monthly ever attempted. Such a thorough study of the subject, Tooker thought, would have appeared in no other American magazine.[62]

Howells, meanwhile, as absorbed in the theory of fiction as Stedman was in that of poetry, wrote an appreciation of Twain (September 1882) that was a manifesto of that humorist's stature as a serious writer and followed this with a sympathetic critique of his friend and fellow realist, James (November 1882). In this latter essay Howells enraged British press critics by saying that fiction in America had "become a finer art in our day than it was with Dickens and Thackeray." Thomas Sargent Perry had earlier (March 1882) paid tribute to Howells. Burroughs, Henry Van Dyke, George E. Woodberrry, and Matthews were other able critics who wrote for Gilder, and Lowell was represented posthumously by a selection from his Harvard lectures (1893–94).[63]

With the aid of Gosse, Gilder also presented his readers with a gallery of great Victorians, their predecessors, and successors. Gosse himself wrote on Robert Browning, Dante and Christina Rossetti, Kipling, and Stevenson. Andrew Lang discussed Matthew Arnold, James dealt with Anthony Trollope, and John Addington Symonds contributed "Recollections of Lord Tennyson." Mrs. M. O. W. Oliphant harked back to earlier prose masters with articles on Daniel Defoe, Jonathan Swift, and Joseph Addison. Continental literature was not neglected. James reviewed the work of his friend Alphonse Daudet, and Daudet sent Gilder his reminiscences of Victor Hugo and Ivan Turgenev.[64]

One of the keys to Gilder's excellence as an editor was his conscientious effort to keep the style as well as the content of his magazine at a high level. Even in features "not purely literary," he insisted on good writing, and in articles like those by General Grant he was confident that "we produce incidentally a sort of literature that will last." In commissioning writers he tried to suit the author to the topic, the manner to the matter. After deciding on a biography, for example, he would read extensively about the subject, then seek the person best equipped to do the individual justice.[65]

Having gained renown by its War Series and the ponderous "Lincoln" of Hay and Nicolay, the *Century* continued to make a specialty of history and biography. The 400th anniversary of the nation's discovery brought a life of Christopher Columbus by Emilio Castelar, translated from the author's "semi-barbaric, semi-archaic" Spanish by Alvey A. Adee, the Department of State's invaluable, sempiternal chief clerk. In 1891 Gilder tried without success to induce Hippolyte Taine, the French historian, to write a biography of Napoleon. He then settled on William M. Sloane, editor of the *New Princeton Review*, who had already begun a study of Bonaparte. The *Century* lent its resources to the completion of the book and published it serially, beginning in 1894, at a time when Napoleonic literature was much in vogue.[66]

This study was followed in 1898–99 by Professor Benjamin Ide Wheeler's "Alexander the Great" which, the monthly's prospectus pointed out, was of special interest "when empire-making projects are engaging the energies of the strongest nations of the earth." Wheeler did not think his work suitable for a magazine, but was persuaded to rewrite it for the *Century*. Its somewhat dull text was enlivened by the powerful imaginative paintings and drawings of the versatile French artist, André Castaigne. A much more readable and also illustrated biography was Paul Leicester Ford's "The Many-Sided Franklin" (1898–99). The monthly's last major biography in the nineteenth century was Lord John Morley's "Oliver Cromwell" (1899–1900), adorned with the usual lavish illustrations, some in color.[67]

Several ambitious projects were planned without coming to fruition. Gilder hoped to get the autobiography of William E. Gladstone—who was said to read the *Century* avidly, chiefly for its American advertisements—but the British statesman declared he could not find time to write it. Otto von Bismarck courteously declined to write his memoirs, on the ground that he must either hurt the living or conceal the truth. In 1900 Gilder planned to take advantage of a meeting with Kaiser Wilhelm to persuade him to write on the campaigns of Julius Caesar, but U.S. Ambassador Andrew D. White warned the editor that this matter was too commercial to discuss at a royal audience. Lengthy negotiations with White himself for a life of Martin Luther eventually came to naught, and a biography of the great religious reformer did not appear in the magazine until 1911.[68]

The editors, conducting a persistent search for historically significant material, printed many previously unpublished letters and memorabilia. Readers, aware of this special interest, plied them with old family documents. Gilder told one volunteer in 1889 that he had more of such manuscripts on hand than he knew what to do with. The editors were leery of these contributions, in part because it was difficult to prove that they had not been previously in print. Nevertheless, Johnson in 1896 remarked, "We need continually good reminiscences," and in 1900 he was still seeking unpublished political documents among the recent accessions to the Library of Congress.[69]

At times Gilder and Johnson tried to strike once again that combination of history and journalism that had distinguished the War Series. Johnson planned a series on California gold hunting, which ran for more than a year, beginning in November 1890, but despite rich illustration and eye-witness narrative, it did not catch on with readers. When war with Spain broke out in 1898, the editors naturally jumped at the chance for another war series. With the important exceptions of Admirals George Dewey and Winfield Schley, the major commanders told their stories for the *Century*. A brief rise in circulation indicated that "The Story of the Captains" won some special attention, but recording only eight months of hostilities and lacking historical perspective, this series could not compare with the earlier war feature. A project somewhat like George Kennan's Siberian venture was E. J. Glave's penetration of central Africa, sponsored by the *Century*, with the aim of gaining information on the intertribal slave trade and then urging its suppression. The English explorer died of fever in 1895 after reaching central Africa. In 1896 the magazine printed excerpts from Glave's journal.[70]

The *Century*'s articles of travel and adventure, in addition to giving readers a panoramic acquaintance with the world, were often worthy specimens of English style. Although the superb engravings were as important as the text, Gilder was not content to have the writing merely embellish the illustrations. Asking his friend and wartime comrade, Charles G. Leland, to "rescue" one contribution that was not up to the mark, Gilder reminded him that "we are trying to solve the problem of bringing a popular illustrated magazine up to the highest literary standard."[71]

The caliber of his authors assured the editor that this goal would be reached in most cases. Men with cultural perception as well as practiced pens brought out the ancient charm of Europe's cities: James wrote on Venice and London, Lang on Old Edinburgh, and Howells on various Italian cities. F. Marion Crawford took readers to Rome and through the Vatican (1896). F. Hopkinson Smith ranged as far as Constantinople (March 1896). Most of these articles carried the hallmark of Joseph Pennell's clean-lined etchings. Teaming up with his wife, Elizabeth Robins Pennell, that artist traveled over the countryside of western and southern Europe, recording picturesque features for the magazine. From 1886 through 1893, this pair contributed illustrated articles to twelve issues of the *Century*.[72]

More remote and exotic civilizations were also explored. From the Far East, the artist John La Farge sent his written impressions of Japan (1890–91 and 1893), while W. W. Rockhill, who had made his way in native costume into previously unknown parts of Tibet, described his narrow escapes and adventures (November 1890 and April 1894). H. Talbot Kelly wrote and strikingly illustrated several articles on the Bedouins and Fellaheen of North Africa (1897–98).

Century readers roamed the oceans vicariously, too, most joyously in Captain Joshua Slocum's "Sailing Alone around the World" (1899–1900), one of the most fascinating sea yarns in American letters. It was Buel, himself an enthusiastic yachtsman, who suggested to Gilder that Slocum "might be able to make a lively story of his tens of thousands of miles in a forty-foot sloop."[73]

Descriptive essays added to the multiform picture of the United States drawn by the local-color writers. The kaleidoscopic development of the nation could be seen in the elegance of Fifth Avenue, as set forth by Mariana G. Van Rensselaer in 1893, and the contrasting ruggedness of western ranch life, as depicted in 1888 by Theodore Roosevelt. Frederic Remington's vividly drawn cowboys were the perfect complement to Roosevelt's vigorous prose. East and West were differentiated, too, in the nature essays of Burroughs and John Muir, both of whom contributed regularly to the magazine during Gilder's editorial term.

Of all the *Century*'s literature during the 1880s and 1890s, nothing seems less alive today than most of its verse. Like all magazine
poetry of the period, it seemed bloodless and derivative even to
contemporaries. "Every singer takes his net and chases a butterfly," said one disparaging critic; "there are none climbing up
to the eagle's eyrie."[74] The *Century* printed a satire by R. K. Mun-
kittrick in September 1890, which summarized the irrelevancy
of its own verse to life in the United States:

'T'is Ever Thus
Ad Astra, De Profundis,
Keats, Bacchus, Sophocles;
Ars Longa, Euthanasia,
Spring, The Eumenides

. . .

Dum Vivimus Vivamus,
Sleep, Palingenesis;
Salvini, Sursum Corda,
At Mt. Desert, To Miss _____

These are part of the contents
Of "Violets of Song,"
The first poetic volume
Of Susan Mary Strong.

Strong was the magazine's composite bard, appropriately female. No wonder that Burroughs found himself reading over and
over a homespun ballad by Riley, thinking, "In the desert of
'Century' poetry, this is a green live thing, if only a weed."
Aldrich, intending praise, inadvertently pointed to one weakness
of the magazine's verse in an 1892 letter to Gilder: "Your May
number is a nest of singing birds. I don't believe any single
number of a magazine ever before contained so much excellent
verse. Not one of the twelve or thirteen poems touches on the
commonplace."[75]

This is not the whole story of the *Century*'s verse, for nothing
lay closer to Gilder's heart than poetry, and he conscientiously
sought out the best work of his time. Though he missed the
recluse genius, Emily Dickinson, he published posthumously

poems by Sidney Lanier and Herman Melville and made up for Holland's snub of Whitman by printing a number of contributions from "the good, gray poet." Whitman himself said: "Gilder takes what I offer unhesitatingly, never interjecting a single word of petty criticism. . . . Do you realize that this is treatment no other magazine editor in America has accorded us?" Not only did the *Century* carry more verse—at good rates of pay—than did any other magazine, but Gilder personally aided and encouraged its writers. He gave liberally to the support of the aging Whitman and also collected considerable sums for him from friends like Andrew Carnegie. He privately subsidized the publication of promising young lyrists.[76]

The motivation for Gilder's zeal in encouraging poets was not only his sympathy with his fellow craftsmen but his belief in the utilitarian function of poetry as the purest expression of ideality. He looked on its creators as custodians of noble thought, "who in the midst of a sordid world are trying to keep alive the harshly blown-upon and flickering flame of the ideal." The reading of poetry was especially desirable in the United States, he thought, as an antidote to the "air of vulgar luxury" which new fortunes had given to society. And yet, the editor had to admit, the public sadly neglected its chanters of the ideal.[77]

Although Gilder was not to blame for the feeble state of American poetry, he undoubtedly overrated the static, delicate creations of poets like Aldrich, Richard H. Stoddard, and Stedman, who, with lesser bards of the same genteel school, dominated the *Century*'s verse written by men. Their work had the quality, as Whitman said, of "porcelain, fine china, dainty curtains, exquisite rugs." They revered and sought to express the ideality for which the magazine stood. They epitomized, in fact, the *Century*'s gradual alienation from what was dynamic in American life.[78]

The *Century*, espousing an idealism that could neither set meaningful standards for fiction nor breathe life into poetry, gave no significant new direction to American literature. But it did provide a broad road by which the traditional forms of writing reached a greater audience than ever before. If Gilder—to use his own disclaimer—"never quite deserved his fame as a distributor of literary destinies," he performed an inestimable service as a dispenser of literary opportunities.[79] While publishing—and intelligently editing—the foremost authors of his time, he spared no pains to discover fresh talent and to bring out the best in his contributors. If he made concessions to the prudishness of his subscribers, he unquestionably cultivated their taste, and he was not afraid to make demands on their intelligence. His magazine was not only a market and proving ground for writers, but an excellent school for two generations of readers.

NOTES

1. In 1883 both Gilder and the editor of *Harper's* preferred pen-and-ink manuscripts. By 1891 Gilder found typewritten contributions easier "on my nerves"; he told an interviewer in that year that while "old-timers" continued to use the pen, most young contributors typed their copy. *Author*, 3 (May 1891):65.

2. William Dean Howells, *Literature and Life: Studies by W. D. Howells* (New York, 1902), 10.

3. Advertising section, Nov. 1882, p. 27; *Author*, 2 (Feb. 15, 1890):30; Irving Bacheller, *Coming Up the Road: Memories of a North Carolina Boyhood* (Indianapolis, Ind., 1928), 268–70.

4. *Writer*, 11 (Oct. 1898): 150; Robert Underwood Johnson, *Remembered Yesterdays* (Boston, 1923), 113, 121, 147; Hamlin Garland, *Roadside Meetings* (New York, 1930), 335; editorials, June 1890 and Apr. 1898.

5. *New York Star*, Mar. 16, 1890; *Author*, 2 (June 15, 1890):93; "Confessions of a Literary Hack," *Forum*, 19 (July 1895):638.

6. The comparison is drawn from the *Century*, 40 (May-Oct. 1890) and the *Atlantic*, 66 (July-Dec. 1890). Of the practice of printing authors' names, the *Journalist*, 12 (Dec. 13, 1890):2, declared, "The Century led and the others were forced to follow."

7. Gilder to Howells, July 31, 1884, and Dec. 27, 1883, Howells Papers, Harvard University, Cambridge, Mass., and *Journalist*, 12 (Dec. 13, 1890):2.

8. Albert B. Paine, *Mark Twain's Letters, Arranged with Comments*, 2 vols. (New York, 1917), 2:687; Gilder to Howells, May 10, 1884, Howells Papers; Aldrich to Gilder, Feb. 27, 1898, Aldrich Papers, Harvard University; Charles Eliot Norton, ed., *Letters of James Russell Lowell*, 2 vols. (New York, 1894), 2:262; "Eleanor Kirk" (Eleanor Maris Ames), *Information for Authors* (Brooklyn, N.Y., 1888), 82; "William J. Bok" (Edward J. Bok) in the *Chicago Journal*, reprinted in *Author*, 1 (Feb. 1889):22–23.

9. Gray to Gilder, Nov. 28, 1897, and Fernald to Johnson, Aug. 5, 1897, and Dec. 5, 1900, CC.

10. Thomas A. Janvier, "A Record of Written Articles Which Have Been Published . . . , " Janvier Papers, Harvard University; Clara Barrus, *The Life and Letters of John Burroughs*, 2 vols. (Boston, 1925), 1:282; Langley to Gilder, Oct. 31, 1891, CC. Twenty dollars a page was the rate paid for the numerous articles by the scholars and ministers collectively known as "The Sociological Group." Richard T. Ely to the Editor, May 23, 1889, CC.

11. Edith Thomas to Johnson, n.d., William P. Dix to the Editor, July 1, 1889, CC; Aldrich to Gilder, Oct. 8, 1891, Aldrich Papers; Horace Traubel, *With Walt Whitman in Camden*, 3 vols. (New York, 1961), 2:480.

12. Gilder to Johnson, Jan. 23, 1886, Gilder to Mrs. R. P. Mulford, Oct. 7, 1886, Gilder to Marion Hamilton Carter, Jan. 23, 1901, GP; Gilder notation to Johnson on Edward A. Atkinson to Gilder, May 21, 1891, Bigelow to Gilder, Mar. 28, 1892, CC.

13. Pope to Johnson, Mar. 20, 1897, Loomis to Johnson, Aug. 24, 1898, Fernald to Johnson, Nov. 5, 1900, CC.

14. J. Henry Harper, *The House of Harper: A Century of Publishing in Franklin Square* (New York, 1912), 319; Gilder to E. C. Stedman, Oct. 28, 1895, GP; W. N. Chamberlin to Gilder, Nov. 9, 1897, and Gilder notation thereon, CC.

15. R. W. Gilder, "An 'Open Letter' about Editing," *Independent*, 48 (Dec. 10, 1896):1669–70; Gilder to the Rev. Percy Browne, Apr. 10, 1888, Gilder to Mrs. Julia Schayer, Nov. 11, 1887, GP; Rosamond Gilder, ed., *Letters of Richard Watson Gilder* (Boston, 1916), 387.

16. Gilder, "An 'Open Letter'"; Fairfax Downey, *Richard Harding Davis: His Day* (New York, 1933), 77–78; L. Frank Tooker, *The Joys and Tribulations of an Editor* (New York, 1924), 209–10.

17. See, for example, the editors' correspondence with Richard Malcolm Johnston, and Johnson to F. Hopkinson Smith, Apr. 10, 1895, CC.

18. John H. Bones to Johnson, Feb. 4, 1897, and Gilder notation on S. E. Benét to Gilder, Aug. 27, 1889, CC.

19. Stewart Chaplin to Johnson, Apr. 19, 1900, Camp to Johnson, June 20, 1893, CC; Tooker, *Joys and Tribulations*, 207–8.

20. Gilder, "An 'Open Letter'"; Johnson, *Remembered Yesterdays*, 114; Mildred Howells, ed., *Life in Letters of William Dean Howells*, 2 vols. (Garden City, N.Y., 1928), 355–56.

21. Gilder, "An 'Open Letter'"; Johnston to Gilder, June 8, 1893, CC; Clara Barrus, ed., *The Heart of Burroughs's Journals* (Port Washington, N.Y., 1967), 86; Julia Collier Harris, *The Life and Letters of Joel Chandler Harris* (New York, 1918), 186.

22. Catherwood to Gilder, May 17, 1888, Long to Gilder, July 8, 1890, Amelia C. Barr to Johnson, Aug. 31, 1896, CC; Maurice Francis Egan, *Recollections of a Happy Life* (New York, 1924), 94.

23. H. H. Boyeson, *Literary and Social Silhouettes* (New York, 1894),

49, and Gilder to Howells, Mar. 25, 1893, Howells Papers. For a longer perspective on how women, in collaboration with ministers, had come to dominate popular literature in America, see Ann Douglas, *The Feminization of American Culture* (New York, 1977). An excellent summing up of nineteenth-century values and the linkage between the ideas of progress and morality in America may be found in Henry F. May, *The End of American Innocence: A Study of the First Years of Our Time, 1912–1917* (New York, 1959), ch. 1.

24. De Vinne to Johnson, Apr. 30, 1895, Johnson to Gilder, Jan. 18, 1898, CC; Tooker, *Joys and Tribulations*, 72–73.

25. Cora S. Stone to Gilder, July 6, 1898, and J. F. William to the Editor, Jan. 14, 1898, CC.

26. Herbert F. Smith, *Richard Watson Gilder*, Twayne U.S. Authors Series no. 166 (New York, 1970), 29.

27. Johnson to Gilder, Jan. 18, 1898, CC.

28. Gilder to Edwards, Nov. 6, 1897, Furman to Gilder, May 8, 1893, Rev. T. M. Griffith to the Editor, July 7, 1887, Gilder to Rev. Griffith, July 13, 1887, CC; Gilder to Foote, Feb. 18, 1885, GP.

29. Advertising section, May 1895, p. 76; Alice French to Gilder, n.d., Arlo Bates to Gilder, Nov. 1, 1891, CC.

30. Gilder quoted in Garland, *Roadside Meetings*, 182–83, and Tooker, *Joys and Tribulations*, 115, 209–10. For satire, see James L. Ford, *The Literary Shop and Other Tales* (New York, 1894), 200.

31. Bernard DeVoto, *Mark Twain's America* (Boston, 1932), 213–16, and Edwin H. Cady, *The Road to Realism: The Early Years, 1837–1885, of William Dean Howells* (Syracuse, N.Y., 1956), 167–68.

32. Gilder to Grant, June 4, 1883, Robert Grant Collection, Houghton Library, Harvard University, and Robert Grant, *Fourscore: An Autobiography* (Boston, 1932), 155–56.

33. Howells in *Harper's Monthly*, 75 (July 1887):318, quoted in Herbert Edwards, "Howells and the Controversy over Realism in American Fiction," *American Literature*, 3 (Nov. 1931):237–48; editorial, Oct. 1882.

34. *Current Literature*, 2 (May 1889):365–67. On the controversy in general, see Edwin H. Cady, *The Realist at War: The Mature Years, 1885–1920, of William Dean Howells* (Syracuse, N.Y., 1958).

35. Gilder to Howells, Aug. 14 and July 5, 1887, Howells Papers.

36. R. W. Gilder, "Certain Tendencies in Current Literature," *New Princeton Review*, n.s. 4 (July 1887):8.

37. Johnson, *Remembered Yesterdays*, 126–27, and Gilder to Wilkins, Oct. 25, 1899, GP. E. C. Stedman used the phrase "law of suggestion" in his essay on Whitman, Nov. 1880.

38. Gilder, "Certain Tendencies," 1–13.

39. Gilder to Howells, Mar. 27, 1882, Howells Papers; Cady, *Road to Realism*, 216, 230; Kenneth S. Lynn, *William Dean Howells: An American Life* (New York, 1971), 286–88.

40. Percy Lubbock, ed., *The Letters of Henry James*, 2 vols. (New York, 1920), 2:498, and Leon Edel, *Henry James: The Middle Years, 1882–1895* (Philadelphia, 1962), 49–50, 137–46.

41. Gilder, "Certain Tendencies," 8.

42. Vernon L. Parrington, *The Beginnings of Critical Realism in America, 1860–1920* (New York, 1930), 173, quoted in Tyler Dennett, *John Hay: From Poetry to Politics* (New York, 1933), 115, and Smith, *R. W. Gilder*, 69–70.

43. Washington Gladden, *Recollections* (Boston, 1909), 274–75, and Charles Howard Hopkins, *The Rise of the Social Gospel in American Protestantism, 1865–1915* (New Haven, Conn., 1940), 140–41.

44. Catherwood to Gilder, Aug. 23, 1893, and May 17, 1894, CC.

45. William Webster Ellsworth, *A Golden Age of Authors: A Publisher's Recollection* (New York, 1919), 187–88, and Tooker, *Joys and Tribulations*, 161–62.

46. Editorial, July 1900. The editors thought so well of Runkle's first attempt at fiction that they made an exception to their rule that serials should be accepted only from writers of proved popularity. Editorial, Aug. 1900.

47. *Critic*, 3 (Jan. 13, 1883):8; Gilder to George M. Smith, July 24, 1895, copy in CC; Tooker, *Joys and Tribulations*, 287.

48. Gosse to Gilder, Feb. 22, 1887, Gosse Papers, Harvard University, and Smith, *R. W. Gilder*, 75–79.

49. Advertising section, June 1880, p. 7. *Nation,* 42 (Jan. 7, 1886):13, noted that brief articles were becoming "a pronounced feature" of the *Century*.

50. Gilder to James Lane Allen, Jan. 28, 1890, GP, and Tooker, *Joys and Tribulations*, 266. "The £1,000,000 Bank Note" ran in Jan. 1893, "The Brushwood Boy" in Dec. 1895.

51. Gilder to James Lane Allen, Jan. 28, 1890, GP.

52. Rubin, *Cable*, 212–24, generally condemned Gilder's editing of Cable as intended to exclude anything of social or political relevance. Smith, *R. W. Gilder*, 67–72, thought Gilder did well by Cable.

53. Grace King, *Memories of a Southern Woman of Letters* (New York, 1932), 58–67, 99–100. Kate Chopin: "A No-Account Creole," Jan. 1894; "Azélie," Dec. 1894; "Regret," May 1895; "Ozeme's Holiday," Aug. 1896.

54. Tooker, *Joys and Tribulations*, 202–3, and Smith, *R. W. Gilder*, 56–59.

55. Johnson, *Remembered Yesterdays*, 383.

56. Smith, *R. W. Gilder*, 59–67. "At Teague Poteet's," May and June 1883; "Trouble on Lost Mountain," Jan. 1886; "Little Compton," Apr. 1887.

57. Oct. 1887 and Apr. 1888, respectively.

58. Furman to Gilder, Apr. 25, 1893, CC, and Gilder to Mrs. M. L. Andrews, Oct. 16, 1888, GP.

59. Garland, *Roadside Meetings*, 119. Four Garland stories appeared in the *Century* in the 1890s: "A Spring Romance," June 1891; "Ol Pap's Flaxen," Mar., Apr., and May 1892; "A Girl of Modern Tyre," July 1897; "'A Good Fellow's' Wife," July 1898. Smith, *R. W. Gilder*, 99–101, citing Donald Pizer, *Hamlin Garland's Early Work and Career* (Berkeley, Calif., 1960), argued that, contrary to some critics, Gilder did not attempt to turn Garland from stories of social protest. See Garland, *A Son of the Middle Border* (New York, 1928), 376, 412, 417.

60. Harte, "The Devotion of Enriquez," Nov. 1895, and "The Passing of Enriquez," June 1898; Wilkins, "Emmy," Feb. 1891; Jewett, "In Dark New England Days," Oct. 1890; "The Hilton's Holiday," Sept. 1893; "The Guests of Mrs. Timms," Feb. 1894; "A Neighbor's Landmark," Dec. 1894; "All My Sad Captains," Sept. 1895; "The Coon Dog," Aug. 1898.

61. Martin I. J. Griffin, *Frank R. Stockton* (Philadelphia, 1939), 63–70. A sequel to "The Lady or the Tiger?" called "The Discourager of Hesitancy" (July 1885) not only left the puzzle unsolved, but propounded a new riddle. Other Stockton stories were "The Transferred Ghost," May 1882, and "A Tale of Negative Gravity," Nov. 1884.

62. Laura Stedman and George M. Gould, eds., *Life and Letters of Edmund Clarence Stedman*, 2 vols. (New York, 1910), 2:476, and Tooker, *Joys and Tribulations*, 37.

63. Lynn, *Howells*, 269–71.

64. James, "Alphonse Daudet," Aug. 1883; Daudet, "Victor Hugo," Nov. 1882, and "Tourgeneff in Paris," Nov. 1883.

65. Gilder to Walter Hines Page, Aug. 8, 1891, GP, and Rodman Gilder, memorandum of conversation with his father, n.d.

66. Adee to Gilder, Oct. 14, 1891, and Taine to the Editor, Aug. 17, 1891, CC. Sloane's work began its serial run in Nov. 1894.

67. Advertising section, Oct. 1898, p. 2, and Wheeler to Gilder, Dec. 17, 1897, CC.

68. Copy of memorandum to Gladstone, n.d., Bismarck (per his secretary) to Gilder, Feb. 22, 1891, CC; Gosse to Gilder, Nov. 6, 1889, Gosse Papers; Johnson, *Remembered Yesterdays*, 226–29.

69. Gilder to W. C. P. Breckenridge, Mar. 29, 1889, GP; Johnson to L. Edwin Dudley, Jan. 31, 1894, Johnson notation to Gilder on letter, John A. Kasson to Johnson, July 3, 1896, Herbert Friedenwald to Johnson, Jan. 18, 1900, CC.

70. Tooker, *Joys and Tribulations*, 315; Robert Howard Russell, "Glave's Career," Oct. 1895; Glave's journal, Aug., Sept., and Oct. 1896. Rodman Gilder recalled that there was a temporary gain in circulation as a result of the Spanish War series; memorandum to the author, n.d.

71. Gilder to Leland, Dec. 16, 1881, GP.

72. James, "Venice," Nov. 1882, and "London," Dec. 1888.

73. Walter Teller, *Joshua Slocum*, rev. ed. (New Brunswick, N.J.,

1971), 159. Slocum was delighted with his treatment, both editorial and financial, by the *Century* editors. Ibid., 165–67.

74. James Buckham, "Some Needs of the Versifiers," *Writer*, 2 (May 1888):114-15.

75. Barras, ed., *Burroughs's Journal*, 145, and Aldrich to Gilder, May 2, 1892, GP.

76. Smith, *R. W. Gilder*, 49–54; Gilder to Whitman, Apr. 19, 1887, Gilder to Horace Traubel, Sept. 6, 1888, and Oct. 31, 1889, GP. Among the young poets whom Gilder befriended were Robert Burns Wilson and John Vance Cheney. Cheney to Gilder, Nov. 23, 1885, CC; Gilder to Houghton, Mifflin and Co., Feb. 17, 1885, to Wilson, Apr. 21, 1887, to John R. Procter, Dec. 20, 1887, GP.

77. Gilder to D. C. Gilman, Jan. 5, 1888, GP, and editorials, June 1896 and Apr. 1900.

78. Traubel, *With Walt Whitman*, 1: 126–27. Gilder professed to believe that his own poetry would survive only in collections, if at all. Gilder to Edmund Gosse, June 1, 1883, GP.

79. Gilder, "The Newspaper, the Magazine, and the Public," *Outlook*, 61 (Feb. 4, 1899):321.

10

A Beacon for the Arts

Richard Watson Gilder could not fully enforce his preference for ideality in literature, but he was well equipped to disseminate his standards in the arts. His rapport with the leading figures of studio, stage, and concert hall strengthened with the years, and in the *Century* he had an excellent instrument for promulgating his conviction that Truth and Beauty were one. Throughout his editorial term, moreover, he had the help of gifted lieutenants as eager as himself to make the magazine a work of art. Alexander W. Drake, the superintendent and inspiring genius of the art department, was joined in the early 1880s by the vigorous William Lewis Fraser, whom Roswell Smith installed as art manager. The division of power between these two chiefs was not explicit, but Fraser evidently handled layouts and helped Drake in negotiations with illustrators; Drake spent more time supervising the production and printing of the wood engravings that he had done so much to improve.[1]

Fraser, a dark-haired Scotch-Canadian of fiery temperament, often battled with the editorial staff over makeup problems, sometimes reducing the women assistants to tears. He also had, as one of his best illustrators recalled, "a trick of writing disagreeable letters without meaning to." Despite cranky moments he was normally genial and cooperative, and his sound knowledge of modern art made him a valuable member of Gilder's team. With Drake, he often accompanied the editor on tours of galleries, and when abroad he was entrusted with the selection of illustrative material.[2]

Meanwhile, Theodore Low De Vinne was establishing the *Century*'s reputation as the best-printed magazine in the world. Versed in the oldest secrets of his craft, he kept abreast of the latest technical developments. In 1886 he supervised the installation of a new web (rotary) press that could do ten times the work of a flatbed press of comparable size. Illustrated forms were run on a flatbed press until 1890, when R. Hoe and Company built a rotary art press that enabled the *Century* to print the first halftone illustrations from curved plates. De Vinne's experiments with various papers, inks, and methods of combining them produced matchless presswork of both illustrations and text. Along with Drake, he gave the *Century* a texture and appearance worthy of its editorial aspirations and won admiration from the master printers of Europe, some of whom sent representatives to study his methods.[3]

The *Century* continued to make a specialty of the wood engravings that Drake and De Vinne had brought to perfection in *Scribner's Monthly*. In 1876 the magazine had spent about $1,500 on the drawings and engravings for one number; by 1890 the cost was about $8,000 for a single issue, of which $2,000 sometimes went into pictures for a single article. Payments to artists and engravers for George Kennan's Siberian series totalled $25,000; virtually the same amount was spent on fine paper, expert printing, and art supervision.[4]

Meanwhile, the *Century*'s chief rival was throwing its funds even more lavishly into pictorial embellishment; the resulting competition did much to bring about a golden age of wood engraving. In 1881 Gilder warned the publishers that *Harper's* was "now competing with us with a prodigality of expenditure unequalled. They have taken every one of our engravers—they have learned several—though not all of our 'tricks' . . . they are spending in ordinary numbers more than we have ever spent in *extraordinary* numbers." Gilder's London agent informed him in 1883 that the Harpers were tempting Joseph Pennell, whom the *Century* had started on the road to fame, with "offers of pay which make one's hair stand on end."[5]

Nevertheless, Drake and Fraser were able to call on the best illustrators of their time. None of them was a salaried staff member, for the *Century* preferred to commission each piece of work separately, but some were closely attached to the magazine. Outstanding among these was Pennell, who drew his first pictures for Drake in 1881 and his last more than forty years later. The relationship was not always smooth; Pennell was sharp-tongued and inclined to imitate the bad manners of his god, James McNeill

Whistler. He was prolific as well as gifted, nearly every volume of the monthly for many years being enriched by the bold and sentient lines of his pen. Gilder at one point suggested Pennell be sent to Neptune for a term, since he would "exhaust this planet inside of two years." Despite their concern over being "too, too full" of Pennell, the editors were thrown into consternation when he accepted a commission from a rival publication.[6] Pennell's etchings for George W. Cable's historical sketches of the Creoles (1883) at once gave him an excellent reputation. The *Century* then sent Pennell to Italy to illustrate William Dean Howells's articles on the Tuscan cities, an assignment on which— even though Howells several times had to bail him out of trouble—Gilder told him he had covered himself with glory. Except for a brief sojourn in the United States in the mid-1880s, when he contributed to the War Series, Pennell worked in Europe for more than thirty years, developing as his forte the portrayal of picturesque architecture. He explored the Continent with his wife and discovered everywhere quaint villages that "must be done for the *Century*." Ordinarily he committed his sketches directly to the etcher's plate, but when he came to illustrate Mariana G. Van Rensselaer's articles on cathedrals, he preferred line drawings because of his uncertain knowledge of church architecture. Returning to New York in 1904, Pennell was inspired by the sight of the towering metropolis to do his famous etchings of skyscrapers, which first appeared in the *Century*.[7]

An illustrator of very different gifts was E. W. Kemble, who gained fame as a delineator of the plantation black. He was only twenty-three when Mark Twain discovered his cartoons in *Life*, the humorous weekly, and promptly engaged him to illustrate *Huckleberry Finn*. When the *Century* editors published advance chapters of the novel, they took the artist with the text, thanking Twain for "unearthing such a gem," and put Kemble under exclusive contract for several years.[8] He created the monthly's stock black, spry, twinkle-eyed, and ungainly, who added flavor to stories by Thomas Nelson Page, Harry Stillwell Edwards, Richard Malcolm Johnston, and James Lane Allen. His only peer in this genre was A. B. Frost, whose illustrations for "Uncle Remus" were outstanding.

At the other extreme were the sophisticated society people drawn by Charles Dana Gibson, whose first contributions to the

Century came in 1889, when he was only twenty-two. These early offerings gave little promise of his future brilliance, but, aided by study in Paris, the young artist developed a distinctive style that soon made him famous. By 1890 the "Gibson Girl"—first mentioned in a *Century* manuscript, but deleted by the editors because her creator was then too little known—had emerged into popularity, and, with her square-jawed male counterpart, was becoming a model of dress and deportment for a generation of middle-class Americans. In his pictures for Constance Cary Harrison's "The Anglomaniacs" (1890) and for Van Rensselaer's "People in New York" (1895) Gibson showed that his idealized figures, slightly overdrawn, could serve the purpose of satire.[9]

Some artists were associated with specific regions. Winslow Homer's sea-filled water colors of Nassau were just right for William C. Church's description of the Bahamas (February 1887). Frederic Remington drew not only the lithe cowboys for Theodore Roosevelt's articles on ranch life in the West but also bronco busters and Indians for his own articles (1889). Howard Pyle and the Frenchman André Castaigne, on the other hand, were gifted with the imaginative power to re-create the past, the former in a thoroughly American manner, the latter in the more exotic style suited to ancient history. In addition to his drawings for "Alexander the Great," Castaigne pictured with soaring imagination the monumental "Seven Wonders of the World" (1898), a project suggested by Gilder and considered by the artist as his best work. Castaigne also contributed to the "Artists' Adventures" Series, which, subordinating text to illustration, also displayed the diverse talents of Walter Shirlaw, Thomas Moran, and F. Hopkinson Smith.[10]

While patronizing American illustrators, the *Century* also enlisted the finest European exemplars of the graphic arts. Henry James's article on "Du Maurier and London Society" (May 1883) featured drawings by that famous *Punch* satirist, as did another article in May 1896, "In Bohemia with Du Maurier." Edmund Gosse in 1884 got permission to print unpublished drawings by William Makepeace Thackeray, although Gilder did not find suitable use for them until many years later in the issues of December 1901 and January 1902. Another fine English contribution came from Phil May, whose studies of English character, along with

Pennell's etchings of streets and structures, added vivacity to Sir Walter Besant's articles on East London (1899–1900).

A Gallic genius of the past was represented in Honoré Daumier's sketches, for which James wrote an explanatory text. Maurice Boutet de Monvel's gift for evoking the simple grace of family life lent charm to Thérèse Bentzon's essay "About French Children" (October 1896) and to Anna L. Bicknell's "French Wives and Mothers" (January 1898). De Monvel's water colors illustrative of the Joan of Arc legend, which Gilder had admired in the painter's Paris studio, were reproduced in November 1896. Another graphic artist famous in France, although Spanish by birth, was Daniel Vierge. Enlisted first in 1880 for "Peter the Great," he appeared again nearly twenty years later when Howells discussed that artist's "Pictures for Don Quixote" (June 1898).

Thoroughly in love with their beautiful wood engravings, the editors were prone to carry decoration too far. Critics at home and abroad occasionally complained that, excellent as the *Century*'s pictures were, they were mannered, too numerous, and often overshadowed the text that they were meant to illustrate. "Ah, your illustrations, your illustrations," James wrote to the editors; "how, as a writer, one hates 'em; and how their being as good as they are makes one hate 'em more!" James particularly resented the magazine's holding back his stories until the artists had time to do their work. In the mid-1880s engravings occupied about 15 percent of the total space in the magazine—not an excessive proportion. But figured borders, tailpieces, the Greek-gowned maidens who sometimes hovered over pages of poetry, and miscellaneous articles on burnt-wood decorations, old Japanese armor, and the like—all these did indeed suggest a certain gratuitous adornment.[11]

Yet it was wrong to imply that Gilder was merely producing a picture magazine for the unthinking. He was endeavoring to promulgate good taste—which to him, as we have seen, was but a manifestation of good morals. What concerned him was "the good influence of art as an offset to the materializing tendencies of the age"; the splendid engravings were cherished as instruments to this end.[12]

The *Century*'s serious view of art was expressed in the essays of Charles Waldstein, the Cambridge classical scholar for whom Gilder helped make a career in the United States. In addition to discussions of ancient archaeological treasures, Waldstein wrote two articles on "The Lessons of Greek Art," which pictured the Americans as the "Magna Graecians of the West," destined to absorb the best of Old World culture and in return to exhibit a fresh development in the arts, just as the colonies in Sicily and southern Italy had enriched the Greek world. He urged a broader education of both artists and public in preparation for this cosmic role. In a hearty endorsement of this thesis, Gilder declared editorially: "The prime necessity is that we should go earnestly and systematically to work to inspire, to develop, to guide and clarify the taste of the people." This expressed one of the great purposes of his magazine.[13]

Over time Gilder showed his readers reproductions from the work of virtually every living artist of stature, European and American. The *Century*'s "American Artists Series," brief biographical and critical sketches of painters with accompanying illustrations, was begun in 1890 and ran in several numbers each year throughout the following two decades. Of the various writers employed on this project, the most prominent was William A. Coffin, art critic for the *New York Evening Post* and its allied weekly, the *Nation*, and an able painter in his own right. In addition to notes for this series, Coffin made full-scale appraisals of John Singer Sargent (June 1896) and Homer (September 1899). Another expert whose essays frequently appeared was Charles de Kay, Gilder's brother-in-law and literary and art critic of the *New York Times*, who often used the pseudonym "Henry Eckford." His "A Modern Colorist" (June 1890) was a tribute to the neglected romantic painter, Albert Pinkham Ryder. Royal Cortissoz, giving special attention to mural painting in America, pointed out that in men such as John La Farge, Edwin Austin Abbey, and Sargent the United States had already produced master muralists.[14]

The *Century* justly celebrated, in picture and text, the striking achievements of American sculptors in this period. De Kay discussed the work of Olin Warner, Coffin hailed young George Grey Barnard as a forceful new master in marble, and both Coffin and John C. Van Dyke submitted admiring estimates of Daniel

Chester French. The highest tributes were reserved for Augustus Saint-Gaudens, Gilder's friend and ally in the promotion of classical standards. Van Rensselaer in 1887 termed his Chicago *Lincoln* "our finest work of monumental art," and ten years later the *Century* called his Robert Shaw Memorial in Boston "the greatest work of plastic art yet produced in America."[15]

In architectural criticism Van Rensselaer was the monthly's mainstay for a generation. Her "Recent Architecture in America" (1884–86) was an elaborately illustrated survey of public and commercial buildings, churches, and dwellings of distinction in both city and country. Subsequently, she kept readers informed about praiseworthy new structures, such as the Madison Square Garden of McKim, Mead and White, and the Boston Public Library, designed by the same partnership. Admiring the Boston Library as a model of symmetry and repose, she saw in it proof that a development from the Renaissance style of Western Europe was the nation's "true line."[16]

The *Century*'s educational effort went beyond American accomplishments to take in the whole Western cultural tradition, of which art in the United States was an offshoot. The survey went back to the sources with Lucy Mitchell's serialized history of antique sculpture (1882) and Waldstein's essays on Greek civilization, in which he discussed the history of art as well as the discoveries in archeology. Kenyon Cox's "Sculpture of the Early Renaissance" (November 1884) carried readers into another great period. It was followed by William Crary Brownell's assessment of French sculpture (1886–90), a part of his rounded study that aroused in the United States an appreciation of French style and craftsmanship. Gosse's two essays on "Living English Sculptors" (June 1883 and November 1885) were so well illustrated as to delight the artists and bring high praise from the British press.[17]

Another aspect of the European heritage was exemplified in Van Rensselaer's history and description of English and French cathedrals, enhanced by Pennell's drawings and etchings. "The Cathedral Churches of England" (1887–92) included thirteen articles; five essays on French churches ran intermittently from November 1894 to September 1899. Author and illustrator were often at odds in this series, for Van Rensselaer conceived of her work as an architectural study, while Pennell's eye instinctively caught the more picturesque angles of the buildings. Nevertheless, their collaboration produced one of the best expressions of the *Century*'s aesthetic zeal.[18]

The numerous and fully illustrated essays on French painters in this period not only gave readers a view of the foremost European school but frequently served as tributes to the Parisian masters who had trained many Americans. Thus, Fanny Field Herring's "Gérôme" (February 1889) was accompanied by a collection of "Open Letters" acknowledging his influence in this country. Similarly, notes by one American pupil of Carolus Duran (January 1886) revealed the lessons that he and his compatriots had learned from that teacher. Among the impressionists, Jean Corot and Claude Monet were represented in engravings and essays, and de Kay characterized the work of "Theodore Rousseau and the French Landscape School" (February 1891). Other subjects of illustrated articles were Eugene Fromentin, Gustave Courbet, and Jean François Millet. Contemporary Dutch, German, and English painters were also included in these pictorial surveys.[19]

The greatest of the *Century*'s art projects was Timothy Cole's series of reproductions from Europe's "Old Masters," begun in the 1880s and carried on into the 1900s. The publishers sent Cole to Europe in 1883, after he had pointed out that he could interpret masterpieces more faithfully from the originals than from photographs. His first destination was the Louvre, where he engraved such famous Italian works as the "Mona Lisa." These were so well received that Gilder dispatched him to Italy for a systematic attack on that country's many treasures; thus began a patient, laborious transcription that continued for twenty-seven years and brought the glories of Europe's churches and galleries to Americans who would never see them first hand.[20]

It was an epic labor with comic undertones. Although "delightfully mellow" in speech and manner, Cole was a stubborn man who regarded his slight stature as a standing invitation to imposition. To the despair of his publishers, he insisted on choosing austere rather than dramatic pictures, and on recording the paintings in the order of their appeal to him, in blithe disregard of carefully laid plans for a more systematic sequence. Devising a new technique that involved a very fine line, he refused to alter it, even though it cut his output from the two blocks per month he had promised to one. To mollify his employers, he agreed to a reduction in his monthly stipend from $300 to $220. Perennially in debt, he labored happily on, entranced by the gaiety of Italian life and enraptured by the splendors of the gloomy chapels. "By heaven," he wrote Fraser in 1887, "I scarcely know what to do between the extascy [sic] of feeling these things . . . on the one hand, and the business department of the Century Co. on the other!"[21]

After several years in Italy, Cole moved successively through the Netherlands, England, Spain, and France, engraving the masterpieces of each country. His method was to transfer a retouched photograph of the painting to the block, then to ply his burin with the original before him—although the poor lighting and the early closing hours of chapels and galleries often meant that he continued to work from the photograph in the evenings. Despite his difficulties with the New York office, he gave the *Century* engravings that combined unsurpassed technical skill with a genuine feeling for great painting. As published with explanatory notes by William James Stillman, Van Dyke, and Cole himself, the Old Masters Series proved to be what it was proclaimed at the outset, a "great educational work."[22]

This course in art was given to a puritanical, as well as a materialistic, nation. Unlike Josiah Gilbert Holland, Gilder was no admirer of Anthony Comstock, whom he thought "densely mistaken" in regarding the nude as immoral. Nevertheless, in art as in literature, he deferred somewhat to the prudishness of his readers. When Cole sent home his engraving of Andrea Mantegna's *Circumcision,* the editors decided to shade the "objectionable" portion of the block, but they ran it unchanged after Cole hotly protested this proposal to "mutilate" his work. When a Bellini painting actually was edited, a group of artists drafted a condemnatory letter, but Gilder's friends among them were able to withdraw it from publication. Later, a detail of Hogarth's "Rake's Progress" was dropped from the Old Masters Series as too sensual.[23]

An indignant delegation of Baptist clergymen once waited on Robert Underwood Johnson because an engraving of a famous Apollo was printed without a fig leaf. Such incidents seemed to justify caution, although the editors' dilemma amused sophisticates. Gosse, answering Gilder's request for a reproduction of a Frederick Watts painting, pointed out that both figures in the picture were entirely nude—"so what would Chaste Connecticut say, not to speak of Virtuous Vermont?" Gradually, however, Gilder did accustom his readers to nudes of a rather genteel kind.[24]

So Gilder made his magazine a sort of illustrated textbook on the arts. But it was not enough to give the people pictures; the form and meaning of art must be brought directly into their daily lives. This was one of the lessons Waldstein had learned from Greek civilization. The *Century,* for instance, persistently advocated a more artistic coinage, and Stillman, launching this campaign, pointed to the Hellenic example. Gilder concurred in Stillman's judgment that U.S. coins were the most "barbarous" and "contemptible" in the modern world. An artistic reform of the nation's hard money would be, he argued, a potent educational influence and an impetus to the art of the medalist. At various times Gilder, Drake, and Saint-Gaudens made written or personal pleas to the director of the mint, but not until 1907 were Saint-Gaudens and other sculptors called in by the government to help transform the coinage.[25]

Another cause persistently urged was "free art." A *Century* editorial, brought to the attention of Secretary of State Frederick T. Frelinghuysen, resulted in the abolition of the special certification fee required of American artists abroad who wished to mail their paintings home. The larger issue was the admission of all works of art duty free. The 15 percent tariff, Gilder editorialized, rested on the delusion that art was a luxury; it was rather a "national necessity." With Frank D. Millet, Gilder drew up a bill embodying the desired exemption. When the reform passed in 1894, an editorial exultantly hailed this response of Congress to "right ideas lucidly expressed and disinterestedly advocated."[26]

On the other hand, the *Century* could never persuade the government to consider wood engravings as works of art. Cole's blocks were seized by U.S. Customs officers at New York and subjected to a duty of about $100 each, causing the editors to observe bitterly that engravings that had won high critical praise from persons like Charles Eliot Norton were nothing but "manufactures of wood" to the Treasury Department. To avoid this duty the Century Company after 1890 had Cole's work transported as electrotypes, the original blocks being stored in Europe.[27]

Gilder's monthly kept a watchful eye not only on government policy but on private institutions charged with the promotion of art. An editorial in 1884 called attention to the needs and shortcomings of the Metropolitan Museum of Art, urging that its limited funds be put into such educational aids as sculptural casts and architectural models rather than concentrated in a few costly collectors' items. In 1892 the monthly praised the museum's progress in this direction and applauded the Sunday opening of its doors. The construction of new museums in Chicago, St. Louis, and Cincinnati brought enthusiastic approval from Ripley Hitchcock in his review of "The Western Art Movement" (August 1886). Another writer described the Corcoran Gallery in Washington as "the most complete individual manifestation" of public-spirited interest in art in the United States.[28]

Edification was to be found, however, not only in such treasures of the past but in the day-to-day environment. Gilder was the prime mover in having Stanford White commissioned to build the Washington Arch in stone, replacing the wooden structure raised for the centennial celebration. To Gilder and his colleagues the design for the new congressional library was a matter for earnest dispute, while proposals for a Grant Memorial offered an exciting opportunity to stimulate art appreciation. The editors made recurring pleas for the creation of national and municipal parks and called in Frederick Law Olmsted, the principal designer of Central Park, to reinforce their arguments for the aesthetic development of urban waterfronts. Acclaiming Olmsted as a genius, they urged young men to emulate him by taking up landscape gardening as a profession.[29]

The desire to cultivate the very folkways of the nation was evident in Constance Cary Harrison's laudatory survey of "American Rural Festivals" (July 1895). The rather synthetic classicism that inspired this essay was accentuated in a number of articles, begun in 1900, on "Civic Festivals and Processions." Barr Ferree, who inaugurated this series, declared that the procession, "properly speaking," was a work of art. The modern American, he said, was "more and more demanding art in the

public festival and parade, just as he is, more and more, demanding art in his public and private life." This series was one
of the many indications of how the *Century*'s stress on classical
standards was carrying it away from the mainstream of American
feelings, for surely the bouyant American of 1900 wanted excitement, not "art," in his parades.[30]

In the World Columbian Exposition at Chicago in 1893, Gilder
and his associates saw the culminating manifestation of art's beneficial relation to society. As early as 1889 the *Century* gave special
attention to the Paris International Exhibition and in the following
year published its director-general's suggestions for the Columbian Fair. As the classic facades rose on the shores of Lake Mich-
igan, Henry Van Brunt described their architectural details in five
articles (May–October 1892), avowedly aimed at awakening popular appreciation of the fair's importance for the nation's aesthetic
development. In an editorial, "What the Columbian Exposition
will do for America," Gilder predicted that the exposition would
show Americans the meaning of art and beauty, inspire the country's artists to nobler efforts, and affirm faith in a democracy
capable of such achievement.[31]

Gilder thought the Chicago fair "the most beautiful thing of
its kind that the world has ever seen." His salutatory rhapsody
to "The White City" (May 1893) represented it as the apogee of
Hellenism in modern America:

> Say not, "Greece is no more."
> Through the clear morn
> On light winds borne
> Her white-winged soul sinks on the New World's breast.
> Ah! happy West—
> Greece flowers anew, and all her temples soar!

Throughout the year of the exposition the *Century*, surveying
this collaborative climax of nineteenth-century American art,
praised its painting, its landscaping, its spectacle. The editor's
valedictory poem affirmed that "The Vanishing City" had been,
"By day, a miracle, a dream by night."[32]

Gilder saw externalized at Chicago the same ideals he embodied
in the *Century*, and it is doubtful if he gave much heed either to

the Transportation Building of young Louis Sullivan or to the
pragmatic view that America needed to form her own architectural standards, not to re-create Greece's. But a different challenge
to ideality in art and life could not have escaped his notice: the
very year of the World's Fair, *McClure's Magazine* (selling at
fifteen cents an issue) and *Munsey's Magazine* (selling at ten cents)
signaled a new era in the publishing of periodicals that would
leave the *Century,* clinging to its classical standards, as far behind
as the twentieth century would soon leave the nineteenth.

The crisis in the *Century's* fortunes brought about by these
inexpensive magazines is discussed later. But to Gilder and Johnson, the cheap photographic reproductions featured in these new
rivals were both an affront to the artistic standards exemplified
by the *Century's* wood engravings and but one of the many signs
of change and decay apparent as the nineteenth century came to
an end.

The theater, for example, was clearly in decline. During the
first decade of Gilder's regime, the *Century* found much to glorify
in the dramatic art. Tommaso Salvini, the Italian tragedian, was
Gilder's particular favorite. Besides many tributes to this Shake-
spearean actor, in article, verse, and picture, the monthly carried
Salvini's own impressions of plays and characters (November
1881 and December 1890) and, in 1892–93, printed passages from
his autobiography. There were also admiring appreciations of
Helen Modjeska, Henry Irving, Constant Coquelin (of the Comédie
Française), and Eleanora Duse, as representative of the finest clas-
sic and contemporary drama. Most of its attention was lavished
on these foreigners, but the *Century* did justice to the work of
American actors like Edwin Booth, John Gilbert, and Joseph
Jefferson, whose autobiography was serialized in 1889–90.[33]

In the 1890s, however, the *Century's* discussion of the American
stage was devoted chiefly to considering its apparent degradation.
The principal critic was John Ranken Towse, drama editor of the
New York Evening Post, who hurled his condemnations both in
signed articles and anonymous editorials. In August 1895 Towse
charged that the theater in the United States was "in a most
forlorn and debased condition. Tragedy, high comedy, the historical and romantic drama, have been virtually banished from
the stage . . . and have been replaced to a large extent by worth-

less melodramas, the extravagant buffooneries of so-called farce-comedies, or the feverish and unwholesome society play, in which the most vicious topics are discussed openly under the pretense of solving social problems." Augustin Daly, said Towse in a later article (June 1898), was "the last surviving representative here of the type of managers who have formed, developed, and preserved the best traditions of the stage, and justified the theater to be numbered among the arts."

To Gilder the sensational theater was a plague that imperiled the stability of American society. As a remedy, he urged a return from chaotic innovation to the ideal standards of the past. Only by the cultivation of the classic drama, he insisted, could the public taste be held to any plane higher than that of "novelty for the sake of distraction." The decline of the theater thus appeared to the *Century*'s editor as one more challenge to the ideality by which the nation ought to live.[34]

Had he lived ten years longer than he did, Gilder would have been aware of a renaissance in American arts and letters and would, presumably, have been less ready to equate change with decline. Yet he would have been astonished that the creative achievements of the twentieth century could take place not only outside the framework of the ideal standards that he believed in, but often in the context of a liberating revolt against those standards. But even if ideality were to prove transient rather than eternal, the educational mission of Gilder's magazine must have had lasting results. Gilder and the *Century* were only a part of a phalanx of purposeful men and publications trying to develop a national culture and a national appreciation of culture, but surely they were an effective part. The magic of art is too subtle for calibration—there is no way of measuring the impact of Cole's Old Masters on a midwestern teacher who had never seen a first-rate oil painting. Contemporary estimates suggest that the impact was not negligible. Intelligent Americans, said the *Christian Union* in 1884, felt a debt to Gilder's magazine for spreading an appreciation of art. Maurice Francis Egan thought the *Century* must be ranked with the Centennial Exhibition of 1876 as one of the two great forces for artistic progress in his time. Nobody, said Egan, could estimate its influence who had not lived through the "reign of the Philistines" that preceded it.[35]

Not all readers took kindly to Gilder's program of edification. A Chicago subscriber in 1892 complained that the *Century*'s art features were alienating it from the "plain people" who had supported Holland's magazine. Gilder, with the earnest good will he invariably showed to sincere critics, pointed out that the monthly's circulation had doubled in the first decade of his editorship and was read by more "plain people" than any periodical of its kind. The magazine's interest, he reminded his correspondent, was not merely in art but in "all that tends to make up the complex civilization of the Nineteenth Century." It was a just rejoinder. The promotion of the arts was simply one aspect of the *Century*'s idealistic urge to improve American public and private life.[36]

NOTES

1. L. Frank Tooker, *The Joys and Tribulations of an Editor* (New York, 1924), 94–95.
2. Elizabeth Robins Pennell, *The Life and Letters of Joseph Pennell*, 2 vols. (Boston, 1929), 1:147. Pennell himself, however, had a temperament that could provoke irritation. For Fraser's role, see Tooker, *Joys and Tribulations*, 83–84.
3. Frank Luther Mott, *A History of American Magazines*, 5 vols. (Cambridge, Mass., 1938–68), 3:467; Theodore Peterson, *Magazines in the Twentieth Century* (Urbana, Ill., 1964), 5; Drake to Gilder, Mar. 12, 1891, and May 2, 1893, Fraser to Johnson, May 3, 1894, De Vinne to the Editors, Feb. 4, 1889, the Royal-Imperial Court and State Press of Vienna to Unwin Brothers [the *Century's* London publishers], Apr. 7, 1887 (translated copy), CC; T. L. De Vinne, "The Printing of 'The Century'," Nov. 1890; Gilder to James Bryce, Nov. 23, 1881, GP.
4. *Journalist*, 12 (Dec. 13, 1890):3.
5. Gilder to Charles Scribner, Jan. 15, 1881, SC, and Edmund Gosse to Gilder, Nov. 7, 1883, Gosse Papers, Harvard University, Cambridge, Mass.
6. Gilder to Johnson, June 17, 1887, CC, and Johnson to Pennell, June 30, 1887, in Pennell, *Pennell*, 1:177.
7. Pennell, *Pennell*, 1:101, 143–44, 228, and Edwin H. Cady, *The Road to Realism: The Early Years, 1837–1885, of William Dean Howells* (Syracuse, N.Y., 1956), 221. Pennell did not like cathedral work. Drake, meeting him at Arles, France, found him dejected about his work and "about ready to throw the whole job over." Drake had to promise him a helper who could draw the basic architecture while Pennell added the artistic detail. Drake to Gilder, May 8, 1890, GP.
8. Arthur Bigelow Paine, *Mark Twaine: A Biography. The Personal*

and Literary Life of Samuel Langhorne Clemens, 3 vols. (New York, 1912), 2:772.

9. Fairfax Downey, *Portrait of an Era as Drawn by C. D. Gibson: A Biography* (New York, 1936), 93–101, 162–63.

10. Castaigne to Gilder, Nov. 19, 1897, CC. For a sample of Pyle's historical style, see his illustrations for article on Paul Jones, Apr. 1895.

11. Leon Edel, *Henry James: The Middle Years, 1882–1895* (Philadelphia, 1962), 156–57, and Mott, *Magazines*, 3:191.

12. Editorial, Sept. 1896.

13. Editorial, Jan. 1886; Gilder to President Barnard of Columbia, Apr. 19, 1882, to President Gilman of Johns Hopkins, Mar. 29, 1883, to R. R. Bowker, Dec. 5, 1884, GP. Waldstein articles, Dec. 1885 and Jan. 1886.

14. Cortissoz, Nov. 1895.

15. Editorial, June 1897, and in the same issue Coffin on Saint-Gaudens and Edward Atkinson on the Shaw Memorial.

16. June 1895.

17. Gosse to Gilder, June 13, 1883, Gosse Papers.

18. Van Rensselaer to Gilder, Feb. 13 and July 31, 1890, copies in CC; Pennell, *Pennell*, 1:151.

19. Corot, July 1889; Monet, Sept. 1892.

20. Alpheus P. Cole and Margaret Ward Cole, *Timothy Cole: Wood-Engraver* (New York, 1935), 36–41; and Robert Underwood Johnson, *Remembered Yesterdays* (Boston, 1923), 131.

21. Cole to Fraser, May 12, 1887, C. F. Chichester (Secretary of the Century Co.) to Gilder, May 15, 1900, Cole to Gilder, Sept. 22, 1900, CC; Cole and Cole, *Timothy Cole*, 35, 49–50, 60–81.

22. Stillman, "Cole and His Work," Nov. 1888; Cole and Cole, *Timothy Cole*, 57–58.

23. Gilder to anon., n.d. [1887], GP; Cole to Gilder, Dec. 1, 1888, and to Johnson, Dec. 2, 1888, John G. Van Dyke to Gilder, Apr. 7, 1890, CC; Cole and Cole, *Timothy Cole*, 72–74.

24. Gosse to Gilder, Sept. 26, 1884, Gosse Papers, and Maurice Egan, *Recollections of a Happy Life* (New York, 1924), 150.

25. Stillman, "The Coinage of the Greeks," Mar. 1887, and editorial, same issue; Gilder to J. P. Kimball (director of the U.S. Mint), Apr. 3, 1888, GP; E. I. Renick to Gilder, Oct. 3, 1890, CC; Johnson, *Remembered Yesterdays*, 101–2.

26. Editorials, July and Oct. 1882, Feb. 1893, and Nov. 1894; Gilder to Congressman Perry Belmont, Jan. 26, 1883, GP. The Dingley Tariff of 1897 restored the duty on works of art, and the cause was again taken up in *Century* editorials.

27. Editorial, Nov. 1891; *Writer*, 4 (Sept. 1890):214; Cole and Cole, *Timothy Cole*, 80.

28. S. G. W. Benjamin, "The Corcoran Gallery of Art," Oct. 1882; editorials, Apr. 1884, Aug. 1886, and Feb. 1892.

29. Olmstead, "Open Letter," Oct. 1886; M. G. Van Rensselaer, "Frederick Law Olmsted," Oct. 1893; editorials, Feb. and Apr. 1884, Oct. 1885, Apr. 1886, June 1887, and July 1895.

30. "Elements of a Successful Parade," July 1900.

31. Editorial, Oct. 1892.

32. Gilder to Edmund Gosse, Aug. 17, 1893, GP, and "The Vanishing City," Oct. 1893.

33. J. R. Towse on Modjeska, Nov. 1883, on Irving, Mar. 1884, on Duse, Nov. 1895; Henry James, "Coquelin," Jan. 1887; article on Gilbert, Jan. 1888; on Booth, Dec. 1897.

34. Editorial, May 1900.

35. Egan, *Recollections*, 138; *Christian Union*, Nov. 27, 1884, quoted in advertising section, Jan. 1885, p. 8.

36. Gilder to Charles H. Gould, Dec. 7, 1892, GP. In a gesture characteristic of his response to honest criticism, Gilder invited this correspondent to visit him when in the East, promising that "we will have it out in a most good-natured way."

11

The Democratic Ideal

Richard Watson Gilder's preoccupation with dispensing high culture to Americans did not absorb all of his exhaustless energy. He continued and vastly expanded the social and political criticism that Josiah Gilbert Holland had made a function of the popular monthly. In his first years as editor Gilder was awakening, along with many of his fellow citizens, to the variety of evils that plagued American democracy. Writing to his British friend James Bryce in 1883, Gilder listed among these evils not only the tariff on art and the lack of international literary copyright, which touched his closest interests, but also corrupt municipal government, the spoils system, and individual and corporate dishonesty.[1]

Gilder stretched himself in these years, impressing his colleagues and friends with his capacity for growth. Walt Whitman observed in 1888: "Gilder seems to be coming on: is a bigger man than he was—by far bigger than when I first knew him." In 1894 the editor, invited to speak at Vanderbilt University, chose a political rather than a literary theme, explaining that "at the present moment in our history I think that the duties of citizenship almost outweigh every other consideration." His conscience drove him ever deeper into public affairs, and he tried to make his magazine a creator of "that nobler public opinion which finally reacts upon the entire machinery of government and the entire life of the community."[2]

The American democratic ideal was defaced in the 1880s and 1890s by sordid and disordered politics, racial prejudice, industrial upheavals, ruthless enterprise and monopoly, and an ominous epidemic of public and private dishonesty. Were there any principles by which some organic harmony could be envisioned behind the clashing interests and the weltering society and brought into being? Gilder tried, with the help of economists, political scientists, ministers, and teachers, to find and promulgate such principles. But the times were out of joint for idealists. The *Century* won or shared in some victories for justice and good government, but more often the realities of power overwhelmed principle. And sometimes the principles conflicted with each other—laissez faire and the Christian ethic, for example.

The *Century* was nonpartisan. Gilder had been brought up as a strict Republican, but he sided with the Mugwumps in 1884, and as private citizen he worked for James G. Blaine's defeat. Nevertheless, he refused to align himself publicly with the independents supporting the Democratic presidential ticket, fearing he might taint his magazine as partisan. Subsequently, Gilder became a warm personal friend and political admirer of Grover Cleveland, but although Cleveland as chief executive sometimes sought Gilder's advice, and occasionally read advance proofs of the *Century*'s articles on governmental affairs, the magazine never supported him as a candidate.[3]

The ostensible reason for a nonpartisan approach to public questions was its appearance of disinterestedness; principles, after all, did not follow party lines. A more practical consideration for Gilder was his disinclination to alienate approximately half of his readers by siding with either major party. Consequently, the *Century*'s crusades were typically for such safe reforms as conservation or the merit system. The tariff, although Gilder personally worked for its amendment, was "too much party politics" for any but equivocal discussion in the magazine.[4] Major new questions that forced themselves on the editor's attention, particularly immigration policy and the government's role in the economy, were not party issues as such; Gilder duly groped with them and found that they had ambiguities for an idealist. But the overshadowing public problem during his early years as editor was the establishment of honest, efficient government, and this was a struggle in which all good citizens, including Gilder, could join enthusiastically.

To reformers in the late nineteenth century, political corruption seemed a Hydra that flourished despite their persistent thrusts. The political boss and his henchmen infested state and municipal governments, and the U.S. Congress served no better masters.

It was, as the *Century* saw it in 1886, "no longer a legislative body. Its degeneration is now admitted. It consists now of a plutocracy at one end, and a mobocracy at the other. The two chronic perils of a democracy have a firm grip on the Congress of the United States." Gilder, deeply depressed by the chicanery and demagoguery in both major parties, feared that the people had "abnegated the government" and that spoilsmen would capture the White House within a few years.[5]

To throw the rascals out and put "the best men" into office, the great panacea was the purification of civil service. This was "the reform before all others," said an editorial of October 1887, for it provided "the machinery by which other reforms are to come." To the constant editorial calls for the merit system were added powerful voices in the contributors' columns: E. L. Godkin (June 1882), Henry Cabot Lodge (September 1890), and Theodore Roosevelt (February 1890). The passage of the Pendleton Act in 1883, providing for classified federal positions and competitive examinations to fill them, was, to the editors, "A Modern Miracle."[6] But this of course was only the beginning. All subsequent presidents, including Gilder's friend Cleveland, had to be encouraged and prodded to extend the classified list. For after all, said a *Century* editorial of August 1895, a pure civil service would mean "the reform of our entire public life."

Gilder and the many other reformers who worked for the merit system certainly nursed exaggerated hopes of what it would bring about. They have also been charged with elitism by some critics, since their aim was to put their own class in control of public affairs. But that was the least of their sins. Their great failure was an inaccurate assessment of American society and its dynamics. Gilder and others among "the best men" were rather vague as to what level of government the merit system should reach, but clearly their ideal was nothing less than the complete divorce of government from politics—a totally unrealistic goal that denied self-interest as a legitimate political motive, rested on a naively optimistic view of human nature, and ignored not only the realities of power in the United States but the inevitability that power would be used to serve the interests of the powerful.[7]

Personally convinced that patronage abuses were "the root of all our trouble" in local as well as national politics, Gilder threw the weight of his magazine behind the extension of the merit system to state and municipal governments. The *Century* also endorsed a model law providing for secret, official ballots and for the citizens' opportunity, through petition, to make independent nominations at the primaries. The editors' enthusiasm for this program was as extravagant as their hopes for civil service reform. With good ballot-reform laws, "we should be rid at one stroke of the assessments upon candidates, of the bribing and bull-dozing of voters, of the nomination of notoriously unfit candidates, of 'deals' and 'dickers' and 'traders' at the polls." By 1892, as a *Century* editorial noted, three-fourths of the states had the Australian ballot; yet the political millennium had not arrived. Too much money in politics was one reason. The editors cheered a New York State law of 1890 that required notarized publication of campaign expenditures, but complained in 1896 that the rest of the country was too slow in following suit.[8]

Most of the reform measures the *Century* advocated were sound steps toward better government, and by and large they were enacted. Yet there was little evidence of progress toward an ideal politics. In one instance, however, Gilder's frustration was relieved by a striking success. In Louisiana a group of New York gamblers, operating the last great legal lottery in the United States, exacted tribute from all parts of the country. When this lottery syndicate boldly applied to the legislature for a twenty-five-year renewal of its charter, a citizens' committee mobilized to fight it. Gilder sent Clarence Buel to Louisiana, and the assistant editor, with the active cooperation of Governor Francis T. Nicholls, presented to the *Century*'s national audience a devastating case against this alliance of greed and politics. The promoters thereupon abandoned their efforts for recharter, and the citizens' committee credited Buel's article with having shamed the lottery into defeat.[9]

The *Century* was most comfortable in promoting causes that were relatively uncomplicated and that could be defined as moral issues. International copyright was a crusade of long standing among people of letters in both England and the United States, who suffered from transatlantic piracy of their works. *Scribner's Monthly* had joined in the battle for one reason, its editors said— to protect "the absolute right of a man to what he has produced."[10] This was the insistent theme of the several "Topics" devoted year by year to the question. In February 1886, the *Century* published several pages of "Open Letters" from a galaxy of American authors favoring congressional action.

Meanwhile, the editors were personally involved in the fight. The Authors Club, formed at Gilder's Studio in 1882, was the nucleus for the American Copyright League, which planned the strategy and lobbied for the desired law. Gilder, a member of the League's executive committee, bombarded his influential friends, including Cleveland, with arguments for the reform and persuaded the president in 1888 to receive an authors' deputation. That winter Gilder devoted "every energy that I possess, and every moment of time that I can spare" to the campaign.[11]

Robert Underwood Johnson was even more deeply absorbed in the movement, especially after 1888, when he was made secretary of the Copyright League and was virtually lent to the cause by the *Century* for nearly two years. He was constantly in Washington during the last weeks before the crucial vote, talking with congressmen and helping to work out compromises with printers, binders, and typographers. Some of his friends insisted that Johnson had "practically created" the successful bill. Actually, the passage of the international copyright act in March 1891 was the culmination of a struggle waged by innumerable individuals and pressure groups, but the *Century* and its editors certainly shared the credit for a notable triumph of justice.[12]

Johnson was also the spearhead of the magazine's campaign for conservation of the nation's forests, carried out in close collaboration with the great naturalist, John Muir. This joint effort began in 1889, when the associate editor accompanied the naturalist on a camping trip through Muir's beloved Yosemite Valley. Enthralled by the scenery, but dismayed at the sight of areas denuded by sheep, Johnson returned to lobby for Yosemite National Park. Muir, writing chiefly in the *Century*, was the chief protaganist for this reservation, which was created in 1890 by President Benjamin Harrison under the prodding of Secretary of the Interior John W. Noble. The victory for conservation in this region was not completed until 1906, when California retroceded to the United States the inner Yosemite Valley that it had previously withheld.[13]

For years the *Century* carried on a lone fight for forest reservation. An outstanding success was scored in 1893, when Noble withdrew from sale the 4,000,000 acres of the King's River Canyon, south of the Yosemite, after an article by Muir in the *Century* (November 1891) had first publicized its treasures. When Cleveland, in one of his last official acts, set aside thirteen reserves of more than 21,000,000 acres, a number of periodicals joined the *Century* in the ensuing battle against private interests which immediately sought to reopen these tracts. Thus Johnson, Muir, and the *Century* helped to lay the groundwork for the greater conservation victories to be gained under Theodore Roosevelt.[14]

The concept of American nationality embodied in a strong Union had a mystic significance for Gilder, which explains why Abraham Lincoln was his ideal statesman. To continue the work of *Scribner's Monthly* in reconciling the South to the Union was a congenial task for the editor. The *Century* attacked both the use of federal patronage and the black vote to perpetuate Republican rule in the South. To prevent the reopening of old wounds, the editors, when serializing John Nicolay and John Hay's "Lincoln," asked the authors to tone down their attacks on the ex-rebels—much to the disgust of Hay, who scorned this mugwump attitude. The *Century*'s continued welcome to southern writers and its keen interest in the South's industrial progress were other manifestations of friendliness.[15]

But Gilder, in turn, demanded loyalty to the nation and refused to court the South by yielding to its special prejudices. Authors who wished to share in the important market to which Gilder held the key might write at length about the charms of antebellum Dixie, but they were not permitted to dispute the fact or the desirability of Union.[16]

The writing of George W. Cable irked the *Century*'s southern readers. His sympathetic treatment of blacks in his Creole stories first alienated leading elements of his native New Orleans. In 1884 he angered more southerners with the statement in "Dr. Sevier"—then appearing as a serial—that even the former rebels now acknowledged the Union cause to have been just. The real tempest broke a short time later when Cable wrote a series of articles urging social and legal justice for the former slaves. "The

Freedman's Case in Equity" (January 1885) was a bitter indictment of Jim Crow laws. Henry W. Grady's sharp retort appeared in April 1885. After denying Cable's right to speak for the South, Grady declared that white domination and the separation of the races were inevitable. "The assertion of that is simply the assertion of the right of character, intelligence, and property to rule." Cable, however, renewed his demands for civil rights, and Gilder showed no reluctance to open his columns to his argument. The editor responded to protests by saying: "The country, the section, or the man that is not infidel to truth, will never fear honest freedom of debate." Gilder refused to print abusive letters about Cable, and he answered them with a form letter, part of which said: "If the South wishes to persecute its brightest literary ornament and leading writer, it is welcome to do so, but the persecution cannot be carried on within our columns." The *Century* continued to combine respect for the South with sympathy for the freedman, Booker T. Washington among others reporting on the progress of the liberated race.[17]

In February 1891 the *Century* unwittingly stung southern pride with criticism of a different sort. Clare de Graffenried, a labor statistician for the federal government, described "The Georgia Cracker in the Cotton Mills." She found him appallingly ignorant and lazy, and although she concluded that he was basically sound as a human being and potentially skillful as an industrial operative, many readers took her article as a "bare-faced slander" of southern factory workers. In the *Charleston News Courier,* the South Carolina superintendent of education replied angrily to the "misrepresentation." The *Manufacturors' Record,* a Baltimore monthly, attacked the *Century* bitterly. The *Atlanta Constitution* complained particularly of E. W. Kemble's "libelous" illustrations. Gilder was upset by these assaults from a region whose friendship he had so carefully cultivated, but Joel Chandler Harris assured him, "All sensible persons here know what the Century has done for the South and Southern writers, and you need not be at all disturbed." The tumult soon subsided.[18]

Gilder was less concerned, however, with appeasing sectional pride than with elevating the idea of American nationality. His patriotism was as intense as his idealism—indeed it was a spark of the same fire—and he resorted unabashedly to symbols and phrases in praise of the Union. One of the avowed purposes of the Civil War Series was to hasten the end of sectional controversy and so to strengthen the Union. Addressing Will H. Thompson, an ex-Confederate who submitted his poem, "High Tide at Gettysburg" as "a stone for the South front" in the War Series, Gilder asked him to add "a word of love for the 'Nation that still lives'"; Thompson complied. Thanks to heroic labors by Gilder, Johnson, and Buel, the narratives of the War Series were remarkably free from sectional animus and doubtless did promote mutual respect between North and South. The *Century* reported approvingly the succession of fraternal meetings in the 1880s between Confederate and Union veterans and encouraged the old soldiers to send in accounts of the battlefield assemblies. The demonstrations of solidarity were climaxed in 1885 at the funeral of General Ulysses S. Grant, where the Blue and the Gray mourned together. Witnessing the brotherly greetings of former enemies on this occasion, L. Frank Tooker, a newcomer to Gilder's staff, felt an immense pride in the *Century* for its part in the great reconciliation.[19]

Gilder, however, was staunchly opposed to the "raid" on the Treasury surplus by Union war veterans and the politicians who catered to them. When the magazine approved President Cleveland's veto of the general pension bill of 1887, outraged "patriots" were up in arms. One New Jersey attorney thought it "a mooted question whether the *Century* is not more *Confederate* than Union." Some readers threatened a veterans' boycott of the monthly. Gilder, undismayed, replied that he would continue to take a disinterested, national position. To a western editor he wrote: "We try not to be patriots for revenue only. If we were sordid in our aims we would not, on the one hand, antagonize the soldier audience by an appeal to their better nature with regard to the pension craze, and, on the other hand, endanger our entire Southern circulation by publishing the 'Life of Lincoln.'"[20]

While keeping a national outlook, Gilder emerged in the 1880s and 1890s as one of New York City's greatest and most active citizens. In its problems and its opportunities, New York was prototypical of fast-growing cities throughout the country. By 1890, with one-third of the nation living in urban centers, compared to one-fifth only twenty years earlier, the *Century* warned that effective municipal government was becoming "more and more the most serious problem" within the United States. The "enormous influx" of untutored immigrants added immensely to the task of good government.[21]

Some prominent contributors to Gilder's monthly urged improvement in the machinery of city government. Roosevelt, convinced that most citizens could not be persuaded to take more than an intermittent interest in municipal affairs, argued (November 1886) that power should be concentrated in the hands of a few officials whose character and actions the voters could scrutinize closely. Seth Low, president of Columbia University, pointed out (September 1891) that the municipality should be organized not as a little state but as a business entity, its council functioning as a board of directors, its mayor wielding broad executive authority. Washington Gladden supported this thesis (March 1893), calling for alterations in city charters to give mayors more responsibility.

The *Century*'s editorial view was that the remedy for misgovernment lay in stirring the voters to place better people in office. The intelligent and honest citizens were in the majority, but they foolishly clung to national party labels, while the ignorant and vicious, supporting whatever faction offered immediate gain, held the balance of power. To encourage independent voting, the magazine repeatedly urged separate municipal elections in which the management of local affairs, rather than broad party questions, would be at issue. In New York State this reform was achieved in 1894.[22]

Another fundamental need was for a permanent organization of earnest, educated citizens to draw up reform proposals and force them on the attention of legislators and officials. In 1893 Gladden outlined, in three articles, a procedure and program for such an association. Members of his "Cosmopolis City Club," pledged to nonpartisan action in local politics, first formed committees to study various aspects of city government; then, on the basis of the committee reports, they framed a new charter calling for an executive with strong appointive powers; and finally, after drumming up support through mass meetings and propaganda, they guided the reform through the state legislature.

Meanwhile, the *Century* heartily endorsed the real counterpart of this hypothetical league, the City Club of New York. After its founding in 1892, victories for good government were scored in a number of cities, and the climax of the reform wave came in 1894 when both Tammany and the New York State machine were defeated. This triumph, the editors jubilantly declared, showed "what an inevitable force the morality of a community constitutes" when united.[23]

This crescendo of interest in municipal politics recorded not only the pressing need for better government but also Gilder's widening vision of the meaning of civic life. "I have a great hope for and belief in this metropolis," he told a friend in 1891, "— a love for it, I may say, for only in it and near it have I found all that is best in this life." He was already one of Manhattan's best known and busiest citizens, although there was still an aesthetic tinge to both his personal and his editorial activities. He had been in the thick of the protracted but vain fight to oust Louis P. di Cesnola as director of the Metropolitan Museum of Art, on grounds of incompetence and dishonesty. He was prominent in clubs, especially those with memberships from literature and the arts. He was secretary of the committee that raised funds for the permanent Washington Centennial arch at Washington Square. He was in demand for commencement addresses, for testimonial dinners to authors, for the reading of commemorative poems, for the dedication of monuments. He worked for a more beautiful and cultured, as well as a better governed, New York.[24]

In the 1890s, however, Gilder acquired a still broader concept of community life. The government of a great city, he saw, could make positive contributions to the welfare of its people not only through honest political administrations and the support of cultural activities but also through social services as well. European experience provided suggestive examples of this larger role. As early as 1890 Albert Shaw began a series of influential articles in the *Century* describing the "municipal housekeeping" of British and Continental cities. Shortly after Shaw's essay on Glasgow appeared (March 1890), Richard T. Ely, the political economist, informed Gilder that it had "already begun to play a part in our state and municipal politics." The *Century*, which regarded federal aid to drought-stricken farmers as dangerously socialistic, went so far as to espouse community ownership of public utilities, pointing out that European cities had not been so foolish as to grant away valuable franchises to private corporations. A personal visit to Europe in 1895 confirmed Gilder's notion that his country had much to learn from abroad about city government. "There is no more conspicuous contrast in the modern world," he told the *New York Tribune* on his return, "than that between the natural advantages and the civic shortcomings of New York as compared with other great cities of the world."[25]

A more profound influence on Gilder's civic education was a painful duty thrust upon him in 1894, when Governor Roswell P. Flower appointed him to an unsalaried state commission for the investigation of New York City tenements, and the commission in turn named him its chairman. He waded "heart-deep in misery" all that hot summer, making house-to-house inspections, dashing to tenement fires in the dead of night, working laborious hours to collate information and prepare reports. He held lengthy hearings and did not hesitate to expose such respectable property holders as the Trinity Church Corporation as owners of some of the city's worst tenements. Armed with the facts, the commission framed bills that Gilder helped guide through the state legislature. These laws were decisive for tenement reform, empowering the city to condemn and raze dangerous or unsanitary dwellings as well as to regulate construction of new buildings, and opening the way for the development of parks and playgrounds where the worst slums had festered. Saluting Gilder for this victory, the *New York Tribune* remarked that "'practical politics' could not have served this community one half so well as it has been served by his perfect rectitude, his unselfish zeal, his tact and his urbanity."[26] This was the practical idealist at his best.

This ordeal left its mark on both the man and the magazine. Gilder was tracing his own expanding humanitarianism when he spoke editorially of the public's changing attitude toward the tenement dwellers: first, they were regarded as subjects for philanthropy; later, as a health menace; and finally had come "the full realization of fellow-citizenship" with these masses. Municipal reform was not merely a "business matter," he reminded his readers. Something like a religious revival was needed, with sacrifice for the common welfare. "There must be some conception of the sacredness of the interests which are involved in good city government, some comprehension of the ideal aims which inspire a genuine civic patriotism."[27]

Tammany must go, the *Century* said in an editorial (November 1894), not only to end corruption but in order that New York could provide more municipal services for its people. In the reform administration of Mayor William L. Strong, elected in 1894, the monthly saw the first fruits of the new civic spirit. Roosevelt and his police board won national attention. The famous "white wings" of Colonel George E. Waring (who told Gilder that when he wished to publicize some municipal problem, "I naturally turn first to you") gave Manhattan clean streets for the first time in its history. The razing of rotten tenements, the construction of better housing, and improvements in schools, libraries, museums, and universities gave the city aspects of greatness, the editors declared. No less an authority than Jacob A. Riis, Gilder's good friend and helpful consultant during the tenement investigation, recorded for the *Century* (December 1896 and December 1898) the transformation of slums into decent dwelling places or breathing spaces in the heart of the metropolis.[28]

Gilder's frail body was henceforth to be "lashed from one public service to another" by his civic spirit. Along with his *Century* associates, he took a vigorous part in the campaign of 1897 to elect Low as mayor, giving up his usual summer sojourn in the country in order to fulfill his editorial duties at the same time. Low was defeated, and the *Century* acknowledged that New York was existing "largely under a system of blackmail." When Low was elected in 1901, however, the idealism of the *Century* and the long educational campaign for which it spoke were triumphantly, if temporarily, vindicated.[29]

If the struggle for good government at home was often discouraging, international events also challenged the *Century*'s hopeful idealism. Despite their cosmopolitan view of literature and culture, the editors in the 1880s and early 1890s were as little concerned with world politics as were most of their readers. Aware of intensifying national rivalries, they were nevertheless surprised by their country's sudden thrust into the roily currents of war and imperialism.

The crisis with Britain over the Venezuelan boundary late in 1895 shocked Gilder and his *Century* colleagues. Recoiling from the "unforgivable wickedness" of war with Britain, the editors made urgent pleas for a board of international arbitration to settle such disputes in the future. Such a step might serve as an example to all of Europe, showing the way to disarmament and peace— "a mission to kindle the imagination and the heart." The *Century* bitterly attacked the U.S. Senate for its rejection of an arbitration treaty with England. "We have fallen on evil days," Gilder lamented to Carl Schurz, and remarked in an editorial that "patriotism" was still the last refuge of scoundrels—referring to politicians who drummed up Anglophobia for their own ends. Articles in the *Century*, including one by Godkin (January 1897), attacked the jingoists and the "absurdity" of war.[30]

When war did come, with Spain, Gilder regarded it with mixed feelings. He had applauded President William McKinley's resistance to the sword-rattlers, and, moreover, he was committed personally and editorially to the principle of arbitration. Yet his patriot heart could be fired with the martial spirit, and he could not believe his country guilty of aggressive war with evil intent. On the Cuban question, the *Century* insisted, there was "an absence of interested motives on the part of the American people, as a whole." Although the editors still approved the arbitration principle, "higher considerations of the justice and righteousness" of our cause might make the use of force acceptable. When the battle was joined, the *Century* approved its purpose as "the rescue of an oppressed people from an incompetent and medieval rule."[31]

As if to demonstrate its devotion to pacific principles, the *Century*, while its new war series celebrated the exploits of men in battle, continued to feature articles glorifying the "Heroes of Peace." Roosevelt called "The Roll of Honor of the New York Police" (October 1897); Riis paid tribute to the city's fire-fighters (February 1898), and other articles honored the voluntary life savers, deep-sea fishermen, lighthouse operators, and railwaymen. Gustave Kobbé was the principal contributor to this series, which lasted into 1899.

To the *Century*, arbitration was the international equivalent of civil service reform as an antidote to power politics. The Hague

Peace Convention of 1899, which created a Permanent Court of Arbitration for international disputes, raised new hopes for an end to war. "The nations are at last in 'the Parliament of Man,'" the *Century* commented in an editorial (October 1899); "it will be only a matter of quarter-centuries, perhaps only of decades, when they will virtually enter 'the Federation of the World.'" But this roseate vision soon dissolved. The close of the century, the magazine acknowledged, was "marked by a recrudescence of international and interracial prejudice and hatred." In foreign affairs, as in so many other fields, the idealist saw a darkening prospect.[32]

Nor could the *Century*'s idealism provide a formula for the disposal of the territories that fell from Spain's feeble grasp. The monthly gave ample space to the great debate on this question, notably in the issue of September 1898, in which Whitelaw Reid argued for American expansion overseas and Schurz against it. Instinctively against imperialism, Gilder distrusted "the Senatorial expanders." But the *Century*'s editorial was equivocal. "If honor, duty, and humanity compel the nation to assume unexpected and unwanted responsibilities, let us not believe it impossible for us to accomplish this new work." In other words, if we must be imperialistic, let us be idealistic about it.[33]

In immigration policy, the guiding principle of American democracy had always been the open door. That principle came under attack in the late nineteenth century as an influx of alien peoples seemed to pose a threat to traditional concepts of American nationality. Between 1880 and 1900 nearly 9,000,000 immigrants poured into the United States—whose population in 1880 was only about 50,000,000—and increasingly they came from southern and eastern Europe. Far more than the English, Irish, Germans, and Scandinavians, these immigrants seemed to present a problem in assimilation, for they were largely unfamiliar with democratic government, with American manners and customs, and with the American standard of living.

Many of Gilder's contributors saw in this tidal stream the poisonous source of many evils, political, economic, and social. Lodge argued for restriction in September 1893, using census figures to show that Americans of foreign birth and parentage made up a disproportionately large part of the pauper and criminal classes.

The bitterest denunciation of the immigrants came in the March 1888 issue from Theodore T. Munger, long an ecclesiastical ally of the *Century*, whom an admiring contemporary called "perhaps the most literary, and at the same time the most Christ-like, figure in the Congregational pulpit" of Connecticut. His correspondence with Gilder about this article measures the rise of nativist sentiment that resulted from, among other factors, industrial strife and incidents like the Haymarket bombing. He submitted the essay two years before its appearance, but had himself withdrawn it as "too harsh and wholesale in its tone." Now, however, he thought that "the times and public temper have come up to it." It was an intemperate outburst, charged with racism and full of extravagant condemnations. Immigration, Munger claimed, was the source of crime, anarchy, political corruption, the pauper problem, the degradation of labor, and spreading atheism. "There is not an evil thing among us, not a vice nor crime, nor disturbing element, which is not for the most part of foreign origin." He called for a "scientific" policy to replace the "grand idealism" which had traditionally admitted all comers.[34]

The magazine's editorial position was much less doctrinaire. An editorial of August 1894, not inimical to immigrants, simply advocated a law to make the foreign-born ineligible to vote until a year after naturalization. Nor were the *Century*'s contributors uniformly hostile to the immigrants. Julian Ralph, describing "The Bowery" for Gilder's readers (December 1891), declared that its polyglot population presented no danger to American institutions; the new immigrants were as desirable as their predecessors. In December 1891 André Castaigne told a graphic and sympathetic picture story of the peasant migration from the Old World to the New, beginning in the fields of Europe and ending in "The Land of Promise."

Gilder's humanitarianism and strong sense of justice brought him to the defense of one particularly wretched alien class. In the early 1880s, persecution in Russia drove great numbers of Jews to refuge in the United States. Shocked by this display of cruelty in a Christian land, the editor nevertheless—in the interest of free speech—permitted one Mme. Z. Ragozin to present the Russian view in April 1882. She declared that the Jews had earned the hatred of her people by their "parasitical" character and their self-imposed "separation" from the rest of the community. In the same number of the magazine, an editorial called these accusations "medieval."

To give a more complete reply, Gilder selected Emma Lazarus, a young Jewish woman whose poems had appeared earlier in the *Century*, but whose sympathy for her kinsmen was now for the first time fully awakened. Her pity for the oppressed—later to find eloquent expression in the invitation to the "huddled masses" inscribed on the pedestal of the Statue of Liberty—was matched by her indignation. Her wrath in this article (May 1882) was all the more effective in that it was directed not merely at the pogroms that inspired it but at the persecution of people anywhere by their fellow human beings.

Nonetheless, as anti-Semitism continued in Europe, Lazarus perceived a special "Jewish problem"; after months of study she concluded, in a *Century* article of February 1883, that her people must establish an independent nation. In 1892 Richard Wheatley, appraising in two illustrated articles (January and February) the character, sentiment, and condition of New York City's fast-growing Jewish population, found much support for this plan. Estimating that there were from 175,000 to 250,000 Jews then in the city, he reported that most of them lived in lower East Side tenements, were "sweated" in the garment industry, and longed for a Jewish homeland.

Many Israelite leaders had the same hope. One of them, Richard Gottheil, professor of Semitic languages at Columbia University, wrote a strongly pro-Zionist article in the issue of December 1899. The *Century*'s friendly interest in this aspiration, and its regard for Hebrew sensitiveness in other respects, won it a loyal following among the Jewish community. "My people owe you thanks, more than they do any other magazine," Gottheil told Gilder.[35]

Meanwhile, the *Century* was making new friends among an older immigrant group, the Irish Catholics. Never so militantly

Protestant as Holland had been, Gilder and his publishers made a conscious effort to cultivate an Irish-American community which was steadily rising in social status and political power. A Boston priest informed the editor in 1886 that the *Century* had successfully "courted Catholic patronage" in his city; that, indeed, "our Catholic clergy here read your magazine almost universally." The rapprochement was abetted by the staff's close personal relations with such New Yorkers as Maurice Francis Egan, poet and editor of religious journals, whose Celtic gaiety, Johnson admitted, "did something to modify the reformer in my blood."[36]

Despite the best of intentions, Gilder's monthly inevitably printed some contributions that angered Catholics. James Lane Allen twice aroused hostility. "The White Cowl" (September 1888), which he had to rewrite twice before satisfying Gilder, was the story of a Trappist monk torn between his vows and his passion for a woman; in "Sister Dolorosa," a three-part story beginning in December 1890, Allen related the similar travail and ultimate tragedy of a young nun who fell in love. The Catholic press and clergy charged Allen with misrepresenting the Trappists and with libelously insulting the sisters of the convent. Mary Hartwell Catherwood's novel of early French Canada was also criticized for its allegedly erroneous portrayal of church doctrines and ceremonies. There were other incidents. One cleric, objecting to an article on "The Ursulines of Quebec" (October 1886), demanded, "Why not leave to the Harpers the monopoly of anti-Catholic bigotry?" He acknowledged, however, that he had never before found anything objectionable in the *Century*. So, too, Joseph H. McMahon, assistant at St. Patrick's Cathedral, although he listed various affronts, absolved Gilder of any intent to offend McMahon's co-religionists.[37]

These were obviously the protests of sensitive well-wishers. The tone and content of the *Century* showed its desire to comprehend the Roman Catholics in its concept of a democratic society. In May 1888 Gilder published a laudatory piece by Egan on "The Personality of Leo XIII"; F. Marion Crawford in 1896 wrote an appreciative series of articles on the pope and his domain.

If anything more were needed to cement the friendship, it came in the mid-1890s when Gladden used Gilder's columns for a telling blow at the American Protective Association. This organization,

and other similar secret societies, represented a recrudescent nativist movement centered in the Midwest. Their crude propaganda included the circulation of counterfeit documents pur-
porting to show a plot to bring public schools, employment, and
government under papal control. Members of the Association
took an oath never to appoint Catholics to political office and
never to employ them in preference to Protestants. Gladden, in
submitting his article, thought the *Century* would "make more
friends among Catholics than you will alienate among your readers" by printing it. Aware, however, that the editor was risking
some circulation, the author told Gilder that his acceptance of
the piece was "the most refreshing and encouraging thing that
I have met with for many a day." Later, Gladden reported that
he had got many letters in response to his article, most of them
"strongly commendatory."[38]

Gilder followed this article with editorial attacks on the Association as subversive of democracy. The *Century* specifically
reproached both the newspaper press for its silence in the face
of this menace and the thousands of Protestant ministers who
had actively supported it. As the nativist movement subsided,
the editors felt they had done much to deflate it.[39]

During these years the magazine was shedding its former prejudice against the Irish on ethnic as well as religious grounds.
Stories of Irish-American life by George H. Jessop, Seumas
MacManus, Chester Bailey Fernald, and others, while sometimes
bordering on caricature, generally indicated an acceptance of the
Irish as a positive addition to the nation. Jennie E. T. Dowe's
songs of Ireland, appearing in the *Century* for several years after
1888, were among the first pieces of their kind to reach an important American audience.[40]

The key to Gilder's attitude toward the foreign-born lay in his
idealized conception of the American nation—peaceful, lawabid-
ing, dedicated to justice. He was deeply stirred when anarchism
or industrial violence marred this ideal state and was quite ready
to blame alien influences. The Haymarket bombing seemed to
have convinced him that, as a *Century* editorial of June 1888
noted, a large percentage of the population was "no longer
American" and "no longer thinks and acts instinctively as Americans have habitually thought and acted." An editorial of August

1893 blamed the Homestead strike riots of 1892 on "the turbulent and anarchistic foreign element which has been admitted to the ranks of American labor so freely during recent years." It was "impossible to think of American-born workingmen rioting and killing as these men did." Again, after the Pullman strike and other violent labor actions in 1894, an editorial (October 1894) asked why workers were "in so many instances seeking to overthrow law and order" and answered that it was because "our laboring class is not as a body American, but anti-American." Not a word of condemnation for the death sentences of anarchists who had been miles from the scene of the Haymarket crime, nor for the armed intervention of the Pinkertons at Homestead, nor for the use of federal armed forces to break the Pullman strike. A quite one-sided view, in short, was presented of the brute power that was distorting Gilder's idealized image of America.

What the United States needed, said a *Century* editorial of August 1892, was citizens of character, ability, and training, with "such complete knowledge of governmental laws and social and economic principles, such familiarity with the history of politics and political systems in all lands and times, that they will be able when occasion offers to stop the progress of 'crazes' and delusions, simply by showing from the working of established laws the impossibility of their success in practice." One of the crazes Gilder had in mind was the movement for free silver. From its earliest years the magazine had stood for sound money, but what had been simply editorial policy became after 1890 a cause driven home to readers in nearly every issue. In that year the Farmers' Alliances of the West and South, determined to stop the deflationary spiral that had brought grain and cotton prices to disastrously low levels, began to pressure Congress. Their pressure pushed through the Sherman Silver Purchase Act, and their leaders made it clear that their goal was the free and unlimited coinage of silver.

The *Century* responded with a full-scale campaign against this "pernicious delusion." In 1891 Joseph Bucklin Bishop began a series of editorial lectures on "Cheap Money Experiments" to demonstrate, first, how inflationary panaceas of the past had invariably spelled disaster, and, second, why the current heresy was also foredoomed to failure. Bishop's historical lessons were gathered into a pamphlet, published by the Century Company, and sold at ten cents a copy. Gilder and his colleagues were delighted by its reception. Western journals reprinted the articles; one Kansas editor reported that they had furnished material for "thousands" of election tracts and speeches in his state, where the Farmers' Alliance met defeat in the fall of 1891. By the end of the following summer the *Century* felt that the free-silver craze had "so nearly disappeared that one wonders if it really ever was formidable."[41]

But the crisis was yet to come. Spurred to furious action as prices of their commodities plunged still further, the debt-ridden agrarians joined with labor elements in a national Populist party, which won twenty-two electoral votes in the presidential election of 1892. The depression of the following year deepened the sectional division. The East, attributing the financial panic to the Sherman Silver Purchase Act, secured its repeal, much to the satisfaction of the *Century*. The silverites captured the Democratic party in 1896 and, with William Jennings Bryan as their candidate, launched their climactic crusade.[42]

Gilder thought Bryan "the wrongest-headed man who in our time has asked to be put in the White House" and his free silver program "the most gigantic swindle and act of repudiation that the world has ever seen." The editor grieved for his country, its dignity affronted by the "turbulent and insane emotion" of the silverites, its "good faith throughout the world" staked on the election.[43]

In equating the gold standard with the right and with national honor, Gilder risked his western circulation. C. S. Thomas of Colorado, a member of the Democratic National Committee, reminded the editor pointedly that he had a large number of readers who believed in free silver, while other westerners threatened to "drop" the *Century* unless it gave them "fair play." Embittered silverites complained that the magazine had abandoned its traditional nonpartisan policy. An Illinois attorney declared that its editorials raised the question as to "whether or not you have degraded The Century from its high place above the political turmoil and caused it to become a sectional political sheet." In reply, the editors expressed regret over the sectional rift, but insisted that there was only one side to the money question. The people of the West and South who took the silver side were "unenlightened and misguided."[44]

When the battle of the standards ended in a triumph for gold, the *Century* hailed the victory. The conviction that the gold standard represented an absolute (or ideal) value had led the editors to speak the black-and-white language of the zealot on this issue. There is no sign that they understood the distress of the farm belt and the need of inflation by some means. Nor did they seem to comprehend that new gold fields, the cyanide process for refining gold ore, and rising commodity prices—that these factors, not the acceptance of right principles—finally ended the sectional division. The editors were learning, however, that many of the great questions of the day were not so easily susceptible to a moral solution.[45]

Near the core of Gilder's genteel value system was a reverence for family life and the concept of woman as an exalted character. In the late nineteenth century, conditions of urban life menaced these pillars of social stability. The boardinghouse and the hotel, Gladden observed (January 1882), were not conducive to a healthy home life. An alarming increase in the divorce rate was an index to loosening family ties, and through Gilder's long reign his magazine attacked divorce in articles and editorials; the clear implication was that divorce was immoral and that unhappy marriages had to be endured as part of "the code."

Gilder and most of his contributors favored a broader education for women and were willing to see their wives and daughters take a more active role in community affairs, especially in humanitarian movements. The *Century* also looked approvingly on the multiplying occupational opportunities for women. When the Johns Hopkins Medical School opened its doors to women, the monthly marked the event with a series of laudatory "Open Letters," one of them from James Cardinal Gibbons.[46]

But Gilder was as strongly opposed as Holland had been to equal suffrage. Unlike his predecessor, however, he admitted the question to the monthly's forum on social problems. In August 1894 he printed a full debate on the subject, Senator George F. Hoar arguing for "The Right and Expediency of Woman Suffrage" and J. M. Buckley pointing to its "Wrongs and Perils."

Hoar pictured the reform as a desirable extension of democracy, while Buckley repeated the oft-heard warning that the vote was "incompatible with the nature of womanhood" and a danger to the family, the safeguard of civilization. Gilder placed his editorial influence firmly against a political change that "would be a revolution of a greater magnitude and effect than any the world has yet witnessed." The editor's privately expressed opinion showed the depth of his feeling. The movement for female suffrage, he wrote, was not a "harmless fad," but a "strong, systematic, well considered attack on the most conservative element of social life, the home woman."[47]

Gilder was concerned over the restless "new woman" and the radical social change of which she was a symbol. A nostalgic *Century* editorial of August 1900 lamented the passing of "the lady"—the "type of woman who meets and greets you in her quiet drawing room as one who has long days of repose behind her, and looks calmly forward to others of the same tenor." Somewhere in the rush of life there must be "stopping-places where one may rest and dream a little"—and it was a feminine function to provide these oases. Thus the *Century* sounded one more clear note of regret for a fading ideal.

As an idealist, Gilder believed that certain eternal verities governed the universe. Increasingly in the 1880s and 1890s these presumed truths were expressed as laws that could be applied to the pressing problems of an industrial age. These laws, the *Century* assured its readers in an editorial of May 1894, were the same in the nineteenth as in the seventeenth century. The great thing was to discover and announce them, so that the public and professional leaders who read the *Century* could diffuse them among the masses. This concept inevitably gave a paternalistic tone to the *Century*'s comments on social problems.

The social law as expounded by some *Century* contributors had a harsh, Darwinian cast. Introducing a series of articles by Professor W. O. Atwater of Wesleyan University on the science of food and nutrition, Edward Atkinson asserted (December 1886) that food in the United States was so plentiful and its distribution so cheap that only wasteful buying and cooking could account for malnutrition among the poor. The rise of "scientific charity," marked by the formation of the State Charities Aid Association in New York, was an effort to prevent duplication of relief and to coordinate attempts at rehabilitation; in July 1882 E. V. Smalley praised this effort as "A Great Charity Reform." Gladden in an "Open Letter" (June 1886) gave a Darwinian sanction to this movement: "The pauper classes go on multiplying; and a careless and sentimental charity protects them from the destruction that their vices and their indolence invoke, and encourages them to increase and multiply and scourge the earth with their bestialized progeny."

Gladden later (December 1892) modified this harsh view, citing Charles Booth's famous London survey to show that poverty was often the cause, rather than the effect, of vice. But the ruthless accent of survival of the fittest sounded in Francis Amasa Walker's analysis of poverty in December 1897. "We must strain out of the blood of the race more of the taint inherited from a bad and vicious pool before we can eliminate poverty. . . . The scientific treatment which is applied to physical disease must be extended to mental and moral disease, and a wholesome surgery and cautery must be enforced by the whole power of the state for the good of all." Rejecting the socialist cures of Henry George and Edward Bellamy, Walker attributed destitution to limited resources, industrial fluctuations, and the "great social and industrial law: 'Unto him that hath not shall be taken away even that which he hath.'"

But other contributors, with Gilder's blessing, were citing different admonitions as guides to social betterment. Although not a church member, the editor admired the Christian ideal and maintained close relations with a phalanx of ministers who preached and practiced "The New Theology." These clergymen placed God in the world, not above it. They stressed the humanity of people to each other more than individual salvation. They easily reconciled science, including the Darwinian theory, with Christianity. They were not dismayed by scholarly analysis of the Bible, accepting the view that the Scriptures were the work of men who were "inspired but also limited by the conceptions of their own times."[48] Leaders of this school, including Munger, Gladden, Newman Smyth, and Lyman Abbott, expounded their liberal views in the *Century*. They sometimes displeased religious conservatives. When Gladden in an editorial (November 1884) urged Sunday school teachers to take into account the recent biblical studies, a leading southern Presbyterian attacked both the writer and the magazine, asking, "Are Christian parents aware of the virulent infidelity which they admit into their homes with this popular monthly?" But Gilder assured a friendly southern correspondent who brought this critical article to his attention that "we seem to have gotten a little beyond that point in the magazine, even if a part of our Southern audience has not."[49]

But the *Century* and the liberal clerics who wrote for it were more concerned with social conditions than theological disputes. An editorial of May 1890 noted that the churches and their wealthy communicants were moving into fashionable districts and abandoning the masses and warned that this kind of class segregation was a danger to democracy. The development in the 1880s and 1890s of the institutional church, carrying education and philanthropy, as well as the gospel, to the tenement districts and slums, was an effort to counteract this divisive trend. Abbott saw a broader challenge to the church. In two articles (August 1888 and December 1890), he preached that the Christian ethic was essential to the success of the American experiment in self-government and that it was the one remedy for social and industrial unrest. All of the great questions of the day, he declared, were bound up in the single, comprehensive problem: "How shall we develop a brotherhood of man?"

The Sociological Group, formed in 1888, was an organized expression of this social Christianity. Its individual members agreed to write essays which, after discussion and modification by the whole Group, Gilder was to publish. The predominantly clerical membership included Bishop Henry C. Potter of Grace Church; the Reverend Charles W. Shields, professor at Princeton University; Munger; Samuel Warren Dike, a Congregational minister and perhaps the nation's leading authority on marriage, divorce, and the family; William Chauncy Langdon, a Protestant Episcopal churchman devoted to the union of the leading Protestant sects; and two conscientious laymen—Low and Ely. Eight more scholars and theologians had joined by 1890.[50]

The Group's praiseworthy objective was, "so far as may be, to bring scientific methods, with a Christian purpose and spirit, to the study of the questions to be considered." These questions covered the whole range of the social problem. The first of the "Present-Day Papers," written by Langdon and appearing in November 1889, proved to be a turgid survey of the social crisis, together with a proposal for the development of an "ecclesiology"—"the science of organic Christianity." Dike's "Problems of the Family," which came next (January 1890), was an equally vague dissertation that suggested further study of sociological problems but offered no meaningful recommendations. With good reason, a contemporary review cited this obscurantist article as an example of "how portentously dull an American can be when he chooses."[51]

Indeed the promise of this high-minded collective effort was never fulfilled. Save for Ely's program for labor reform (April 1890), the Group's articles hardly came to grips with economic and political realities. Gilder understandably lost interest in the experiment, which eventually gravitated into a movement for church unity.[52] Nevertheless, the *Century* continued to voice the idea of a social Christianity, frequently through men like Ely and Gladden who had belonged to the Sociological Group.

At the heart of the social crisis was the clash between capital and labor. Individually helpless against the might of the corporations who employed them, industrial workers in the 1880s combined more effectively than ever before in an effort to win shorter hours, better wages, and an improvement in working conditions. A nation schooled in the dogmas of free competition looked on these organizations with disquiet or, when they became militant, with alarm.

Hay's novel, "The Bread-Winners," serialized in 1883–84, plunged the *Century* into the controversy over the role of labor unions. Hay, then a business executive in Cleveland, insisted that the story be published anonymously, which increased public discussion of the novel and helped make it a popular success. Hay's "Brotherhood of Bread-Winners" was a secret society, led by an unscrupulous criminal, which terrorized an entire city to enforce its strike demands until subdued by a citizen's law-and-order league. The author mentioned, but did not stress, that this conspiratorial group was not a trade union. That the distinction was a small one in Hay's view was shown by his two anonymous

"Open Letters" in answer to a "chorus of vituperation" from critics. Strikes always ended in violence, he said, and the "inner circle of petty tyrants who govern the trades-unions expressly forbid the working-man to make his own bargain with his employer."[53]

The *Century*'s editorial position was more impartial. "Unqualified denunciation of unions shows ignorance," said the magazine, even while Hay's novel was in progress. Even Professor William Graham Sumner, the apostle of Social Darwinism, had acknowledged that unions were "right and useful, and perhaps necessary."[54] In February 1887, commenting on the appearance of labor parties in politics, an editorial pointed out that they sought neither anarchy nor socialism but simply the improvement of labor's condition. But they had an "imperfect idea" of how to accomplish their ends, so that it was up to the educated classes to guide the movement. "It is the duty of the best men among us to do all they can to help the working-men in their legitimate aspirations, and at the same time to show them their errors and rebuke them when they go wrong."

The rebukes, of course, were numerous as the *Century* performed its paternalistic duty. Organized labor's attempts to coerce nonunion workers in the interest of collective bargaining excited especially stern disapproval. The right of a man to work for whom and for what wages he would, said an editorial of August 1886, was "the corner-stone of our free institutions."

As the depression of the mid-1880s brought a "Great Upheaval" of labor to combat wage cuts and unemployment, union tactics increasingly antagonized the public at large. The Knights of Labor, reaching the peak of its power, led great railroad strikes that paralyzed traffic in the heart of the nation. The *Century* was particularly alarmed when the Knights used the indirect boycott to coerce individuals or groups who patronized the union's opponents. The editors feared that this weapon, by provoking an ever-spreading warfare, threatened the social order itself.[55] The national conscience, an editorial of November 1886 declared, was with labor when it organized to repeal unjust laws or gain an equal footing with employers, but not with its assumption of "power to punish its enemies through agencies outside of and unknown to the laws."

Gilder's grasp of the capital-labor confrontation was weakened by his persistent belief that natural law, rather than government intervention or raw power, ultimately determined labor's situation. Thus, labor's demand for an eight-hour workday was to the *Century* a desirable goal, which should be reached by the natural process of technological advance. To enact it by legislation, said an editorial of December 1886, would be to give labor a "forced, artificial and unfair advantage" and would simply drive industry to new locations in states without such restrictions.

In the 1890s the capital-labor conflict broke out again in pitched battles, notably at the Carnegie steel mill in Homestead, Pennsylvania, and in the Pullman Company strike at Chicago. Appalled by the bloodshed at Homestead, Gilder felt that the workers had "put themselves fearfully in the wrong." That armed Pinkerton strikebreakers provoked the workers seemingly made no impression on Gilder. Again, he strongly supported President Cleveland's dispatch of federal troops to quell the disorders following the strike of Eugene V. Debs's railway union in 1894; that the troops also broke the strike was evidently not worthy of his remark. "The nation does not exist if anarchy and destructive despotism take the place of law," he wrote to the president. In an editorial obviously aimed at Governor John Peter Altgeld of Illinois, who had refused to call for federal troops, the *Century* declared (October 1894) that the public would not tolerate officials who would not uphold and execute the laws.[56]

This bitterness against the strikers and Altgeld stemmed in part from Gilder's conviction that alien influences inspired the costly class warfare. But there was something more: Cleveland's drastic step upheld the power of the Union so idealized by the editor. Commenting ten years after the Pullman strike on Cleveland's published *Presidential Problems*, a *Century* editorial referred to "the great service rendered not only to his country but to 'ordered liberty' . . . in the manner of dealing with the Chicago riots." Cleveland's move, the editorial said, was an important step in the growth of nationality and national supremacy. And the Supreme Court's denial of an appeal from Debs, who had been sentenced to prison for defying an injunction against the strike, created a debt of gratitude to the Court by the American people for its part in "the creation of a true nation."[57]

Anarchism was another threat to "ordered liberty," and anarchism was abroad in the land in the 1880s, its leaders, many
of them European-born, advocating terrorism as a means to
utopian ends. Gilder reflected the conservative dread of this menace when, in 1885, he stopped the presses to delete a reference
to "dynamite war-fare" in England, fearing that it would "doubtless have been copied by dynamite journals as an endorsement
of their methods." Asking William Dean Howells to change a
passage in "The Rise of Silas Lapham," Gilder explained that his
objection was to "the very word, *dynamite,* that is now so dangerous for any of us to use, except in condemnation." None but
a crank, he admitted, would misinterpret the intent of the phrase,
"but it is the crank who does the deed."[58]

Such fears seemed confirmed for Gilder when the Chicago
Haymarket bombing in 1886 took place amid anarchist agitation.
For the anarchist leaders who were hung or imprisoned for allegedly inciting this terrorist act, Gilder felt no sympathy. Seven
years later the *Century* printed a defense of their trial and sentence
written by Joseph E. Gary, the presiding judge in the case. Gilder
concurred in Gary's conclusion "that not only philosophically,
but legally, words are deeds, and that for words leading to a
crime a man must suffer the extreme penalty of the law." Gilder
deeply resented Governor Altgeld's later pardon of the imprisoned
anarchists. In a sardonic mood he once remarked privately, "I
think we shall have to change the Constitution, so that Altgeld
[who was foreign-born] will be eligible to the Presidency. Then
we will have Debs for Vice-President, and . . . all the pardoned
anarchists ought to have places in the cabinet."[59]

Such uncharacteristic vindictiveness may have reflected Gilder's
frustration at the waning power of the *Century* in particular and
of "the best men" in general to influence the course of public
policy in the direction of right principles. He could not see, or
at least could not admit, that ideal standards of government could
not be realized in the face of powerful interests. An editorial of
March 1897, on the occasion of McKinley's inauguration, remarked that the president of the United States "should be open
to the influence of that body of expert and cultivated citizens
which in the last resort must shape and order events in a democracy, if they are to be shaped and ordered for the public

good. The intelligence of the few is the safeguard of the many."
This editorial view showed no awareness that McKinley owed
his entire political career to the support of big business.

Gilder did take note of the ominous growth of trusts. However
efficient these giant consolidations might be, said an editorial of
August 1888, they crushed small businessmen, and there should
be legal guarantees of "full, fair and free competition." Such
criticism was far too mild to please one friend of Gilder and the
magazine. John Burroughs wrote the editor in 1896:

> I have always known that as a man your sympathies were with
> the poor and the unfortunate. . . . But as an editor you are far
> less outspoken on the wrongs of the people, the greed of monop-
> olies, the insolence and tyranny of railroads and other corporations
> than I should be. I would pour hot shot into them all the time. . . .
> I would show them up just as Kennan showed up the Russian
> despots. I would give the people a true history of the oil trust,
> and the sugar trust. . . . I believe any magazine would make its
> fortune that dared to do it.

Years later, Burroughs recalled that both Gilder and Johnson were
aghast at this suggestion of a policy that was to be pursued
successfully by the muckraking magazines of the early twentieth
century.[60]

Gilder in reply said that the *Century* had published "article after
article, and editorial after editorial, attacking known wrongs by
certain corporations and interests. But we always want to be sure
when we strike, and not to go into careless generalities when
they may do great harm,—because it will be a great while, if
ever, before we shall be in a socialistic state and throw away all
the benefits of individual action and private property." The editor
said he had been looking into the charge that "the poor are getting
poorer and the rich richer" and had found it false. The mass of
the people were much better off than they had been fifty years
earlier.[61]

Nevertheless, Gilder came to recognize that big business combinations posed a threat to democracy. In May 1900 Andrew
Carnegie argued that the formation of trusts was an inevitable
and desirable phase of an evolutionary process. By obeying "the
great law of aggregation," business was able to make cheaper
products and add to the happiness of rich and poor alike. The

magazine's editorial rejoinder, in the same number, was that Carnegie's claims ignored the "moral" issue. "Our social order is based on the principle that we should try to give every man a fair chance." The trend to concentration of capital "puts into the hands of a few men a power over the industrial life of the country such as they never possessed before." Here was another case, then, where Gilder clung to a standard—in this case that of free competition—without discerning or acknowledging that changing conditions had made it obsolete for much of American industry.

While Gilder's standards were conservative, he opened his columns to men who saw the need for sweeping changes in the economic ground rules. In "Is It Peace or War?" (August 1886), Gladden held that strikes, lockouts, riots, and boycotts were the natural outcome of pure competition. "Competition means war." And as long as the war persisted, labor must be granted "belligerent rights" to form unions and to strike in order to avoid a social degradation similar to slavery. Gladden predicted that peace would only come when some form of cooperation replaced raw competition as a social ideal. Thanking Gilder for "the privilege of putting this word of peace into the mouth of that mighty Angel, The Century," Gladden exclaimed, "God speed the word! and God bless the messenger!"[62]

In another article in that same year, Gladden argued that the state must check the abuses of unrestrained capitalism: it should control monopoly and speculation, regulate the railroads, and possibly employ a progressive income tax to halt the tendency toward the concentration of wealth in the hands of a few powerful individuals or corporations. In the November 1885 issue, Abbott, declaring that "neither Herbert Spenser nor Professor Sumner can stay the forward march of humanity," listed housing construction and the operation of the nation's railroads and telegraph lines as proper activities of the Federal government."

Ely made the boldest argument for extending the role of government. "Paternalism," he said (March 1898), was an epithet used to frighten the people from using the commonwealth for social ends. He demanded laws to regulate the employment of women and children, to insure factory sanitation and protection from dangerous machinery, and to fix employer liability for industrial accidents. He advocated federal savings banks. He favored government ownership of such "natural monopolies" as gas, water, and electricity and the rigid regulation of the railroads. There was "no self-help for the masses like state action," Ely declared. "The state is a suitable field for the co-operation of ordinary men with ordinary means."

The editorial position of the *Century* was generally for the unimpeded operation of economic laws, however, and it resisted the use of federal power to offset individual and corporate wealth and influence. The magazine objected vehemently to proposed inheritance, gift, and graduated income taxes, and Gilder privately damned the income tax of 1894 as "class legislation."[63] As late as 1896 an editorial listed the great public issues as sound finance, a reformed currency, conservation, and the merit system and called for congressional leadership to assert the "right side" of these questions.

But by 1900 the time was at hand when the government was to play a more dynamic part in the national life. "The truth is," the *Century* admitted in that year, "that we have witnessed a survival, into an age of combination, of legal and moral ideas which were based on the existence of free competition." If selfish interests were to flout the traditional rules of the game, the commonwealth must step in to insure fair play.[64]

Once the government role widened, however, public policy was to emerge as the outcome of conflicting pressure groups rather than the enactment of moral and economic "laws." What were to Gilder and the *Century* causes based on supposed ideal standards then became simply alternative programs. Gilder could never be comfortable with this pragmatic concept of government. But it was clear that the attempt to erect ideal standards would be no more successful in politics, economics, and social life than it had been in literature and the arts.

NOTES

1. Rosamond Gilder, ed., *Letters of Richard Watson Gilder* (Boston, 1916), 115–18, hereafter cited as Gilder, *Gilder*.

2. Horace Traubel, *With Walt Whitman in Camden,* 3 vols. (New York, 1961), 2:485; Gilder to Chancellor J. H. Kirkland, Mar. 8, 1894, GP; editorial, Oct. 1897.

3. Gilder to G. W. Curtis, June 9, 1884, to E. L. Godkin, same date, to Theodore Roosevelt, June 10, 1884, GP; Allan Nevins, ed., *Letters of Grover Cleveland, 1850–1908* (Boston, 1933), 226, 352. Cleveland wrote his first inaugural address at Gilder's summer home in Marion, Mass. *Christian Science Monitor*, June 4, 1934.

4. Gilder to Cleveland, Dec. 18, 1893, GP.

5. Editorial, Nov. 1886, and Gilder to Hamilton Wright Mabie, Aug. 22, 1891, GP.

6. Editorial, Mar. 1883.

7. See John Tomsich, *A Genteel Endeavor: American Culture and Politics in the Gilded Age* (Stanford, Calif., 1971), 86–92.

8. Gilder to Bishop H. C. Potter, Jan. 13, 1894, GP; editorials: July 1887, Dec. 1888, July 1890, Apr. 1892, and Jan. 1896.

9. Buel, "The Degradation of a State," Aug. 1891; Gilder to Nicholls, Mar. 14 and Nov. 2, 1891, GP; Robert Underwood Johnson, *Remembered Yesterdays* (Boston, 1923), 123–24.

10. Editorial, Jan. 1872.

11. Gilder to W. M. Baskerville, Jan. 6, 1888, and to Secretary of State Frederick Frelinghuysen, Nov. 21, 1884, GP; Brander Matthews, *These Many Years* (New York, 1917), 224; Allan Nevins, *Grover Cleveland: A Study in Courage, 1850–1908.* . . . (Boston, 1933), 452; Cleveland to Gilder, Mar. 11, 1888, in Nevins, ed., *Letters of Cleveland,* 176.

12. Maurice F. Egan, *Recollections of a Happy Life* (New York, 1924), 109; Edmund Gosse in *Author,* 3 (July 1891):96; Johnson, *Remembered Yesterdays,* 242–43.

13. Muir on the Yosemite, Aug. and Sept. 1890; editorials, Jan. 1890, Jan. 1893, and Apr. 1896; Linnie Marsh Wolfe, *Son of the Wilderness: The Life of John Muir* (New York, 1947), 249–51, 272–73; Johnson, *Remembered Yesterdays,* 291–93.

14. Johnson, *Remembered Yesterdays,* 296–300, and John Swett, "John Muir," May 1893.

15. Tyler Dennett, *John Hay: From Poetry to Politics* (New York, 1933), 140–41; Helen Nicolay, *Lincoln's Secretary: A Biography of John G. Nicolay* (New York, 1949), 298–300; editorial, Apr. 1882. Howard Mumford Jones, *The Age of Energy: Varieties of American Experience, 1865–1915* (New York, 1970), 33–36, pointed out that Whitman and other poets after the Civil War interpreted the American nation as "possessing a sacrosanct character." Gilder certainly was one of these "other poets."

16. L. Frank Tooker, *The Joys and Tribulations of an Editor* (New York, 1924), 41. The advertising section, Feb. 1885, quoted the *Memphis* (Tenn.) *Appeal* as follows: "The people of the South owe it [the *Century*] special thanks not only for the fairness of its spirit towards this section; but because it opened its pages to many of our best writers and made them known to the world." See the treatment of southern industrial expositions in issues of Feb. 1882, May and June 1885, Jan. 1888, Jan. 1896, and May 1897.

17. Editorial, May 1885, and Herbert F. Smith, *Richard Watson Gilder*, Twayne U.S. Authors Series no. 166 (New York, 1970), 71. Other criticisms by Cable of the South appeared in "The Convict Lease System in the Southern States" (Feb. 1884) and "The Silent South" (Sept. 1885). Washington articles, Jan. and Aug. 1900.

18. Harris to Gilder, Mar. 23, 1891, F. A. Connor to the Century Company, Feb. 27, 1891, W. J. Thackston to the Editor, Feb. 7, 1891, Henry R. Bennett to the Century Company, Feb. 7, 1891, de Graffenried to Gilder, May 28, 1891, clipping from the *Sheffield* (Ala.) *Enterprise*, enclosed in Henry King to Johnson, June 27, 1891, CC.

19. Thompson to Gilder, June 18, 1887, and to Johnson, Aug. 8, 1903, CC; Tooker, *Joys and Tribulations,* 46–47; editorial, Oct. 1884; "Open Letter," Dec. 1887. Charles A. Dana of the *New York Sun,* who seldom went out of his way to speak a good word for the *Century,* praised Thompson's contribution as "the noblest battle poem of our day or perhaps of any day." See Edward P. Mitchell, *Memories of an Editor: Fifty Years of American Journalism* (New York, 1924), 268.

20. James F. Rushing to Buel, June 26, 1891, CC; Gilder, *Gilder,* 169–73; editorials, May and Oct. 1887.

21. Editorials, July 1891 and Mar. 1890.

22. Editorials, Mar., Sept., and Oct. 1890, Jan. 1889, and Feb. 1894.

23. Editorial, Jan. 1895. See also editorials of July 1892 and June 1895.

24. Gilder to George E. Woodberry, June 4, 1891, GP, and Gilder, *Gilder,* 107–12, 180–81.

25. Ely to Gilder, Mar. 13, 1890, CC, and Gilder to the editor of the *New York Tribune,* Oct. 9, 1895, GP.

26. Gilder, *Gilder,* 254–72; editorial, *New York Evening Post,* Nov. 19, 1909; Louise Ware, *Jacob A. Riis: Police Reporter, Reformer, Useful Citizen* (New York, 1938), 102–29.

27. Editorials, Dec. 1897 and July 1895.

28. Waring to Gilder, Aug. 9, 1893, CC; editorials, Dec. 1895 and Nov. 1896.

29. Editorial, *New York Evening Post,* Nov. 19, 1909; Gilder to George E. Woodberry, Sept. 15, 1897, GP; Gilder, *Gilder,* 318–28; editorial, May 1899.

30. Gilder to Schurz, Jan. 20, 1897, GP; editorials, Mar. and Apr. 1896 and Aug. 1897.

31. Editorials, May, June, and July 1898.

32. Editorial, Oct. 1900.

33. Gilder to Gladden, Jan. 13, 1899, GP, and editorial, Aug. 1898.

34. Munger to Gilder, Nov. 17, 1887, CC, and *Hartford Post,* quoted in *Author,* 2 (Mar. 15, 1890):42–43.

35. Gottheil to Gilder, Nov. 22, 1899, CC.

36. William H. Duncan (pastor of St. Mary's Church, Boston) to the Editor, Oct. 13, 1886, CC, and Johnson, *Remembered Yesterdays,* 403.

37. William H. Duncan to the Editor, Oct. 13, 1886, McMahon to

Gilder, Feb. 3, 1891, I. B. Ashton to the Editor, Mar. 7, 1899, CC; Allen, "Open Letter," May 1891; Grant C. Knight, *James Lane Allen and the Genteel Tradition* (Chapel Hill, N.C., 1935), 72, 89–91.

38. Gladden to Gilder, Dec. 11, 1893, Jan. 2, 1894, and n.d. [1894], CC.

39. Johnson, *Remembered Yesterdays,* 137, and editorial, May 1896.

40. Dowe to Gilder, May 31, 1888, CC.

41. Editorials, Feb. and Aug. 1892, and Herbert Myrick to Gilder, Aug. 3, 1891, CC.

42. Editorials, Nov. 1893 and June 1894.

43. Gilder to Herbert Walsh, Oct. 4, 1900, to Jane E. Robbins, Oct. 12, 1896, GP; editorial, Oct. 1896.

44. W. H. Warder to the Century Company, July 2, 1896, C. S. Thomas to the Century Company, May 2, 1893, F. P. Crews to the Editor, June 5, 1893, Charles A. Raymond to the Editor, June 5, 1893, CC; editorial, Aug. 1896.

45. Editorial, Jan. 1897.

46. Feb. 1891.

47. Gilder to H. C. Bunner, June 7, 1894, GP, and editorials, July and Aug. 1894.

48. The phrase is from Theodore T. Munger, quoted in William R. Hutchison, *The Modernist Impulse in American Protestantism* (Cambridge, Mass., 1976), 95–96. Hutchison discusses the New Theology, ibid., 79ff.

49. Clipping of article by Dr. Robert Dabney, n.d., in the *Central Presbyterian*, and Gilder to Gordon Pryor Rice, Mar. 3, 1885, both in CC.

50. W. C. Langdon to Gilder, Nov. 23, 1888, Bishop Potter to Gilder, Nov. 7, 1888, CC; introduction to "Present-Day Papers," Nov. 1889. The additional members were Bishop Hugh Miller Thompson of the Protestant Episcopal Church; Professor Charles A. Briggs of Union Theological Seminary; Gladden; Edward J. Phelps, diplomat and professor of law at Yale University; Professor William M. Sloane of Princeton University; Charles Dudley Warner; William F. Slocum, Jr.; and Francis G. Peabody.

51. *Review of Reviews,* 1 (Feb. 1890):66, and introduction to "Present-Day Papers."

52. Langdon to Gilder, Mar. 21, 1894, CC, and *Dictionary of American Biography*, s.v. Langdon, W. C.

53. Hay's "Open Letter," Nov. 1883, and Johnson, *Remembered Yesterdays,* 119–20. See also Hay's subsequent "Open Letter" responding to attacks on this work, Mar. 1884.

54. Editorial, Feb. 1884.

55. Editorial, June 1886.

56. Gilder to Cleveland, Aug. 30, 1892, GP, and Gilder to Cleveland, n.d., cited in Nevins, ed., *Letters of Cleveland,* 625.

57. Editorial, Dec. 1904.

58. Gilder to Howells, Feb. 18, 1885, Howells Papers, Harvard University, Cambridge, Mass.

59. Gary, "The Chicago Anarchists of 1886," Apr. 1893, and editorial same issue; Gilder to Henry T. Thurber, July 8, 1896, GP.

60. Clara Barrus, *The Life and Letters of John Burroughs*, 2 vols. (Boston, 1925), 1:360–61; 2:372.

61. Gilder to Burroughs, Sept. 22, 1896, GP.

62. Gladden to Gilder, May 24, 1886, CC.

63. Gilder to George F. Parker, Mar. 31, 1894, GP, and editorial, Apr. 1888.

64. Editorial, May 1900.

CHAPTER

12

Loss of Preeminence

The *Century* had an average monthly circulation of 222,000 in
1887. This level, mainly a result of the Civil War Series, could
not be held, but circulation stayed on a plateau of nearly 200,000
for several years, well ahead of *Harper's* and *Scribner's Magazine*.
In the 1890s, however, the *Century* dropped to about 150,000 and
after 1900 struggled to stay around 125,000.[1]

The primary reason for this decline was an influx of new, less
expensive, and livelier competitors. The essence of the magazine
revolution was the discovery of a mass readership hitherto un-
reached by periodicals and the exploitation of this mass market
by means of national advertising. Revenues from advertising assured profits to publishers even though costs of production exceeded income from subscriptions and newsstand sales. Once this
mass audience was discovered, it was inevitable that most magazine editors would cater to its tastes. No doubt just as inevitably,
the *Century* and its established peers—*Harper's*, *Scribner's Magazine*, and the *Atlantic*—resisted the popularization of editorial content, and in so doing, they removed themselves ever further from
the mainstream of American life and accelerated their own
decline.[2]

Samuel S. McClure was a key figure in this revolution in the
production of magazines. In the 1880s he put together a newspaper syndicate that bought stories and features from the world's
best authors and brought them to millions of readers. Through
such syndicated features the newspapers, especially the enlarged
Sunday editions, began to rival magazines, not only in com-
manding good writers but in their ability to present thorough,
coherent discussions of issues. It was his success in editing for
a million families of readers over ten years through his syndicate
that convinced McClure there was an audience for an inexpensive

magazine. He launched *McClure's* in 1893 at a price of fifteen cents per issue at a time when the *Century* and *Harper's* sold at thirty-five cents and *Scribner's* at twenty-five cents. By 1900 *McClure's* had a circulation of nearly 365,000. *Munsey's Magazine* cut its price to ten cents in 1893 and by 1900 was selling about 700,000 copies each month. *Cosmopolitan*, which had sold at twenty-five cents, halved its price in 1894. A host of new, low-priced monthlies followed, and Robert Underwood Johnson could remark that by 1910 the *Century* had forty or fifty competitors.[3]

Magazine advertising, which more than doubled in the period 1880–1900, naturally flowed to the new periodicals with mass—larger—readership. As these new magazines grew wealthy from advertising revenues, they were able to offer more money than the *Century* and its older competitors for established writers and expensive features. *McClure's*, for example, outbid the *Century* for Rudyard Kipling's "Captains Courageous," which it serialized beginning in 1896.[4]

For a time the *Century* held on well. Advertising in its pages more than doubled in quantity in the 1890s, despite the depression that lasted through much of the decade. Yet Richard Watson Gilder's magazine during these years was passing up an opportunity to adapt to changing times in order to win new readers. With the Spanish-American war and the succeeding wave of prosperity, the low-paid competitors took off in both circulation and advertising while the *Century* became hard pressed to make ends meet. By late 1899 the magazine had reached a financial crisis. To avert "a possible debacle," Johnson told Gilder in August of that year, the *Century* had to cut expenditures. Management must search the art and advertising departments, as well as the editorial side, for "leakages." In such a crisis, Johnson said, "the first thing Mr. Roswell Smith would have done would be to *stop needless outlay*." Gilder resisted Johnson's proposal to reduce the magazine's staff, but Johnson argued that if employees were to be kept on, it was "imperative considering the congestion of our force that we should immediately undertake some large enterprise." Unfortunately, there was now no Smith to conceive and carry out such an enterprise.[5]

The Century Company weathered this crisis, but in the same

it produced a rather blurred image at first, it was rapidly improved with the employment of the halftone screen. With this process the new magazines could print as many pictures as their older rivals at perhaps one-tenth the cost. *Harper's* and the *Century* each spent about $5,000 a month for wood engravings; *McClure's* began with total resources of about $7,000. Under the new conditions of illustration, Ellery Sedgwick recalled, "Starting a magazine was like stocking a pushcart."[9]

As the special exponent of wood engraving, the *Century* was the last of the leading periodicals to adopt photographic illustration. (Paradoxically, it was the first quality magazine to use the halftone, to reproduce a brush drawing.)[10] Beginning in 1889, the editors used photographs occasionally, but only when their suitability was warranted. For example, they twice printed photographs of celestial bodies taken at Lick Observatory, recognizing that scientific phenomena demanded literal reproduction. But Gilder and his art department deplored and resisted the changing method of illustration. "The process can copy outlines," said an editorial of June 1890, "but it cannot interpret tones; it cannot think." Five years later (October 1895), an editorial reiterated, "There is a distinct difference between picture-making and art," and predicted that "the rage for cheap work" would never eradicate the love of finer illustration. The *Century* boasted that it used more wood engravings than any other magazine, serving the "truest ends of art" at a cost of hundreds of thousands of dollars. As late as 1899 the editors promised "something like a revival in wood-engraving." But they were championing a dying craft, for even the artists were coming to favor mechanical reproduction of their work. The *Century* had to adapt, although it kept engravers employed in retouching photographs to bring out the tone of the original.[11]

To Gilder, the cheap illustration was the symbol of a revolution that threatened the whole ethos for which the *Century* stood. It was symptomatic of a "recording tendency" in all of American life which could be seen "in fiction, in verse, in picture and sculpture, even in music." There was "a sort of religion of the commonplace, as well as a religion of the beastly, the putrescent, and the obscene." Cheap printing had combined with photography to produce a glut of books and periodicals. The time was at hand "when every man will be his own publisher, author, and editor, illustrating his work with his own snap-shots." But then "we shall all begin again, and the art of selecting from the world's thought and doings what is really worthy of record and worthy of examination will once more be exalted among men."[12]

But the glory days of the *Century* were now waning; the changes in American life and taste, as in illustration, were irreversible. The reading public showed an increasing appetite for reality in illustration. Perusing the early numbers of *McClure's*, one sees that photoengravings were not simply less expensive than woodcuts but also produced quite different and more striking effects. Beginning with his first number, McClure ran a series of "Human Documents," photographic layouts showing famous men like Thomas Edison, Edward Everett Hale, and William Dean Howells at various stages of their lives, from infancy to maturity. Used in this way, the photographs gave a sense of reality and immediacy unmatched by wood engravings. *Munsey's* went to even more journalistic lengths, featuring page after page of photographs of actors, actresses, and opera stars currently on the New York stage.

The *Century* tried to adapt the new illustrative technique to its own ideal purposes. Photography *could* be art, the editors decided, and they had Alfred Steiglitz explain (October 1902) how art societies around the world were opening their doors to photographic exhibits.[13] In May 1907 the *Century* ran "a group of ideal subjects posed and produced by F. Benedict Herzog." These "decorative photographs," said Christian Brinton in an accompanying commentary, were in the "grand style," reminding one of Raphael, Tintoretto, or Veronese. In short, instead of accepting the revolutionary implications of photography for magazine illustration, the *Century* chose to emphasize the continuity of its own artistic tradition.

Gilder and his editorial colleagues similarly refused to come to terms with other changes in American life and taste which to them meant a lowering of standards. They lamented trends in morals, manners, and culture that undermined the old ideals, and it seems clear that they identified the *Century*'s loss of preeminence with these trends. Whether indicting divorce, the vulgarity of the newly rich, or the lack of manners in the young—all frequent editorial themes in the late nineteenth and early twentieth centuries—the editors usually managed to suggest that the debasement of the printed word and of illustration was somehow a cause of these and other evils. "The rotary press and the cheap 'process' produce a profusion in the literary and pictorial 'output' which has a tendency to befog the intellect and lower the standards of taste" ("Topics," March 1898). "The age of reflection seems to have passed, and to have been succeeded by the age of agitation. . . . Fast trains and cheap print spread the agitation far beyond its limits" ("Topics," May 1898). Divorce threatened the destruction of society, and no force combating this evil was likely to be more effective than "the literature produced by men and women who are true to an art solidly based upon the eternal verities, and consciously or unconsciously celebrating the sanctive and ever-lasting virtues of self-control, forbearance, devotion, and honor" ("Topics," June 1902).

The *Century*'s editors, then, continued to bear aloft the flame of the ideal in an ever more raucous and changing world. There was no thought of cheapening the magazine to slow the steady drifting away of subscribers. To manifest the eternal verities in print and picture was a duty that must be carried out, even if readership were reduced only to those capable of appreciating and sharing the editorial ideals.

As the *Century*'s circulation declined, its prestige remained high, especially among those who shared its belief in standards. "I don't think there were ever two such beautiful issues of a magazine as the Nov. and Dec. [1899] numbers of *The Century*," Thomas Bailey Aldrich told Gilder. Mark Twain, writing from Vienna in 1899, praised virtually everything in the most recent issue of the magazine and added, "Continue! You are editing very well." Arthur Twining Hadley, president of Yale University, wrote to Johnson in 1900, "I do not know of any medium which is carefully read by so many people as the Century." As late as 1908, Maurice Francis Egan, then U.S. minister to Denmark, remarked that he read all the important American magazines, and "I do not think there is any publication in the world that better lives up to the highest possible standard" than the

Century. That such tributes were deserved is borne out by close examination of the *Century*'s pages from 1900 until Gilder's death in 1909.[14]

In these years, for example, the magazine continued to feature authoritative histories and biographies. John Morley's biography of Oliver Cromwell concluded in October 1900, and the next month J. B. McMaster's serialized study of Daniel Webster began. In 1901 Woodrow Wilson wrote on Edmund Burke and the French Revolution, Grover Cleveland gave his own version of the Venezuelan boundary controversy with Britain in 1895, and Emerson Hough began a three-part series on "The Settlement of the West." From November 1902 through March 1903, Justin H. Smith wrote four articles on the American Revolution. From May through November 1904, S. Weir Mitchell's life of the young George Washington ran serially. Andrew D. White's "Chapter from My Diplomatic Life," stressing his experiences with Otto von Bismarck and in Russia, ran episodically from August 1903 through February 1905.

Beginning in November 1906, the eminent historian Ellis Paxson Oberholtzer contributed serial articles on Jay Cooke, the financier of the Civil War. "The Reminiscences of Lady Randolph Churchill" started its serial run a year later, the former Jennie Jerome relating her experiences in various courts and societies without mentioning her son, Winston. Robert Fulton's life and his invention of the steamboat were recounted by his granddaughter with the aid of manuscripts "never before published and with Plans by Himself Newly Discovered." There were reminiscences of Andrew Johnson and of Rutherford Hayes in the White House, and just before Gilder's death appeared a review of the Hayes administration by James Ford Rhodes—a kind of postscript, the editors remarked, to the author's monumental history of the United States. Gilder's own "Grover Cleveland: A Record of Friendship" began a serial run in August 1909, the author observing in an introductory note that it seemed to him not only "an obligation of friendship but of patriotism to make some record of the personality of Mr. Cleveland as revealed in an intimacy of many years."

And always there was Abraham Lincoln. The more materialistic and pragmatic American life became, the more Gilder seemed to feel the need to hold up the Great Emancipator as the incarnation of the ideal statesman. Every February in Gilder's last years a rash of Lincolniana broke out in the *Century*'s pages, culminating in 1909. The February issue that year had a drawing of Lincoln on the cover, a miniature of him as a frontispiece, and twenty-two Lincoln portraits. Most of these were used to illustrate the lead article—a good one—by Gilder himself on "Lincoln the Leader." Also pictured in this issue was a cast of Lincoln's hands, as drawn by J. Alden Weir from the original made by Leonard W. Volk in 1860. The cast, together with a life mask of Lincoln also by Volk, had come into Weir's possession many years earlier. Visiting Weir in his Paris studio, Gilder had been shocked to see these venerated symbols lying amid the painter's casual clutter. He organized a subscription list to buy these treasures and present them to the Smithsonian Institution (where they still are). Each subscriber received copies in plaster or bronze, depending on the size of his donation.[15]

Symbols and relics of the past were a passion with Gilder. Thus, when the bones of John Paul Jones were discovered in France and returned to America, the magazine celebrated elaborately. In addition to a "rare portrait" of Jones, the September 1905 number featured a poem by Edmund C. Stedman, "Homeward Bound"—referring, of course, to the body of Jones. The cover for October 1905 pictured the battle between *Serapis* and *Bon Homme Richard* and announced, in large capital letters, that the issue contained an article on the recovery of the body written by the man who had conducted the search, former U.S. ambassador to France, Horace Porter. There was also an editorial on this patriotic coup.

Gilder had an obsession with special occasions, such as anniversaries, centennials, and the deaths of notable men. Most of his poems in the *Century* commemorated such occasions—the assassination of William McKinley, the death of Cleveland, the bicentennial of La Salle's great expedition. Gilder seems almost to have assumed the mantle of unofficial poet laureate. He needed little excuse to apostrophize poets and patriots; in October 1905 he contributed to his own magazine an essay on the romance of Robert and Elizabeth Barrett Browning, and in an editorial note he remarked that the article was timely—the 100th anniversary of Mrs. Browning's birth was near! At a time of thronging immigration, booming prosperity, and a sweeping reform movement, Gilder remained as preoccupied as ever with Keats, Dante, and the heroes of the American past.

The elegiac note in Gilder's later work and thought, the search for the sweet essence of past greatness, seems to have deepened after his long illness in 1903 and 1904. A curious instance of this trait is found in his account, in the February 1906 issue, of his discovery of two life masks of Keats and how these had served as illustrations in later editions of that poet's work. Toward the end of this article, Gilder added the irrelevant sentence: "While Mr. Lowell was United States Minister to Madrid he looked up, at my suggestion, Senora Llanos, Keats's sister." The irrelevancy is so glaring as to suggest early senility—yet Gilder's later prose pieces on Lincoln and Cleveland were strongly and lucidly written. The more frequent intrusion of his own name and experiences into the magazine during his later years may have been partly a response to upstarts like Munsey and Bok, who advertised themselves extensively in their own periodicals. It is of some significance, in any case, to the story of the *Century* to note that the past, especially its greatness, had become more fascinating to its editor than the clangorous present.

Despite its editor's passionate devotion to art, the *Century* was not strong in significant art criticism in Gilder's later years; it was its rival, *Scribner's*, which "excelled in its intelligent devotion to the various art movements."[16] But clearly the profuse reproduction in Gilder's magazine of paintings, sketches, drawings, statuary, cathedrals, and monuments was intended for something more than illustration or entertainment. It was intended, after 1900 as before, to bring education, inspiration, and uplift to the reader.

Wherever Gilder found art news—the opening of a new museum or gallery, the unveiling of a new monument, the dedication of a worthy new building—he seized on it to run a pictorial display. The Isabella Stewart Gardner Museum in Boston was hailed, in the January 1904 issue, as "An American Palace of Art." Three years later the installation of the Charles L. Freer collection as part of the Smithsonian was celebrated in prose and picture, some of James McNeill Whistler's paintings being among those illustrated. A photograph of the *Fountain of the Five Great Lakes*, a sculpture designed by Lorado Taft, was featured in July 1906. The four marble *Groups of the Continents*, designed by Daniel Chester French, were given to readers in four striking photo-illustrations (January 1906), with Charles de Kay writing that they were the "strongest work of one of our greatest sculptors." In August 1904, André Castaigne pictured the Louisiana Purchase Exhibition in St. Louis, and an editorial reminded readers that he had contributed a similar series of drawings to the *Century* in celebration of the Columbian Exposition, the Universal Exposition of Paris in 1900, and the Pan-American Exposition in Buffalo in 1901.

Monuments of the past always furnished subjects for illustration. Joseph Pennell did a notable series on French cathedrals in 1906–7, the textual commentary being furnished by his wife, Elizabeth Robins Pennell. Jules Guérin, a Frenchman, provided illustrations for Richard Whiteing's four articles on the chateaus of France in 1905; later, for a series on "The Spell of Egypt," he painted five haunting, full-color frontispieces, beginning with the Sphinx in February 1908. Edith Wharton's "Italian Villas" began in November 1903 and ran episodically until 1907, providing vehicles for many excellent Maxfield Parrish illustrations.

On the American scene, Pennell's striking etchings of New York's skyscrapers, all six in the March 1905 number, became famous. The November 1902 issue led off with seven color paintings by Parrish to illustrate Baker's article on "The Great Southwest." An intermittent but effective series after 1900 were sketches—always in groups of four—showing representative Americans at work; particularly powerful were Thornton Oakley's series on the anthracite coal miners (September 1906) and "In the Railway Yard" (January 1907).

Something less than art, yet charming as illustrations, were Howard Chandler Christy's graceful young ladies. "Glimpses of the Summer Girl" showed her in four sketches playing tennis, motoring, canoeing, and on the beach (August 1905), while Christy's frontispiece in color for August 1906 displayed "The Sweet Girl Graduate."

The artist who most frequently contributed the frontispiece in this period was Sigismond De Ivanowski, who painted two series of portraits especially for the *Century*. One series, painted from life, was of actresses and opera stars costumed for roles with which they were identified: Maude Adams as Peter Pan; Blanche Bates as Madame Butterfly; Ethel Barrymore as Madame Trentino in Clyde Fitch's *Captain Jinks*; Mary Garden as Melisande in Claude Debussy's *Pelléas et Mélisande*; and others. Heroines of fiction provided another Ivanowski series, including imaginary portraits of Becky Sharpe, Lorna Doone, and Jane Eyre. All these frontispieces were in color.[17]

The "American Artists Series" continued in these years—illustrations of individual works by native painters, with commentary usually in the "Open Letters" department. Another series that ran intermittently was "Examples of American Portraiture," and there was still another on Gilbert Stuart's portraits of men.

In short, the *Century*, as its circulation declined, remained a magazine of lavish, high-quality illustrations that were intended to inspire as well as to please. More explicit efforts to elevate public taste were also retained under the general heading of "civic improvement." Sylvester Baxter wrote a series of illustrated articles to demonstrate that street signs and lamps, railway stations, and public squares could be beautiful and functional. Baxter warned, however, that amateur enthusiasts should not enact their own whims. There were "certain standards of beauty that are commonly agreed upon by persons of recognized good taste"; Americans trying to improve their environment should ascertain what these standards were and "conform to them."[18]

But it proved difficult to make Americans understand and conform to such standards. Writing in 1902, Baxter saw the United States as "manifestly at the dawn of a great civic awakening. Never before has there been such a general sense of the value of beauty in the life of a people." And yet a *Century* editorial of August 1909 sadly concluded: "The public simply has not yet learned to honor the function of beauty."[19]

Gilder's enthusiasm for music and drama was equal to his passion for painting and sculpture—he would, a close friend observed, go into rhapsodies about musical performances—but coverage of these art forms was limited, since they did not readily lend themselves to illustration. As in other fields, Gilder's personal and professional roles intertwined when he came to celebrate music. The *Century* was proud of having introduced Ignace Paderewski to America, and that pianist was much at home with the Gilders. So was another famous pianist of that era, Ossip Gabrilowitsch, husband of Twain's daughter Clara—herself a good friend of the Gilders. In Gilder's last year the *Century* published interviews with Paderewski and Gabrilowitsch, the former critical and technical, the latter light-hearted and anecdotal.

From time to time the magazine published personal reminiscences of great composers, usually by critics or concert managers who had known them. Occasionally a new star of concert or opera was singled out for attention. The versatile young James Huneker, for example, hailed "A New Isolde: Olive Fremstad" in November 1908. Richard Aldrich in February 1905 paid tribute to the Boston symphony, which had "raised the standard of orchestral playing in this country immeasurably."

There was no regular department of dramatic criticism in the *Century*, doubtless because there was little theater on the American stage in these years worthy of review. Good theater ranked, in Gilder's mind, with art and music as a medium for embodying ideal standards; individual dramatic artists like the Shakespearian actor Edward H. Southern, Julia Marlowe, and Alla Nazimova were presented in the magazine's columns as inspiring performers. But the United States was "most lacking" in drama, an editorial of 1909 concluded. In contrast to France, the support of the stage in America "largely comes from an unthinking and inartistic world"; the theater had remained a mere amusement, not a vehicle for the projection of artistic standards.[20]

By 1909 Gilder had been trying for some 35 years to educate and inspire his magazine audience through discussion and illustration of the fine arts. The two underlying assumptions were, first, that an elevated public taste would encourage, even demand, more ideal creations, and second, that good art would have a tonic effect on American life. Nothing fired Gilder's indignation more than the tariff on works of art, which had been abolished in 1890 but restored in 1897. Not only should this be ended, said an editorial of December 1908, but the government must adopt a policy of caring for art. A national art commission was needed to help select works for government galleries and to screen out the mediocre. The government "must cease to look upon Art as a luxury of the rich and come to regard it as an educator and refiner, a solace and an inspiration, and the elevating recreation and luxury of the poor."

Toward the end of this long crusade to elevate public taste, the *Century* seemed to despair of the outcome. America undervalued its artists, said an editorial in August 1909. "They do these things better in France, where the service of art is distinguished by the dignity that attaches to formality." By this time both Gilder and Johnson were members of the American Academy of Arts and Letters, founded in 1904—Johnson, appropriately enough, was its secretary. The need to form such an establishment was a sign that the champions of ideal standards were on the defensive. There had once been a discriminating minority in America, the critic William C. Brownell observed a few years later, which had been arbiter of the arts comparable to the Academy in France. But "democracy had enlarged the 'intellectual and aesthetic electorate' until it was useless to hope for standards." This accurately explained the plight of the *Century* by 1909.[21]

Gilder's magazine entered the twentieth century still maintaining that government should be based on right principles and administered by expert, honest men uninfluenced by political considerations. The *Century*'s editors were still unconvinced that new forces, especially the power of big business, made such a system unworkable. Civil service reform, said an editorial in 1901, was still "the fundamental political reform, the success of which is essential to the honest determination of any other political question." Gilder would not acknowledge the role of practical politics in running the government. A friend and admirer of Theodore Roosevelt, he nevertheless was severely critical of the president for appointing unfit men to office—quite oblivious of Roosevelt's need to use patronage in wresting control of his party from Mark Hanna and big business. "American statesmen," argued a 1901 editorial, "should be sustained by public opinion in doing the absolutely right thing." Public men should be encouraged not to do evil in the hope that good might come of it, "but to do right, and right only, that good may come." The assumption that public officials would always recognize the "absolutely right thing" and act accordingly was typical of the *Century*'s failure to cope with the pragmatic world of the twentieth century.[22]

In any case, developing enlightened public opinion to support the right was not easy, since millions of Americans did not read the *Century*. They read instead the inexpensive magazines and the sensationalist press, the latter one of the few objects of Gilder's hatred. The yellow press, the *Century* noted at various times, deluded the workingman, set the poor against the rich, and fouled the political process. Gilder had a public feud with William Randolph Hearst in 1906, when Hearst ran for governor; Gilder labeled Hearst an unscrupulous self-seeker using his *New York Journal* to advance him to the presidency. The *Journal*, in turn, called Gilder a "quivering mouse" and an "incubator chick." In an editorial postmortem on Hearst's unsuccessful campaign, Gilder referred to "the crime of corrupting public opinion."[23]

Not only were right principles jeopardized by the yellow press, demagogues, and pressure groups; the principles themselves were increasingly hard to define unambiguously. The *Century* had long insisted, for example, on the principle of "the right to work" and on this basis had generally criticized labor unions. An editorial in 1902 denounced the "tyranny" of labor unions that took reprisals against those who sought to work without being members. "There are principles which are eternal," said the editorial, "and no immediate and apparent benefit, no so-called 'victories,' can atone for the loss of a principle." (An article on the steel industry in the same issue of the magazine noted that steel laborers worked twelve-hour days, which evidently did not cause the editors to reflect on the cost of principle to the worker.) Yet in March 1904, the *Century* opened its columns to a worker who explained what labor union principles were in the face of big business power. An introductory note by the editor said: "The article which follows gives the views of a stone-cutter on the fundamental principles at stake. They are expressed with such plainness, and the writer's conclusions are drawn with such blunt frankness, that the article has a significance worthy the consideration of those holding opposite opinions." By 1906 the *Century* acknowledged in an editorial that trade unions had accomplished enough good to justify their existence.[24]

In the 1880s and 1890s, the *Century*'s more emotional outbursts against labor unions had been linked to the influence on labor of radical foreign elements, whose words and leadership led to violence. This fear subsided in the prosperous years of the early twentieth century, although there was a temporary recurrence of panic when an American of Polish descent assassinated President McKinley. Commenting on this tragedy, Joseph M. Buckley wrote (November 1901): "The capacity of the United States to assimilate all creeds, nationalities, and races has been overworked in orations, in the press, and in public confidence." In 1904 Henry Cabot Lodge expressed his concern in the *Century* about the new immigrants from southern and eastern Europe, who were "utterly alien to us, not only ethnically, but in civilization, tradition, and habits of thought." But three years later the *Century* carried an article sympathetic to these immigrants, and followed this with an argument by Brander Matthews that these newcomers would be Americanized just as the older immigrants had been.[25]

A more enduring question of assimilation concerned blacks, and on this subject the *Century* generally reflected the conventional wisdom of the time, which held that blacks were inferior to whites. The assertion of inferiority came principally from two sources. One source was from the South. Southerners explained that there was no race problem so long as blacks knew and kept their place. Harry Stillwell Edwards, long a contributor of black dialect stories, summed up his paternalistic argument with this verdict: "We know to the youngest college boy that this country will never in part or in whole be governed or directed by other than the white race." The second source of the argument was from science. Robert Bennett Bean summarized anthropological research in comparative brain measurements (October 1903 and September 1906), concluding that the larger frontal lobe of white people proved their superiority. Charles Francis Adams, after two winters in Egypt and the Sudan, presented a social Darwinist view that the African was inferior to the Anglo-Saxon, whether in Africa or America (May 1906).[26]

Gilder, with his innate decency and concern for justice, did not let these views go unchallenged. In a period when Progressives were virtually ignoring blacks, the *Century* showed a good deal of interest in them. Booker T. Washington, whom the magazine praised as "the Moses of His People," contributed articles on "Heroes in Black Skins" and on efforts by blacks to become respectable homeowners. The *Century* periodically attacked lynchings, sometimes with bitter satire on southern society. To the Adams article mentioned above, the magazine offered an editorial rebuttal, citing Franz Boas as an authority for black achievements in Africa and potential accomplishments in America and concluding that "the race . . . will produce here, as it has done in Africa, its great men; and . . . will contribute its part to the welfare of the community." The editorial argued that the American people owed the blacks a special consideration in education and uplift.[27]

Racism was closely linked with imperialism in these years. The *Century* was not given to assertions of Anglo-Saxon superiority, but this theme did emerge occasionally in its fiction. "The Sign of the Jumma," a short story appearing in 1903, concerned a young subaltern of the Yorkshire Lancers, who takes a furlough to seek treasures of Oriental literature in Himalayan monasteries. Disguised as a monk, he penetrates a secret order, is discovered, and looks into the face of death without a tremor. "He it was of all that company who in the hour of trial had proved his mastery of passion. Here in tableau was shown forth the victory of the West over the East, the victory of Christian philosophy over pantheistic." When the hero is rescued by his regiment, the monks try to kill the man who will leave with their secrets, but swords drive back "the rabble."

Gilder himself remained an anti-imperialist who was reluctant to believe his country could do wrong. He thought there was "a taint of pure sordidness" in the American annexation of the Philippines, but he still felt that "we will yet take a generous position in history and a consistent and righteous one." When American forces left Cuba, Gilder, ignoring the Platt Amendment and the economic leverage that left that island a virtual dependent of the United States, wrote to his brother: "With all its faults, don't you feel proud of your country for letting go of Cuba?" The *Century*, while skeptical of imperialism, never condemned it in an editorial, but it did stand up for the patriotic motives of the anti-imperialists.[28]

In foreign as in domestic affairs, the idealistic editors had no stomach for *realpolitik*. Their exaggerated hopes for civil service reform were paralleled by their faith in international arbitration. "Every arbitration treaty is worth a hundred battleships," said an editorial in February 1904. (One can imagine how Theodore Roosevelt, a *Century* contributor as well as subscriber, felt about that!) The magazine, in fact, took little note of the new and dangerous balance of power in the world and its deadly potential as armaments grew. A striking exception was Stedman's article in May 1908, in which he pointed out the military significance of air power and specifically noted that German zeppelins menaced Britain's supremacy. Alexander Graham Bell, commenting on Stedman's paper, agreed that the nation controlling the air "will ultimately rule the world." An article in February 1909 urged the United States to prepare for aerial defense.

In 1908 the *Century* was involved in a minor cause célèbre. William Bayard Hale, a well-known journalist, interviewed the German emperor, hoping to sell the story to the *New York Times*. The German foreign office, however, cleared the interview only for "the leading magazine of America," and Hale offered it to the *Century* for $1,000. The story contained some of the kaiser's usual indiscreet remarks, but the *Century* was preparing to publish it when a more sensational and anti-British interview with William II appeared in the *London Times*. In the ensuing uproar, the German foreign office asked the *Century* to suppress the earlier interview, and the magazine obliged. The German government reimbursed the *Century* for costs already incurred on plates, printing work, and paper; the proofs were destroyed, and the final sheets already in print—some 33,000 copies—were picked up and taken away in a German cruiser.[29]

The new interest in Asia was, of course, reflected in the *Century*. There were eye-witness accounts of the Boxer Rebellion and a number of articles on Japan. But there was little suggestion in the magazine that an ominous new chapter in American diplomatic history had opened in the Far East. One writer did warn that the Japanese had a will-to-power as well as picturesqueness, but the dominant note, insofar as there was any besides the purely descriptive, was that of missionary opportunity. This was the theme of Bishop H. C. Potter's "Impressions" of Japan as well as other Asian countries that appeared in a series of articles in 1901.[30]

The *Century*'s optimistic idealism concerning the role of the United States in world affairs was perhaps in keeping with the mood of the country, but the editors were much less in tune with events and opinion within the United States. Through the years of a vigorous Progressive movement, the *Century*'s position was detached rather than participatory. The magazine did not join in the muckraking that brought fame to many of its contemporaries, including *McClure's*. Its major series of articles on the trusts was descriptive rather than accusatory and was accompanied by editorial disclaimers of any intent to blame. Even the titles of these articles—"The So-Called Beef Trust," "The So-Called Tobacco Trust"—reflected this approach.[31] To Gilder, who seems to have had little interest in economics, the danger from great industrial and business combinations lay less in their power to control markets and suppress competitors than in their tendency to corrupt the political process by paying off politicians. That was, of course, a fact as well as a danger, but what one misses in the *Century*'s criticism is the sense of an irresistible dynamic by which the power accruing to the giant combinations would inevitably be used. Gilder could not come to terms with the concept of power used pragmatically. He insisted on individual honesty and morality as the cure for national ills. Perhaps this was because the principle of laissez faire could no longer be relied on. The *Century* editorialized on the need to return to "the standard of an earlier time when justice and private probity were more prized and praised than the agglomeration of national or personal wealth."[32]

One index of Gilder's disenchantment with American public life was an increasing reluctance to discuss it in the magazine. According to spot checks, public affairs coverage—exclusive of editorials—had amounted to about 6 percent of the *Century*'s reading matter throughout the 1890s, and to a somewhat lower but still appreciable level in the first years of the new century. By 1906, however, the *Century* had virtually abandoned the treatment of public affairs, while its fiction content soared to an all-time high of 46 percent. There were fewer editorials on public questions, too, and these—apart from those on conservation—were perfunctory.

In the last year of his life, Gilder may have become aware of this shift in emphasis, for the magazine made an apparently conscious effort to resume its critique of great economic and political questions. In December 1908 Andrew Carnegie argued against the need for a protective tariff in an article that predictably stirred much controversy. (Carnegie, who had made part of his fortune in the sale of armor plate, concluded his article with an attack on a big army and a big navy.) In 1909 there were several articles on regulation of railroads or street railways, one on President William H. Taft's opportunity to crack the Solid South, and one by the Honorable Joseph G. Cannon on "The Power of the Speaker." ("Is He an Autocrat or a Servant?" ran the subtitle of Cannon's contribution. Servant, of course, said Uncle Joe.)[33]

The *Century* remained a champion of conservation, a cause in which it had pioneered; most of its advocacy now was in editorials, although John Muir continued to point out beauty spots endangered by private interests.[34] When Roosevelt called a conference of governors in 1908 to consider conservation of national resources, the *Century* published a comprehensive editorial on the subject (November 1907). "We are proud to know," the editors remarked in the February 1908 issue, "that, through an advance copy sent to the President, this article has been contributing to favorable action on what he rightly calls 'probably the most weighty question now before the people of the United States.'" The *Century* had solicited comments from the governors on this editorial and printed responses from several of them (February 1908), most of which praised not only the cause but the magazine.

Despite its interest in conservation and in municipal reform, the *Century* was never caught up in the Progressive movement. The moral tone of Progressivism should have appealed to Gilder, and he certainly admired both Roosevelt and Taft. Gilder was, however, a conservative, and one suspects he would have favored Taft over Roosevelt in 1912. In any case he did not seem to equate the accomplishments of Progressives with victories for idealism. When in the last year of Gilder's life, the *Century* looked for examples of idealism in government, it could cite only the international copyright bill, the return of Boxer indemnity money to China, and "our retirement from control of Cuba."[35]

The *Century*'s fiction after 1900 was undistinguished, but it is doubtful that this had much to do with the magazine's loss of preeminence, for its competitors did little better. "The years from 1902 to 1912 form the single most dreary decade in the nation's letters," Larzer Ziff has written. And Howells in 1910 remarked that in fiction and drama "there never was a more imbecile time, perhaps." Gilder, after welcoming the new realism of Howells and Henry James, had been repelled by the more sordid themes of the younger generation. He had rejected Stephen Crane's "Maggie, a Girl of the Streets" and "The Red Badge of Courage." Frank Norris was represented in the *Century* by several suitably moral potboilers among his short stories, but his novels would have been unacceptable.[36] In any case, Crane was dead by 1900 and Norris by 1902. James labored on, his artistry recognized, but "the laborious beetle flight" of his prose was not suited to magazines.[37] Nobody, certainly not the *Century*, would print Theodore Dreiser's early novels. Dreiser did try out a short story on the editors, who rejected it, whereupon the impulsive author charged them with not having read his story. After Johnson wrote to dispute this, Dreiser replied contritely that he had received both attention and courtesy from the *Century*. "A kind answer turneth away wrath!" was Gilder's notation on this letter; to which Johnson added complacently, "Yes, and a gentle snub bringeth the young man to his senses."[38]

The serialization of London's "The Sea Wolf," for which Gilder paid $4,000, was evidently a conscious effort to add a masculine tone to the magazine. The wary Gilder, noting in the author's synopsis that two lovers were left alone on an island for some time, warned London that the magazine retained the right to modify the manuscript. This comparatively bold venture by the editors evidently paid off, for the serial—which began its run in January 1904—had a dramatic impact on the reading public.[39]

For the most part, however, sentimentalists and romanticists dominated the *Century*'s serialized novels after 1900. Many of them were contributed by women: Alice Hegan Rice ("Sandy,

Mr. Opp"); Kate Douglas Wiggins ("Rose o' the River"); Mrs. Humphrey Ward ("Fenwick's Career"); Frances Hodgson Burnett ("The Shuttle"); and "Mary Adams," a *nom de plume* for Elizabeth Stuart Phelps ("The Confessions of a Wife"). The alternative was the historical romance, with Mitchell continuing as the *Century*'s mainstay. His "A Diplomatic Adventure," a story of French espionage against the American embassy during the Civil War, began in February 1906, and "The Red City," about Philadelphia during the second Washington administration, appeared two years later. Irving Bacheller's "D'ri and I," a novel set in the St. Lawrence valley during the War of 1812, began its serial run in March 1901. The *Century* also serialized an adventure story by A. E. W. Mason, "Running Water," beginning in August 1906.

Short stories—which became noticeably shorter during this period—evidenced more variety and occasionally more merit. James appeared in December 1900 ("Broken Wings"); Howells in February 1901 ("At Third Hand"); Twain in November 1901 ("Two Little Tales"); George W. Cable in August 1901 ("Pere Raphael"); Kipling in August 1905 ("An Habitation Enforced"). London contributed several short stories, mostly about the Yukon gold rush. Young Willa Cather made her *Century* debut in August 1907 with "The Willing Muse." Hamlin Garland remained an occasional contributor. But most of the stories were no more than anecdotes. The stream of local color diminished but persisted, with divers country folk portrayed in their regional dialects and their rustic virtues. Dialect stories of blacks continued, Edwards appearing most frequently as their author. The New York melting pot provided milieu and themes for other stories. One regular was Margherita Arline Hamm, who wrote about the Egyptian colony in Manhattan. An unusually good short story was Israel Zangwill's "The Yiddish 'Hamlet'" (January 1906), very knowledgeable about the Yiddish theater and its audience, with tough-minded characters and sharp dialogue.[40]

The search for ideality in American literature had led nowhere, unless the reiteration of old values by stereotyped characters could be accepted as a form of idealism. The stereotypes were unchanging. In October 1903 there appeared a short story about an Irish steamboat engineer who is fired for drunkenness but who takes over the flaming engine room during a fire and, at the cost

of his own life, saves all hands. In the same issue another drunk-
ard, this one a Scot, redeems himself by saving a trawler during
a storm. In a story of the Boxer Rebellion appearing in September
1904, Corporal Sweeney deserts his unit, flees across the desert,
is caught in a sandstorm, and gives up his life to save a Chinese
boy. Examples of self-sacrifice apparently gave the readers, or
at any rate the editors, a warm glow.

Gilder, once caught up in the exciting prospect of blending the
new realism with ideality, had ceased to cope seriously with
contemporary fiction. After 1900 the *Century* attempted no regular reviews of current literature, and Gilder's few literary comments merely rationalized the escapist stories of the time. In
"Topics" for April 1903, he remarked that the success of writers
like Wiggins and Rice showed that Americans now wanted "the
genial" in literature. The tragic has its audience, he said. "But
in the rush and strain of modern life is the distinctly genial especially valued." Once concerned about his magazine's heavy
emphasis on dialect stories, he now justified their continuance
by noting that the history of dialect went back to William Shakespeare and was valuable as history and folklore.[41]

With an increasing interest in municipal affairs and his continued absorption in the fine arts, Gilder seemed to have yielded
much of the editorial responsibility for fiction to Johnson. Gilder
wanted to take up Edith Wharton. He saw her as a fine writer
on the eve of popular success whose fame the *Century* could build
up and share. But Johnson objected, and Gilder deferred to his
associate's feelings. (Johnson's antipathy to Wharton may have
been personal. He was present one evening in March 1903, when
she was a guest of the Bernard Berensons in Florence. Mrs.
Berenson recorded in her diary that Wharton's behavior had been
hateful—she had been rude, self-absorbed, venomous.) Gilder
was on leave at the time, suffering a long illness, and perhaps
was reluctant to overrule the man he had left in charge. Yet one
gains the impression that Gilder in his late years never re-asserted
his control in determining what fiction to admit to the magazine.
Wharton was represented in the *Century* only by her essays on
"Italian Villas" and by a single short story. It is hard to conceive
of a novelist better suited to the *Century* than she, for she had
a sophisticated awareness of changes in society and yet wrote

about them with concern for traditional values. The case is symptomatic of Johnson's stubborn insistence on his standards even at the cost of the magazine's vitality.[42]

Poetry remained the literary medium through which Gilder and his genteel contemporaries best expressed the ideal, so it is not surprising that Gilder's magazine carried more verse than its new competitors. Most poems continued to apostrophize abstract beauty or its embodiment in statues, cathedrals, and other poems, especially those of Keats. Women still predominated among the *Century*'s verse writers, and the male submissions were often so dainty and derivative that one writer in the magazine, Lee Wilson Dodd, urged his fellow-poets to sing in a manlier way:

> Far better mute
> Were the emasculate lute,
> Far better silent, than thus chirping on
> An echo of things gone—[43]

But Gilder, who had published Walt Whitman's poems on the average of one a year for many years, was willing to listen to new accents and to a younger generation of poets. Contributors after 1900 included Edward Arlington Robinson ("Uncle Ananias," August 1905); William Vaughan Moody (a seven-page fragment from his poetic drama, "The Death of Eve," December 1906); Joaquin Miller ("Missouri"—a tribute to the river, February 1907); Edward Markham ("The Jugglers of Touraine," a long Christmas poem, December 1907); and the young Harriet Monroe ("A Power Plant," about a turbine engine station in Chicago, February 1906). Paul Laurence Dunbar, the distinguished black poet, usually contributed dialect verse, but his "The Forest Greeting" (September 1903) was serious and powerful.

Its poetry, indeed, was the principal feature that entitled the *Century* to think of itself as a literary periodical. Occasional literary reminiscences and unpublished letters from major figures like William Makepeace Thackeray, Sir Walter Scott, and Edgar Allan Poe hardly compensated for the absence of serious and systematic literary criticism. Among the highlights of these years were excerpts (1905–7) from Horace Traubel's manuscript, "With

Walt Whitman in Camden." But it is fair to say that the *Century*'s literary pretensions were overwhelmed by its attention to the fine arts. This remained Gilder's passion, and there was never any weakening in his drive to make each issue both a celebration of the arts and a work of art in itself. In the latter aim he surely succeeded. The printing and illustration remained outstanding. Bound volumes in libraries attest to this, and more than one veteran of the publishing industry has recalled what sheer pleasure it was to page through and handle what may have been the most beautiful general periodical ever published regularly in this country.

Rather surprisingly for such a decorous publication, the *Century* maintained a high level in its humor columns. George Ade contributed "The Modern Fable of the Old Fox and the Young Fox" (March 1902) and Finley Peter Dunn wrote "A Little Essay on Books and Reading by Mr. Dooley" (May 1902). The best regular feature was the light verse, which appeared in the long-standing department, "In Lighter Vein." This was consistently good. In addition to Ellis Parker Butler and John Kendrick Bangs, who were regular contributors, new names began to appear, which would become familiar, some even famous, later in the twentieth century: Carolyn Wells, Arthur Guiterman, Wallace Irvin, Alfred Damon Runyon, and Franklin P. Adams. "F.P.A." wrote to Johnson: "My minimum wage is a dollar a line. I don't say that it's worth it, but that's what these prodigal magazines are paying me. And my Children Cry for Bread."[44]
In four consecutive numbers in 1908, Oliver Herford's verse and drawings about "The Mythological Zoo" anticipated Dr. Zeuss. In September 1908 Sinclair Lewis made his first contribution to the *Century*—a short, punning rhyme about "My Lady's Maid" who, after watching her mistress apply cosmetics, professed to know how "My Lady's made." The editors were justified in keeping and even expanding somewhat the space available for such innocent merriment.

The genteel writers and critics usually had a limited interest in science and technology, but the *Century*'s coverage in these fields was at least adequate in the first decade of the twentieth century. Zoology, natural history, and astronomy were the subjects most frequently addressed, perhaps because they lent themselves to pictorial illustration. Henry Fairfield Osborn, curator of the American Museum of Natural History, and a professor at Columbia University, was a star contributor. He wrote on "Fossil Wonders of the West," including the remains of the dinosaur, on the evolution of the horse in America, and later, after leading an expedition to Africa, on "Hunting the Ancestral Elephant."[45]

In astronomy the leading writers were Timothy Pickering of the Harvard Observatory, who discussed the moon, and Percival Lowell, director of the Lowell Observatory at Flagstaff, Arizona, who in 1907 and 1908 gave the magazine a series of six articles on "Mars as the Abode of Life." The canals on Mars, Lowell felt, could not be natural and must be the product of intelligent life.

Famous individual scientists both wrote and were written about in the *Century*. In January 1904, an article by a physicist from Cornell University on "The New Element Radium" was followed by Mme. Marie Curie's discussion of "Radium and Radioactivity." Luther Burbank—once considered a charlatan, the editors pointed out—was praised in an article and himself contributed descriptions of his experiments in scientific horticulture, as well as a speculative piece urging eugenic experiments to improve the human race.[46]

Frank J. Sprague, father of the trolley car, described his early experiments in one article and summarized the present state of the art in another. The September 1908 issue featured "The Wright Brothers Aeroplane," written by Orville and Wilbur Wright, and was prefaced by an editorial comment which claimed that this was "the first popular account of their experiments prepared by the inventors."[47]

There was no hint in the *Century* of the revolution in physics that was sweeping away the Newtonian universe, probably because the new physics had not reached the stage where its concepts could be popularized. Still, there is a certain poignancy in considering that the absolutes for which the *Century* stood were being undermined by relativity in Gilder's last days.

Brief mention should be made of contributions to the *Century* after 1900 that are not readily categorized. James Cardinal Gibbons favored the *Century* when he chose to publish. His contributions included essays on "The Moral Aspects of Suicide" (January 1907), on divorce (May 1909), and on "The Character of Leo XIII," in a number (September 1903) that had a drawing of the pope as frontispiece. The January 1907 issue led off with an essay by Roosevelt on the ancient Irish sagas, for which Gilder paid the president of the United States $1,000.[48]

Albert Bigelow Paine specialized in New York City scenes, among them "The New Coney Island" (August 1904) and an article on pawnbrokers' auctions in the city. Fanciful and illustrated prose-poems by Maurice Maeterlinck appeared in December 1903 and January 1904. John Burroughs continued to write for the magazine, usually about animals, and so did Muir. Four numbers during 1905 carried articles about the Associated Press by its manager, Melville E. Stone. Dr. Wilfred T. Grenfield wrote about his experiences as surgeon and missionary in Labrador (June 1909).

Gilder, who did charitable work with the blind, had great admiration for Helen Keller, whom he had known since her childhood. Keller was a frequent contributor of both verse and essays and was featured on the cover for January 1905. The editor's introduction to her article on "Sense and Sensibility" (February 1908) is an example both of Gilder's admiration for her and of the decorous, stilted accents in which the editors described special features: "In the maturity of her intellectual powers, Miss Helen Keller had concluded to give to her friends and the world the most intimate and detailed account she has yet prepared of her experiences in an existence where, deprived of the senses of sight and hearing, she is restricted to the three other senses of touch, taste, and smell." Her contribution was "unique in literature."

These highlights of the *Century*'s contents after 1900 show that, despite undistinguished fiction and a weakened voice in public affairs, there was no appreciable decline in the monthly's quality and standards, even though its circulation and its revenues were dropping. This record also is indicative of Gilder's steadfast editorial vision and purpose as he faced adversity and changing public tastes. Nor was the editorial vision a narrow one. Although the *Century* continued to exemplify high culture, it was not Gilder's aim to produce a magazine for a wealthy elite. Five years after Gilder's death the Century Company did indeed stress a appeal to class in its promotional advertisements: "THE CENTURY CLASS is the typical American class, the kind of people who travel, motor, invest and buy all those good things that $^{44}/_{45}$ths of the people think of as luxuries."[49] This was not exactly the appeal to the solid middle class with which Holland had begun the monthly, but in Gilder's lifetime the aim remained to win and uplift the educated middle-class audience. Only a relatively few articles on horse-breeding, hunting, and racing could be said to appeal essentially to the leisured rich. Notations and words of "Old College Songs," with accompanying drawings, began naturally enough with those of Harvard, Yale, and Princeton universities, but the second series featured the military academies, West Point and Annapolis.[50]

Nor did Gilder intend to concentrate his magazine's attractions on the "effete" East. He held to his purpose of producing a truly national magazine. The South continued to provide many of the *Century*'s writers and themes, and Gilder made a special effort to give the West adequate representation. The June 1904 issue was a "Western Number" in which, the editors pointed out "every trans-Allegheny State and territory is represented, either by topic or by contributor." Except for London's "The Sea Wolf," continuing as a serial, every piece of fiction had a western locale.

The *Century* made a studied effort to interest the rural areas. In October 1904, Gilbert Grosvenor described for readers a method developed by the Department of Agriculture for "inoculating" the soil with nitrogen-producing bacteria. "No single paper THE CENTURY has ever printed has called forth so much inquiry from those directly engaged in tilling the soil," the editors remarked a few months later. The editors promised—and delivered—other articles of interest to farmers on fighting disease among herds and improving breeds, on saving fruit crops from insects, on how to make a living out of a single acre, and a series on how to educate farm youth and how to make farming more attractive to young people. Beginning in August 1908, there was also a series of illustrations called "Scenes from American Rural Life."[51]

Gilder seems to have been relatively successful in holding his trans-Allegheny readers. The earliest figures available for the geographical distribution of the *Century*'s subscriptions and sales are for 1914, but it seems safe to presume a considerable continuity in the spread of readership in the less than five years following Gilder's death. These figures show that of a total circulation of 92,000, only 34,000 sales were in the Middle Atlantic states and another 14,000 in New England, while there were nearly 11,000 in the Far West and nearly 26,000 in the Midwest from Ohio to Kansas.[52]

It is true that not all midwestern readers appreciated Gilder's portrayal of the ideal through celebration of history and the fine arts. The editor of the Topeka, Kansas, *Daily Capital* wrote in 1905: "You doubtless think things are pretty dull here in Topeka. If you do you ought to read the current [August] number of the Century magazine."[53] (The *Century* did seem to undergo a mild slump in editorial excellence at this time, probably due to Gilder's lengthy illness preceding it.) But the charge that the *Century* had grown dull in comparison with its new competitors was not confined to one region. In New York, as in Kansas, readers were tiring of Gilder's efforts to inspire them through the traditional; but nothing could stop Gilder, while he lived, from continuing the effort.

It is the thesis of this study that the decline of the *Century* was fated by the erosion of the "eternal verities" for which it stood. But certain rigidities in its editorial and business management undoubtedly hastened its loss of preeminence. The death of Smith on the eve of the challenge from new competition was surely a crucial factor in the *Century*'s ultimate failure to meet that challenge. Smith, like McClure, was usually ahead of his competitors. (It is interesting to note that Smith fired young McClure from the Century Company because, instead of performing his routine duties, he put in his time dreaming up new departures in publishing for the attention of his boss. Smith advised McClure that he would do better to start his own business.)[54] It cannot, of course, be known precisely what Smith would have done had he lived in the age of the new competition. That he would have done something effective, either to enliven the *Century* or to produce revenues through other publishing ventures, is a safe conjecture. In times of crisis, the editors always asked themselves, "What would Roswell Smith have done?" They never found the answer.

In one respect Smith's foresight did not reach far enough. When in his lifetime and again in his will he had arranged for key personnel of the editorial, art, and business departments to acquire stock in the Century Company, he guaranteed the continuity of a successful publishing team. As the years went by, however, this very continuity blocked the advent of fresh talent into the editorial and policy-making councils. Holland had benefited from an energetic young Gilder. The aging Gilder had no such galvanizing force at his right hand; he had, instead, Johnson.[55]

More than Gilder, Johnson epitomized genteel values. His idealism, more than Gilder's, had crystallized around traditional forms and hardened into prejudice. The postimpressionist painters, to him, were not artists at all but charlatans degrading the public taste. Van Wyck Brooks left a description of Johnson— many years after his editorship—rising at an Institue of Arts and Letters dinner "to read aloud a poem of Sandburg's, on shaving in a pullman car, to show that the election of such a man would represent the ruin of the ancient faith." Johnson was the last man likely to urge any change in the *Century*'s customary mixture or to give an editorial home to any new movement in literature and the arts.[56]

Gilder's poor health in the last ten years of his life surely weakened his editorial grip and increased Johnson's influence. As early as 1879–80 Gilder had been forced to leave the magazine for fifteen months, most of which time he spent in Europe, suffering from nervous and physical exhaustion.[57] He seems to have flourished in the 1880s, but in the 1890s his correspondence is studded with references to minor ailments. In February 1895, for instance, finding himself "under the weather" while in Washington, he moved, at President Cleveland's insistence, into the White House, where he was "nursed and doctored for several days." In 1899 he wrote: "I have been over-working again—and am sent away for a shorter 'let up.'"[58]

In 1903 Gilder was seriously ailing again. He told Roosevelt that "inflammation of the cells of the muscles is my infernal affliction." He was ill all that fall and winter, went to Florida for recuperation in February 1904, and in December 1904 was just getting back to his desk.[59] He always had an inability to relax—all his holidays were enforced by doctors. He had acquired a summer place near Marion, Massachusetts, where Stanford White had designed another Studio for Gilder and and his wife and where he enjoyed the company of neighbors such as Cleveland and Joe Jefferson and visits from literary and artistic acquaintances, including James. It was a pleasant society at Marion, but Gilder always carried with him a briefcase full of manuscripts and the cares of the office. He did not know how to rest, and he was simply burnt out at the age of sixty-five.

One may wonder whether Gilder's illnesses and nervous exhaustion signified a kind of psychic crisis. Was there a subconscious sense of personal failure associated with his inability to keep his magazine preeminent, to make his ideals prevail in American life, or even, a loss of faith in the ideals themselves? If Gilder nursed a secret burden of anxiety and unhappiness, it was probably related to his loss of religion. His agnosticism, which he acknowledged in 1905, did not come easily. He revered the memory of his minister-father, and no doubt experienced guilt feelings as his own faith slipped away. He was quick to rebuke any potential contributor who wrote anything offensive about Christianity. His poem "The Parthenon by Moonlight" (1897) contained the line: "For Beauty is of God, and God is true." As late as 1903, the Gilder family held Sunday services at their Massachusetts farm—although these consisted principally of "the singing of hymns, accompanied by the children's violins and assisted by their music teacher on the piano."[60] It is clear that Gilder was reluctant to relinquish his religious beliefs, and once he did, he may have recognized subconsciously that with the removal of his faith in God, the foundation of his faith in ideals was also shaken. How could one be sure of "eternal verities" if one could not be sure of God?

Yet Gilder did not seem to be affected with the advanced pessimism and disillusion that beset so many of the genteel poets and critics—Henry Adams and Charles Eliot Norton, for example—in the late nineteenth and early twentieth centuries. To the last he enjoyed work and society, worshipped beauty, and proclaimed his idealistic faith as stoutly as ever. He wrote to a young poet in 1907:" I *know* that the only sane aim of life is the noble, the well-nigh unattainable best." His last letter, written to his daughter hardly an hour before his death, extolled the glories of Shakespeare, whom he had been reading in his sickbed. Even recumbent he pursued the ideal, and it was this pursuit that wore out his nerves and his body. George Santayana's observation is apropos: "To understand oneself is the classic form of consolation; to elude oneself is the romantic." Gilder had no interest in systematic philosophy. He forgot himself and followed the gleam like the romantic he was, and whatever inner doubts he may have felt did not appear in the *Century*.[61]

A more pertinent question is what effect Gilder's prolonged health problems had on his magazine and its fortunes. Every Gilder absence tended to entrench Johnson's editorial influence. Johnson's successful veto of Wharton as a major fiction contributor has already been noted. There are other signs that Gilder relaxed his editorial grip in these later years. He seems, for example, to have written fewer editorials. And a great deal of his presumably diminishing energy went to noneditorial work. His reminiscences of Cleveland and his shorter work on Lincoln were both written in his later years. Since Gilder always considered himself first a poet, there is no likelihood that he reduced the hours he spent on his verse. Although he tried to curtail his social and cultural obligations, or at least to decline new ones, he was still caught up in many affairs—for example, he always planned the literary dinners Carnegie liked to sponsor on his periodic retreats from Skibo Castle to America.[62]

Finally, there is the hint of the editor emeritus in the tone of Gilder's own late contributions to the magazine, a preoccupation with the past that seemed not only historical but also personal: memories of Cleveland, commemorative poems, the recollection of how he procured the death mask of Keats. Conversely, there is the absence in his later correspondence of any excitement about new discoveries in fiction. There is no suggestion of an editor looking—as the younger Gilder had looked—for new worlds to conquer.

It can he said with some assurance that Johnson's editorial

influence, always strong, was stronger after 1903, and that meant more rigidity of editorial policy in the face of a changing world. And yet the decision, renewed month by month, to retain the *Century*'s essential characteristics was surely as much Gilder's as Johnson's. Together they ignored, rejected, or deplored many of the new currents in American life. It is doubtful if they understood the deeper forces that were undermining their nineteenth-century values. Gilder was personally friendly with William James, and the *Century* once quoted him approvingly, but otherwise the editors paid no attention to this prophet of a new empiricism which brushed aside the absolute values of religion and of idealistic philosophy. They were probably unaware that James had, in Santayana's words, given a "rude shock" to the genteel tradition within which they lived.[63]

In 1904 Sarah Platt Decker, president of the General Federation of Woman's Clubs, told the assembled ladies: "Dante is dead. He has been dead for several centuries, and I think it is time that we dropped the study of his *Inferno* and turned our attention to our own."[64] Gilder did not agree. Brander Matthews recalled meeting the editor at a time when the *Century* was publishing two series of papers, one on Dante and one on the wanderings of Ulysses. When Matthews expressed doubt whether the average reader would have any interest in such articles, Gilder responded, "When I can't print that sort of thing in the *Century*, I'll resign!" Nobody asked Gilder to resign, and nobody altered his will to project ideal values through his magazine.[65]

So the *Century* continued on its course, a stately argosy bearing treasures of the past out of the nineteenth century into the twentieth, to dwindle, to disappear—but to be remembered.

Richard Watson Gilder died November 18, 1909, of angina pectoris—the same disease that had killed Holland—and, after a simple but impressive funeral, was buried at Bordentown, New Jersey. Andrew Carnegie, coming into New York later by ferry could only think, "Gilder is not there, Gilder is not there." The tributes to Gilder then and in subsequent weeks justified the *Nation*'s comment that "rarely has any single New Yorker been beloved in so many places and circles." Gilder's life, said the

Nation, was a "message to the world, that, for all its shortcomings, in its finest citizenship America remains a land of lofty ideals."[66] That was a fitting epitaph for the editor as well as the citizen.

NOTES

1. *N. W. Ayer and Son's Directory of Newspapers and Periodicals* (New York, 1887), p. 81; Frank Luther Mott, *A History of American Magazines*, 5 vols. (Cambridge, Mass., 1930–68), 3:475; L. Frank Tooker, *The Joys and Tribulations of an Editor* (New York, 1924), 306.

2. Frederick Lewis Allen, "The American Magazine Grows Up," *Atlantic Monthly*, 180 (Nov. 1947):78–80, and Frank S. Presbrey, *The History and Development of Advertising* (Garden City, N.Y., 1929), 470–71.

3. Peter Lyon, *Success Story: The Life and Times of S. S. McClure* (New York, 1963), 74, 133–37, 251; Frank A. Munsey, "The Making and Marketing of Munsey's Magazine," *Munsey's Magazine*, 22 (Dec. 1899):323–43; Robert Underwood Johnson, *Remembered Yesterdays* (Boston, 1923), 138.

4. Lyon, *McClure*, 146, and Mott, *Magazines*, 4:41.

5. Johnson to Gilder, Aug. 30, 1899, CC, and Mott, *Magazines*, 3:475. See Table 5.

6. Gilder to "Dear Molly" [Foote?], Nov. 30, 1899, GP.

7. Edward W. Bok, *The Americanization of Edward Bok* (New York, 1922), 156–80, 190–203, and James Playsted Wood, *Magazines in the United States: Their Social and Economic Influence* (New York, 1949), 109–20.

8. Gilder to McClure, Dec. 29, 1902, GP, and Lyons, *McClure*, 134.

9. Ellery Sedgwick, *The Happy Profession* (Boston, 1946), 107–8; Mott, *Magazines*, 4:153; J. Henry Harper, *The House of Harper: A Century of Publishing in Franklin Square* (New York, 1912), 202–3; *Nation*, 48 (Apr. 18, 1889): 325–26.

10. Mott, *Magazines*, 4:153.

11. Editorials, Oct. 1899 and Jan. 1899; advertising section, Nov. 1895, pp. 29–31; W. L. Fraser, "Open Letter," Jan. 1895; Alpheus P. Cole and Margaret Wood Cole, *Timothy Cole: Wood-Engraver* (New York, 1935), 96–97.

12. Editorial, Feb. 1897.

13. Steiglitz proposed the article and the reproduction of "pictorial photographs," saying, "Recognition from the 'Century' is worth much to those battling for the cause." Steiglitz to Gilder, Mar. 15, 1902, CC. (A recent check by the Manuscript Division of the New York Public Library did not locate this letter in the Century Collection, but I do affirm that it was there when I took notes from it some years ago.)

14. Aldrich to Gilder, Dec. 11, 1899, Aldrich Papers, Harvard Uni-

versity, Cambridge, Mass.; Twain to Gilder, Feb. 2, 1899, Egan to
Gilder, June 6, 1908, GP; Hadley to Johnson, May 14, 1900, CC.

15. Louise Hall Tharpe, *Saint-Gaudens and the Gilded Era* (Boston,
1969), 188.

16. Mott, *Magazines*, 4:146.

17. The two Ivanowski series alternated, beginning with "Becky
Sharpe" in Sept. 1906 and extending to May 1908.

18. Baxter, "The Beautifying of Village and Town," Apr. 1902.

19. Baxter, "A Great Civic Awakening in America," June 1902. In
launching this series of articles, the editors remarked that "the advancing
tide of civic improvement now passing over the United States" was
not only aesthetic but "a phase of patriotism." Editorial, Mar. 1902.

20. Editorial, Aug. 1909.

21. Brownell, *Standards* (New York, 1917), quoted in May, *The End
of American Innocence: A Study of the First Years of Our Time, 1912–1917*
(New York, 1959), 352.

22. Gilder to Dr. [Lyman?] Abbott, Nov. 14 and Nov. 17, 1902, to
Roosevelt, Nov. 21, 1902, GP; editorials, May and June 1901.

23. Editorial, Jan. 1907; Gilder to the Editor of the *New York Times*,
Oct. 16, 1906 (published Oct. 18). Both the *Times* (Oct. 19, 1906) and
the *New York Tribune* (Oct. 29, 1906) defended Gilder and attacked
Hearst.

24. Editorials, Dec. 1902 and Oct. 1906.

25. Lodge, Jan. 1904, and Matthews, July 1907.

26. Edwards, "The Negro and the South," June 1906.

27. Editorial, Sept. 1903; Washington, Sept. 1903 and May 1908.

28. Gilder to President Arthur Twining Hadley of Yale, May 24,
1902, to Joseph B. Gilder, May 21, 1902, GP; editorial, Apr. 1902.

29. Johnson, *Remembered Yesterdays*, 229–37, and William Webster
Ellsworth, *A Golden Age of Authors: A Publisher's Recollection* (New
York, 1919), 283–93.

30. Richard Barry, "Underlying Japanese Humanities," Sept. 1907.

31. The overall title of the series, which began in Nov. 1902, was
"The Great Business Combinations of Today." Henry Loomis Nelson,
writing on "The So-Called Steel Trust" for Dec. 1902, said: "It is no
part of the purpose of this article to assist in a search for evils the
existence of which is often asserted, but which are difficult to define."

32. Editorial, Oct. 1903.

33. Cannon, June 1909.

34. See, for example, Muir, "The Endangered Valley," Jan. 1909.

35. Editorial, June 1909.

36. Larzer Ziff, *The American 1890s: Life and Times of a Lost Generation*
(New York, 1966), 228; Howells quoted in Edwin H. Cady, *The Realist
at War: The Mature Years, 1885–1920, of William Dean Howells* (Syracuse,
N.Y., 1958), 236; R. W. Stallman, *Stephen Crane: A Biography* (New
York, 1968), 91, cited in John Tomsich, *A Genteel Endeavor: American*

Culture and Politics in the Gilded Age (Stanford, Calif., 1971), 122. One of Norris's *Century* stories, "The Passing of Cock-Eye Blacklock" (July 1902), concerned a man killed by a stick of dynamite which a dog had retrieved. Jack London published a similar story at about the same time, leading to mutual suspicions of plagiarism. It developed that both men had based their stories on a news account of an actual event. Warren French, *Frank Norris*, Twayne U.S. Authors Series no. 25 (New York, 1962), 31.

37. The phrase is attributed to John Addington Symonds by Leon Edel, *Henry James: The Treacherous Years, 1895–1901* (New York, 1969), 124. "*Scribner*, the *Century*, the *Cosmopolitan*, will have nothing to say to me—above all for fiction." James wrote Howells in 1895, ibid., 95.

38. Dreiser to Johnson, Jan. 16, 1900, with notations, CC.

39. Robert Baltrop, *Jack London: The Man, the Writer, the Rebel* (London, 1976), 100–1, 106–8.

40. London: "Trust," Jan. 1908; "To Build a Fire," Aug. 1908; "The Seed of McCoy," Apr. 1909. Garland: "Her Mountain Lover," serial beginning Dec. 1900; "Two Stories of Oklahoma," June 1904; "A Night Raid at Eagle River," Sept. 1908.

41. Editorial, Feb. 1902.

42. Herbert F. Smith, *Richard Watson Gilder*, Twayne U.S. Authors Series no. 166 (New York, 1970), 154–55; R. W. B. Lewis, *Edith Wharton* (New York, 1975), 269; Wharton, "The Choice," Nov. 1908.

43. Dodd, "Frail Singers of Today," Sept. 1905.

44. Adams to Johnson, Apr. 24, 1907?, CC.

45. Jan. 1905, Nov. 1904, and Oct. 1907, respectively. Horses had been quite common in America before they mysteriously disappeared, to be re-introduced by the Spanish.

46. William S. Harwood, "A Wonder-Worker of Science," Mar. and Apr. 1905, and Burbank, "The Training of the Human Plant," May 1906.

47. Sprague, "The Electric Railway," July 1905, and "Later Experiments and Present State of the Art," Aug. 1905.

48. Maurice F. Egan, *Recollections of a Happy Life* (New York, 1924), 209. Egan was the middle-man in the transaction.

49. *Century* promotion sheet, 1914, CC.

50. "Old College Songs," June 1908 and June 1909.

51. Editorial, June 1905. L. H. Bailey, director of the College of Agriculture, Cornell University, contributed four articles in 1906–7 on educating farm youth. James M. Hill, president of the Great Northern Railway, wrote on "Government Model Farms" for Dec. 1906.

52. Circulation sheet, 1914, CC.

53. W. D. Ross (superintendent of schools, Jefferson County, Kans.) to the Century Co., Sept. 29, 1905, CC.

54. Lyon, *McClure*, 48–50.

55. See Smith, *R. W. Gilder*, 154.

56. Robert E. Spiller, ed., *The Van Wyck Brooks–Lewis Mumford Letters: The Record of a Literary Friendship, 1921–1963* (New York, 1970), 97–98. In *Remembered Yesterdays*, 145, Johnson noted: "We gave this post-impressionist school, if school it can be called, the justice of printing a dozen or more examples of work by its most prominent practitioners, which might be called childish were this not an imputation on the work of the average child."

57. Rosamond Gilder, ed., *Letters of Richard Watson Gilder* (Boston, 1916), 88–99, hereafter cited as Gilder, *Gilder*. Characteristically, however, Gilder, as his correspondence showed, spent much of his time in England running down material for his magazine.

58. Gilder in "Grover Cleveland: A Record of Friendship," Sept. 1909, pp. 694–95, and Gilder to J. M. Bruce, Dec. 19, 1899, GP.

59. Gilder to Roosevelt, Nov. 7, 1903, to T. B. Aldrich, July 14, 1904, to Chester E. Lowell, Dec. 13, 1904, GP.

60. Gilder to the Reverend Robert P. Kreitler, Apr. 1, 1903, GP.

61. Gilder to George Silvester Viereck, June 24, 1907, quoted in Smith, *R. W. Gilder*, 145–47; Gilder, *Gilder*, 497–98; George Santayana, "The Genteel Tradition in American Philosophy," in Douglas L. Wilson, ed., *The Genteel Tradition: Nine Essays by George Santayana* (Cambridge, Mass., 1967), 37–64; Tomsich, *Genteel Endeavor*, 8. Here and elsewhere in his study, Tomsich attributes the despair of the genteel authors as a group to their loss of religious faith.

62. Joseph Frazier Wall, *Andrew Carnegie* (New York, 1970), 952.

63. Editorial, Feb. 1910, and Wilson, ed., *The Genteel Tradition*, 53–54.

64. Quoted in William L. O'Neill, *Everyone Was Brave: A History of Feminism in America*, rev. ed. (Chicago, 1971), 150.

65. Matthews tribute in *Century*, Feb. 1910, p. 636.

66. Henry Holt, *Garrulities of an Octagenarian Editor. . . .* (Boston, 1923), 245, and *Nation*, 89 (Nov. 25, 1909):505–6. A memorial meeting that filled Mendelsshon Hall was held on Feb. 20, 1910, with Governor Charles Evans Hughes presiding.

Postscript

Upon Richard Watson Gilder's death, Robert Underwood Johnson became the editor. Considering himself "the apostolic as well as the editorial successor of Holland and Gilder," he carried on the *Century*'s traditional policies. He did his best to enliven his pages with shorter articles, novellas, and humor, but the *Century* continued to lose circulation. Johnson suggested that the Century Company start a new, inexpensive magazine to meet the competition while continuing the *Century* as it was. The trustees would not approve this idea, and in 1913, after the death of Frank H. Scott, the dignified conservative who had succeeded Roswell Smith as president of the Century Company, Johnson resigned. He remained busy with his poetry and the affairs of the American Academy of Arts and Letters; in 1920 he was appointed as ambassador of the United States to Italy.

In contrast to the calm continuity of policy and personnel that characterized the magazine until 1913, its later history was marked by sudden shifts in content, format, and editorial direction. Robert S. Yard, a former newspaperman, succeeded Johnson and tried to make the *Century* more journalistic, but he resigned in 1914 after participating in an abortive attempt to purchase control of the magazine. He was followed by Douglas Z. Doty (1915–18); Thomas H. Smith (1919); W. Morgan Shuster (1920–21), who had also become president of the Century Company; Glenn Frank (1921–25); and Hewitt H. Howland (1925–30).

These men preserved the high literary tone of former days and carried on the tradition of interest in public affairs. Under Frank, especially, the *Century* won a new reputation for its lively editorials on current events. During Frank's regime, illustrations were curtailed, and after his departure they were completely eliminated, a change that symbolized the decline of the *Century* from the glory days of Gilder and Alexander Drake.

In 1929, the *Century* became a quarterly. In 1930, with circulation at 20,000, the *Century* was bought by the owners of *Forum* and merged with that magazine, its independent existence at an end after sixty years.[1]

NOTE

1. Information in the postscript is from Frank Luther Mott, *A History of American Magazines*, 5 vols. (Cambridge, Mass., 1930–68), 3:477–79; Samuel C. Chew, ed., *Fruit among the Leaves: An Anniversary Anthology* (New York, 1950), 122–31; Robert Underwood Johnson, *Remembered Yesterdays* (Boston, 1923), 138–39, 513–14.

Appendix

Correspondence between Volume Number and
Year and Month in Issues of
Scribner's Monthly and the *Century Magazine*

Volumes run from November through April and from May through
October, each volume having six numbers. Thus the November and
May issues are always Number 1, the December and June issues always
Number 2, and so on.

Volume No., Month and Year	*Volume No., Month and Year*
1. Nov. 1870–Apr. 1871	20. May 1880–Oct. 1880
2. May 1871–Oct. 1871	21. Nov. 1880–Apr. 1881
3. Oct. 1871–Apr. 1872	22. May 1881–Oct. 1881
4. May 1872–Oct. 1872	★23. Nov. 1881–Apr. 1882
5. Nov. 1872–Apr. 1873	24. May 1882–Oct. 1882
6. May 1873–Oct. 1873	25. Nov. 1882–Apr. 1883
7. Nov. 1873–Apr. 1874	26. May 1883–Oct. 1883
8. May 1874–Oct. 1874	27. Nov. 1883–Apr. 1884
9. Nov. 1874–Apr. 1875	28. May 1884–Oct. 1884
10. May 1875–Oct. 1875	29. Nov. 1884–Apr. 1885
11. Nov. 1875–Apr. 1876	30. May 1885–Oct. 1885
12. May 1876–Oct. 1876	31. Nov. 1885–Apr. 1886
13. Nov. 1876–Apr. 1877	32. May 1886–Oct. 1886
14. May 1877–Oct. 1877	33. Nov. 1886–Apr. 1887
15. Nov. 1877–Apr. 1878	34. May 1887–Oct. 1887
16. May 1878–Oct. 1878	35. Nov. 1887–Apr. 1888
17. Nov. 1878–Apr. 1879	36. May 1888–Oct. 1888
18. May 1879–Oct. 1879	37. Nov. 1888–Apr. 1889
19. Nov. 1879–Apr. 1880	38. May 1889–Oct. 1889

★First volume of the *Century*.

Bibliographical Essay

The most important source for this study was the magazine itself—the seventy-eight volumes of *Scribner's Monthly* and the *Century Magazine* from November 1870 through October 1909, in which every item has been examined. Most of the bound volumes of the periodical in the Library of Congress include the advertisements that it carried; these pages, besides suggesting the social and economic ambience in which publication took place, provide some index of the magazine's prosperity. The advertising pages also include an occasional publishers' section containing circulation claims and other useful information. From time to time the editors themselves reviewed the history and progress of the monthly, most fully in "The Rise and Work of a Magazine. The History of the *Century Magazine (Scribner's Monthly),*" published as a supplement to the first number of the *Century* (November 1881).

In the notes, items appearing in *Scribner's Monthly* or the *Century* are usually cited only by year and month, except that editorials and other departmental material such as "Open Letters" are so labeled. The appendix provides a cross-reference between the year and month of issue and the corresponding volume and number of the magazine. Page numbers are omitted except in citing material in the advertising section or publishers' department, which are not covered by the table of contents found with each number and additionally with each volume. To avoid endless repetition and to economize on space, the title of the magazine under study is also omitted, save in a few instances where it seemed necessary to avoid confusion with the other sources cited. Thus, a reference in the notes to Jan. 1882 means that the item appeared in the *Century* for that year and month. All other periodical references are cited by title, volume, and page.

The indispensable manuscript source is the Century Collection in the New York Public Library (cited as CC in the notes). There are approximately 50,000 letters in the collection, dated from 1870 to 1914, the great majority of them *to* the editors from contributors or potential contributors. Many autograph items from outstanding authors have been removed from the collection and sold at auction, but a significant number of major writers, scholars, and public figures are represented. There are also valuable papers over the signatures of the various editors of the magazine or officials of the Century Company. Moreover, editorial annotations on the letters, even on those otherwise unimportant, give insights into the functioning of the *Century* editorial staff and the standards—both literary and moral—by which policy was guided. There are also several volumes of manuscripts and proofs in the Century Collection.

The Richard Watson Gilder Papers (cited as GP in the notes) are also in the New York Public Library. Most of the 6,000 items are letters *to* Gilder. However, there are letterbooks containing copies of letters written by Gilder. With a few exceptions, these do not relate to Gilder's editorial duties but are concerned with his manifold activities as poet, citizen, and friend of arts and letters, but since the magazine reflected its editor's personal ideals and interests, this correspondence provides a useful background to editorial policy. There is also a list of editorials and other departmental material written by Gilder. The Robert Underwood Johnson Papers in the New York Public Library are relevant mainly for the period after Gilder's death when Johnson became editor.

The archives of Charles Scribner's Sons, now in the Princeton University Library, contain excellent documentary information on *Scribner's Monthly*. Among the papers in this collection (cited as SC in the notes) are letters of Charles Scribner, Josiah Gilbert Holland, and Roswell Smith relating to the founding of the magazine; memoranda regarding its circulation and financial position; and a detailed record of the dispute that brought about a change of ownership and the emergence of the *Century*.

Seventy letters to Holland were lent to the author by Holland's granddaughter, the late Mrs. Theodora Van Wagonen Ward. This correspondence, centered in the years 1870–75, recorded Holland's attempts to enlist contributions from British and American authors.

Manuscripts consulted at the Houghton Library, Harvard University, include the Thomas Bailey Aldrich Papers and the William Dean Howells Papers. The sixty Gilder letters in the Howells Papers are especially revealing of Gilder's literary theories, editorial methods, and political and cultural interests. Also at Harvard are more than one hundred letters to Gilder from Sir Edmund Gosse, the London literary agent of the *Century*.

Other manuscripts used are cited in the notes.

The many books and articles useful for this study are listed in the notes as appropriate, but some of them deserve special mention as being, at least in part, primary sources. Rosamond Gilder's *Letters of Richard Watson Gilder* (Boston, 1916) is in effect a biographical sketch of the editor assembled by his daughter from his correspondence and his journal; the letters bearing directly on the magazine, although relatively few in number, are well chosen to illustrate Gilder's editorial aims and ideals. Robert Underwood Johnson's *Remembered Yesterdays* (Boston, 1923) includes authoritative passages about the *Century* and its personnel, written by the longtime associate editor who ultimately succeeded Gilder. L. Frank Tooker's *The Joys and Tribulations of an Editor* (New York, 1924) pictures the staff, policies, and milieu of the *Century* from a junior editor's point of view. Herbert F. Smith's *Richard Watson Gilder* (New York, 1970), an excellent study emphasizing Gilder's creative contributions as a literary editor, contains excerpts from letters not otherwise available to me. Mrs. H. M. Plunkett's *Josiah Gilbert Holland* (New York, 1894), a sentimental and uncritical biography by a friend of the Holland family, has useful firsthand information on the magazine's first editor. Harry Houston Peckham's *Josiah Gilbert Holland in Relation to His Times* (Philadelphia, 1940) has much of interest on Holland's character and career, supplementing Plunkett's work with information from Holland's descendants.

Mention should be made of other books that I have cited only infrequently in the reference notes but that provided valuable cultural and intellectual background to this study. Henry F. May's *The End of American Innocence: A Study of the First Years of Our Time, 1912–1917* (New York, 1959) emphasizes challenges to the system of values inherited from the nineteenth century, but begins with an admirable description of those values, summed up as morality, culture, and progress. Howard Mumford Jones's *The Age of Energy: Varieties of American Experience, 1865–1915* (New York, 1971) is a view of a period that overlaps the years of Holland and Gilder and includes (in Chapter 6) a perceptive defense of the genteel critics and creators. In *The Feminization of American Culture* (New York, 1977), Ann Douglas illustrates how a combination of women and ministers achieved dominance over popular literature in America, a dominance that the *Century* editors chose to live with and respect. Stow Persons in *The Decline of American Gentility* (New York, 1973) describes the code, the aims, and the disillusion of the cultural elite of which Gilder was representative. John Tomsich's *A Genteel Endeavor: American Culture and Politics in the Gilded Age* (Stanford, Calif., 1971) deals specifically with Gilder as one of eight writers and critics who espoused genteel aims and values.

Index